2017
SUN SIGN
BOOK

Forecasts by
Kim Rogers-Gallagher

Cover Design by Kevin R. Brown
Editing by Andrea Neff
iStockphoto.com/6682368/©linearcurves
iStockphoto.com/9051595/©Vjom
iStockphoto.com/44372890/©Hollygraphic
iStockphoto.com/59359876/©shoo_arts

Copyright 2016 Llewellyn Publications
ISBN: 978-0-7387-3764-5
A Division of Llewellyn Worldwide Ltd., www.llewellyn.com
Llewellyn is a registered trademark of Llewellyn Worldwide Ltd.
2143 Wooddale Drive, Woodbury, MN 55125
Printed in the USA

Contents

2017 Sun Sign Book Forecasts

2016

SEPTEMBER
S	M	T	W	T	F	S
				1	2	3
4	5	6	7	8	9	10
11	12	13	14	15	16	17
18	19	20	21	22	23	24
25	26	27	28	29	30	

OCTOBER
S	M	T	W	T	F	S
						1
2	3	4	5	6	7	8
9	10	11	12	13	14	15
16	17	18	19	20	21	22
23	24	25	26	27	28	29
30	31					

NOVEMBER
S	M	T	W	T	F	S
		1	2	3	4	5
6	7	8	9	10	11	12
13	14	15	16	17	18	19
20	21	22	23	24	25	26
27	28	29	30			

DECEMBER
S	M	T	W	T	F	S
				1	2	3
4	5	6	7	8	9	10
11	12	13	14	15	16	17
18	19	20	21	22	23	24
25	26	27	28	29	30	31

2017

JANUARY
S	M	T	W	T	F	S
1	2	3	4	5	6	7
8	9	10	11	12	13	14
15	16	17	18	19	20	21
22	23	24	25	26	27	28
29	30	31				

FEBRUARY
S	M	T	W	T	F	S
			1	2	3	4
5	6	7	8	9	10	11
12	13	14	15	16	17	18
19	20	21	22	23	24	25
26	27	28				

MARCH
S	M	T	W	T	F	S
			1	2	3	4
5	6	7	8	9	10	11
12	13	14	15	16	17	18
19	20	21	22	23	24	25
26	27	28	29	30	31	

APRIL
S	M	T	W	T	F	S
						1
2	3	4	5	6	7	8
9	10	11	12	13	14	15
16	17	18	19	20	21	22
23	24	25	26	27	28	29
30						

MAY
S	M	T	W	T	F	S
	1	2	3	4	5	6
7	8	9	10	11	12	13
14	15	16	17	18	19	20
21	22	23	24	25	26	27
28	29	30	31			

JUNE
S	M	T	W	T	F	S
				1	2	3
4	5	6	7	8	9	10
11	12	13	14	15	16	17
18	19	20	21	22	23	24
25	26	27	28	29	30	

JULY
S	M	T	W	T	F	S
						1
2	3	4	5	6	7	8
9	10	11	12	13	14	15
16	17	18	19	20	21	22
23	24	25	26	27	28	29
30	31					

AUGUST
S	M	T	W	T	F	S
		1	2	3	4	5
6	7	8	9	10	11	12
13	14	15	16	17	18	19
20	21	22	23	24	25	26
27	28	29	30	31		

SEPTEMBER
S	M	T	W	T	F	S
					1	2
3	4	5	6	7	8	9
10	11	12	13	14	15	16
17	18	19	20	21	22	23
24	25	26	27	28	29	30

OCTOBER
S	M	T	W	T	F	S
1	2	3	4	5	6	7
8	9	10	11	12	13	14
15	16	17	18	19	20	21
22	23	24	25	26	27	28
29	30	31				

NOVEMBER
S	M	T	W	T	F	S
			1	2	3	4
5	6	7	8	9	10	11
12	13	14	15	16	17	18
19	20	21	22	23	24	25
26	27	28	29	30		

DECEMBER
S	M	T	W	T	F	S
					1	2
3	4	5	6	7	8	9
10	11	12	13	14	15	16
17	18	19	20	21	22	23
24	25	26	27	28	29	30
31						

2018

JANUARY
S	M	T	W	T	F	S
	1	2	3	4	5	6
7	8	9	10	11	12	13
14	15	16	17	18	19	20
21	22	23	24	25	26	27
28	29	30	31			

FEBRUARY
S	M	T	W	T	F	S
				1	2	3
4	5	6	7	8	9	10
11	12	13	14	15	16	17
18	19	20	21	22	23	24
25	26	27	28			

MARCH
S	M	T	W	T	F	S
				1	2	3
4	5	6	7	8	9	10
11	12	13	14	15	16	17
18	19	20	21	22	23	24
25	26	27	28	29	30	31

APRIL
S	M	T	W	T	F	S
1	2	3	4	5	6	7
8	9	10	11	12	13	14
15	16	17	18	19	20	21
22	23	24	25	26	27	28
29	30					

MAY
S	M	T	W	T	F	S
		1	2	3	4	5
6	7	8	9	10	11	12
13	14	15	16	17	18	19
20	21	22	23	24	25	26
27	28	29	30	31		

JUNE
S	M	T	W	T	F	S
					1	2
3	4	5	6	7	8	9
10	11	12	13	14	15	16
17	18	19	20	21	22	23
24	25	26	27	28	29	30

JULY
S	M	T	W	T	F	S
1	2	3	4	5	6	7
8	9	10	11	12	13	14
15	16	17	18	19	20	21
22	23	24	25	26	27	28
29	30	31				

AUGUST
S	M	T	W	T	F	S
			1	2	3	4
5	6	7	8	9	10	11
12	13	14	15	16	17	18
19	20	21	22	23	24	25
26	27	28	29	30	31	

Meet Kim Rogers-Gallagher

Kim fell in love with astrology in grade school and began her formal education close to thirty years ago. She's written hundreds of articles and columns for magazines and online publications, contributed to several astrological anthologies, and has two books of her own to her credit, *Astrology for the Light Side of the Brain* and *Astrology for the Light Side of the Future*, both available from ACS/Starcrafts Publishing. Kim is the author of daily e-mail horoscopes for astrology.com, and her work appears in the introductory sections of *Llewellyn's Astrology Calendar*, *Llewellyn's Witches' Datebook*, and *Llewellyn's Witches' Calendar*.

At the moment, Kim is having great fun on her Facebook page, facebook.com/KRGFenix, where she turns daily transits into fun celestial adventures. She's a well-known speaker who's been part of the UAC (United Astrology Conference) faculty since 1996 and has lectured at many other international conferences.

An avid animal lover, Kim occasionally receives permission from her seriously spoiled fur-kids (and her computer) to leave home for a while and indulge her ninth-house Sagg Sun by traveling for "work"— that is, talking to groups about astrology (which really isn't work at all). In typical Sagg style, Kim loves to laugh, but she also loves to chat, which comes in handy when she does private phone consultations.

She is a twenty-year "citizen" of Pennsic, an annual medieval event, where she gets to dress up in funny clothes, live in a tent, and pretend she's back in the 1300s for two weeks every year—which, oddly enough, is her idea of a good time.

Kim can be contacted at KRGPhoenix313@yahoo.com for fees regarding readings, classes, and lectures.

New Concepts for Zodiac Signs

The signs of the zodiac represent characteristics and traits that indicate how energy operates within our lives. The signs tell the story of human evolution and development, and all are necessary to form the continuum of whole-life experience. In fact, all twelve signs are represented within your astrological chart.

Although the traditional metaphors for the twelve signs (such as Aries, the Ram) are always functional, these alternative concepts for each of the twelve signs also describe the gradual unfolding of the human spirit.

Aries: The Initiator is the first sign of the zodiac and encompasses the primary concept of getting things started. This fiery ignition and bright beginning can prove to be the thrust necessary for new life, but the Initiator also can appear before a situation is ready for change and create disruption.

Taurus: The Maintainer sustains what Aries has begun and brings stability and focus into the picture, yet there also can be a tendency to try to maintain something in its current state without allowing for new growth.

Gemini: The Questioner seeks to determine whether alternatives are possible and offers diversity to the processes Taurus has brought into stability. Yet questioning can also lead to distraction, subsequently scattering energy and diffusing focus.

Cancer: The Nurturer provides the qualities necessary for growth and security, and encourages a deepening awareness of emotional needs. Yet this same nurturing can stifle individuation if it becomes too smothering.

Leo: The Loyalist directs and centralizes the experiences Cancer feeds. This quality is powerfully targeted toward self-awareness, but can be shortsighted. Hence, the Loyalist can hold steadfastly to viewpoints or feelings that inhibit new experiences.

Virgo: The Modifier analyzes the situations Leo brings to light and determines possibilities for change. Even though this change may be in the name of improvement, it can lead to dissatisfaction with the self if not directed in harmony with higher needs.

Libra: The Judge is constantly comparing everything to be sure that a certain level of rightness and perfection is presented. However, the Judge can also present possibilities that are harsh and seem to be cold or without feeling.

Scorpio: The Catalyst steps into the play of life to provide the quality of alchemical transformation. The Catalyst can stir the brew just enough to create a healing potion, or may get things going to such a powerful extent that they boil out of control.

Sagittarius: The Adventurer moves away from Scorpio's dimension to seek what lies beyond the horizon. The Adventurer continually looks for possibilities that answer the ultimate questions, but may forget the pathway back home.

Capricorn: The Pragmatist attempts to put everything into its rightful place and find ways to make life work out right. The Pragmatist can teach lessons of practicality and determination, but can become highly self-righteous when shortsighted.

Aquarius: The Reformer looks for ways to take what Capricorn has built and bring it up to date. Yet there is also a tendency to scrap the original in favor of a new plan that may not have the stable foundation necessary to operate effectively.

Pisces: The Visionary brings mysticism and imagination, and challenges the soul to move beyond the physical plane, into the realm of what might be. The Visionary can pierce the veil, returning enlightened to the physical world. The challenge is to avoid getting lost within the illusion of an alternate reality.

Astrology Basics

Astrology is an ancient and continually evolving system used to clarify your identity and your needs. An astrological chart—which is calculated using the date, time, and place of birth—contains many factors that symbolically represent the needs, expressions, and experiences that make up the whole person. A professional astrologer interprets this symbolic picture, offering you an accurate portrait of your personality.

The chart itself—the horoscope—is a portrait of an individual. Generally, a natal (or birth) horoscope is drawn on a circular wheel. The wheel is divided into twelve segments, called houses. Each of the twelve houses represents a different aspect of the individual, much like the facets of a brilliantly cut stone. The houses depict different environments, such as home, school, and work. The houses also represent roles and relationships: parents, friends, lovers, children, partners. In each environment, individuals show a different side of their personality. At home, you may represent yourself quite differently than you do on the job. Additionally, in each relationship you will project a different image of yourself. For example, your parents may rarely see the side you show to intimate friends.

Symbols for the planets, the Sun, and the Moon are drawn inside the houses. Each planet represents a separate kind of energy. You experience and express each energy in specific ways. The way you use each of these energies is up to you. The planets in your chart do not make you do anything!

Signs of the Zodiac

The twelve signs of the zodiac indicate characteristics and traits that further define your personality. Each sign can be expressed in positive and negative ways. What's more, you have all twelve signs somewhere in your chart. Signs that are strongly emphasized by the planets have greater force. The Sun, Moon, and planets are placed on the chart according to their position at the time of birth. The qualities of a sign, combined with the energy of a planet, indicate how you might be most likely to use that energy and the best ways to develop that energy. The signs add color, emphasis, and dimension to the personality.

The Twelve Signs

Aries	♈	The Initiator
Taurus	♉	The Maintainer
Gemini	♊	The Questioner
Cancer	♋	The Nurturer
Leo	♌	The Loyalist
Virgo	♍	The Modifier
Libra	♎	The Judge
Scorpio	♏	The Catalyst
Sagittarius	♐	The Adventurer
Capricorn	♑	The Pragmatist
Aquarius	♒	The Reformer
Pisces	♓	The Visionary

Signs are also placed at the cusps, or dividing lines, of each of the houses. The influence of the signs on the houses is much the same as their influence on the Sun, Moon, and planets. Each house is shaped by the sign on its cusp.

When you view a horoscope, you will notice that there appear to be four distinct angles dividing the wheel of the chart. The line that divides the chart into a top and bottom half represents the horizon. In most cases, the left side of the horizon is called the Ascendant. The zodiac sign on the Ascendant is your rising sign. The Ascendant indicates the way others are likely to view you.

The Sun, Moon, or a planet can be compared to an actor in a play. The sign shows how the energy works, like the role the actor plays in a drama. The house indicates where the energy operates, like the setting of a play. On a psychological level, the Sun represents who you think you are. The Ascendant describes who others think you are, and the Moon reflects your emotional self.

Astrologers also study the geometric relationships between the Sun, Moon, and planets. These geometric angles are called aspects. Aspects further define the strengths, weaknesses, and challenges within your physical, mental, emotional, and spiritual selves. Sometimes patterns also appear in an astrological chart. These patterns have meaning.

To understand cycles for any given point in time, astrologers study several factors. Many use transits, which refer to the movement and positions of the planets. When astrologers compare those positions to the birth horoscope, the transits indicate activity in particular areas of the chart. The *Sun Sign Book* uses transits.

As you can see, your Sun sign is just one of many factors that describe who you are—but it is a powerful one! As the symbol of the ego, the Sun in your chart reflects your drive to be noticed. Most people can easily relate to the concepts associated with their Sun sign, since it is tied to their sense of personal identity.

Meanings of the Planets

The Sun

The Sun indicates the psychological bias that will dominate your actions. What you see, and why, is told in the reading for your Sun. The Sun also shows the basic energy patterns of your body and psyche. In many ways, the Sun is the dominant force in your horoscope and your life. Other influences, especially that of the Moon, may modify the Sun's influence, but nothing will cause you to depart very far from the basic solar pattern. Always keep in mind the basic influence of the Sun and remember all other influences must be interpreted in terms of it, especially insofar as they play a visible role in your life. You may think, dream, imagine, and hope a thousand things, according to your Moon and your other planets, but the Sun is what you are. To be your best self in terms of your Sun is to cause your energies to work along the path in which they will have maximum help from planetary vibrations.

The Moon

The Moon tells the desire of your life. When you know what you mean but can't verbalize it, it is your Moon that knows it and your Sun that can't say it. The wordless ecstasy, the mute sorrow, the secret dream, the esoteric picture of yourself that you can't get across to the world, or that the world doesn't comprehend or value—these are the products of the Moon. When you are misunderstood, it is your Moon nature, expressed imperfectly through the Sun sign, that feels betrayed. Things you know without thought—intuitions, hunches,

The Planets

Sun	☉	The ego, self, willpower
Moon	☽	The subconscious self, habits
Mercury	☿	Communication, the intellect
Venus	♀	Emotional expression, love, appreciation, artistry
Mars	♂	Physical drive, assertiveness, anger
Jupiter	♃	Philosophy, ethics, generosity
Saturn	♄	Discipline, focus, responsibility
Uranus	♅	Individuality, rebelliousness
Neptune	♆	Imagination, sensitivity, compassion
Pluto	♇	Transformation, healing, regeneration

instincts—are the products of the Moon. Modes of expression that you feel truly reflect your deepest self belong to the Moon: art, letters, creative work of any kind; sometimes love; sometimes business. Whatever you feel to be most deeply yourself is the product of your Moon and of the sign your Moon occupies at birth.

Mercury

Mercury is the sensory antenna of your horoscope. Its position by sign indicates your reactions to sights, sounds, odors, tastes, and touch impressions, affording a key to the attitude you have toward the physical world around you. Mercury is the messenger through which your physical body and brain (ruled by the Sun) and your inner nature (ruled by the Moon) are kept in contact with the outer world, which will appear to you according to the index of Mercury's position by sign in the horoscope. Mercury rules your rational mind.

Venus

Venus is the emotional antenna of your horoscope. Through Venus, impressions come to you from the outer world. The position of Venus by sign at the time of your birth determines your attitude toward these experiences. As Mercury is the messenger linking sense impressions (sight, smell, etc.) to the basic nature of your Sun and Moon, so Venus is the messenger linking emotional impressions. If Venus is found in the same sign as the Sun, emotions gain importance in your life and have a direct bearing on your actions. If Venus is in the same sign as the Moon, emotions bear directly on your inner nature, add self-confidence, make you sensitive to emotional impressions, and frequently indicate that you have more love in your heart than you are able to express. If Venus is in the same sign as Mercury, emotional impressions and sense impressions work together; you tend to idealize the world of the senses and sensualize the world of the emotions to interpret what you see and hear.

Mars

Mars is the energy principle in the horoscope. Its position indicates the channels into which energy will most easily be directed. It is the planet through which the activities of the Sun and the desires of the Moon express themselves in action. In the same sign as the Sun, Mars gives abundant energy, sometimes misdirected in temper, temperament, and quarrels. In the same sign as the Moon, it gives a great capacity to make use of the innermost aims, and to make the inner desires articulate and practical. In the same sign as Venus, it quickens emotional reactions and causes you to act on them, makes for ardor and passion in love, and fosters an earthly awareness of emotional realities.

Jupiter

Jupiter is the feeler for opportunity that you have out in the world. It passes along chances of a lifetime for consideration according to the basic nature of your Sun and Moon. Jupiter's sign position indicates the places you will look for opportunity, the uses to which you wish to put it, and the capacity you have to react and profit by it. Jupiter is ordinarily and erroneously called the planet of luck. It is "luck" insofar as it is the index of opportunity, but your luck depends less on what comes to you than on what you do with what comes to you. In the same sign as the Sun or Moon, Jupiter gives a direct and generally effective response to opportunity and is likely to show forth at its "luckiest." If Jupiter is in the same sign as Mercury, sense impressions are interpreted opportunistically. If Jupiter is in the same sign as Venus, you interpret emotions in such a way as to turn them to your advantage; your feelings work harmoniously with the chances for progress that the world has to offer. If Jupiter is in the same sign as Mars, you follow opportunity with energy, dash, enthusiasm, and courage; take big chances; and play your cards wide open.

Saturn

Saturn indicates the direction that will be taken in life by the self-preserving principle that, in its highest manifestation, ceases to be purely defensive and becomes ambitious and aspiring. Your defense or attack against the world is shown by the sign position of Saturn in the horoscope of birth. If Saturn is in the same sign as the Sun or Moon, defense predominates, and there is danger of introversion. The farther Saturn is from the Sun, Moon, and Ascendant, the better for objectivity and extroversion. If Saturn is in the same sign as Mercury, there is a profound and serious reaction to sensory impressions; this position generally accompanies a deep and efficient mind. If Saturn is in the same sign as Venus, a defensive attitude toward emotional experience makes for apparent coolness in love and difficulty with the emotions and human relations. If Saturn is in the same sign as Mars, confusion between defensive and aggressive urges can make a person indecisive. On the other hand, if the Sun and Moon are strong and the total personality well developed, a balanced, peaceful, and calm individual of sober judgment and moderate actions may be indicated. If Saturn is in the same sign as Jupiter, the reaction to opportunity is sober and balanced.

Uranus

Uranus in a general way relates to creativity, originality, or individuality, and its position by sign in the horoscope tells the direction in which you will seek to express yourself. In the same sign as Mercury or the Moon, Uranus suggests acute awareness, a quick reaction to sense impressions and experiences, or a hair-trigger mind. In the same sign as the Sun, it points to great nervous activity, a high-strung nature, and an original, creative, or eccentric personality. In the same sign as Mars, Uranus indicates high-speed activity, love of swift motion, and perhaps love of danger. In the same sign as Venus, it suggests an unusual reaction to emotional experience, idealism, sensuality, and original ideas about love and human relations. In the same sign as Saturn, Uranus points to good sense; this can be a practical, creative position, but more often than not it sets up a destructive conflict between practicality and originality that can result in a stalemate. In the same sign as Jupiter, Uranus makes opportunity, creates wealth and the means of getting it, and is conducive to the inventive, executive, and daring.

Neptune

Neptune relates to the deep subconscious, inherited mentality, and spirituality, indicating what you take for granted in life. Neptune in the same sign as the Sun or Moon indicates that intuitions and hunches—or delusions—dominate; there is a need to rigidly hold to reality. In the same sign as Mercury, Neptune indicates sharp sensory perceptions, a sensitive and perhaps creative mind, and a quivering intensity of reaction to sensory experience. In the same sign as Venus, it reveals idealistic and romantic (or sentimental) reactions to emotional experience, as well as the danger of sensationalism and a love of strange pleasures. In the same sign as Mars, Neptune indicates energy and intuition that work together to make mastery of life—one of the signs of having angels (or devils) on your side. When in the same sign as Jupiter, Neptune describes an intuitive response to opportunity along practical and money-making lines. In the same sign as Saturn, Neptune indicates intuitive defense and attack on the world, which is generally successful unless Saturn is polarized on the negative side; then there is danger of unhappiness.

Pluto

Pluto is a planet of extremes, from the lowest criminal and violent level of our society to the heights people can attain when they realize their significance in the collectivity of humanity. Pluto also rules three important mysteries of life—sex, death, and rebirth—and links them to each other. One level of death symbolized by Pluto is the physical death of an individual, which occurs so that a person can be reborn into another body to further his or her spiritual development. On another level, individuals can experience a "death" of their old self when they realize the deeper significance of life; thus they become one of the "second born." In a natal horoscope, Pluto signifies our perspective on the world, our conscious and subconscious. Since so many of Pluto's qualities are centered on the deeper mysteries of life, the house position of Pluto, and aspects to it, can show you how to attain a deeper understanding of the importance of the spiritual in your life.

Astrological Glossary

Air: One of the four basic elements. The air signs are Gemini, Libra, and Aquarius.

Angles: The four points of the chart that divide it into quadrants. The angles are sensitive areas that lend emphasis to planets located near them. These points are located on the cusps of the first, fourth, seventh, and tenth houses in a chart.

Ascendant: Rising sign. The degree of the zodiac on the eastern horizon at the time and place for which the horoscope is calculated. It can indicate the image or physical appearance you project to the world. The cusp of the first house.

Aspect: The angular relationship between planets, sensitive points, or house cusps in a horoscope. Lines drawn between the two points and the center of the chart, representing the earth, form the angle of the aspect. Astrological aspects include the conjunction (two points that are 0 degrees apart), opposition (two points, 180 degrees apart), square (two points, 90 degrees apart), sextile (two points, 60 degrees apart), and trine (two points, 120 degrees apart). Aspects can indicate harmony or challenge.

Cardinal Sign: One of the three qualities, or categories, that describe how a sign expresses itself. Aries, Cancer, Libra, and Capricorn are the cardinal signs, believed to initiate activity.

Chiron: Chiron is a comet traveling in orbit between Saturn and Uranus. It is believed to represent a key or doorway, healing, ecology, and a bridge between traditional and modern methods.

Conjunction: An aspect or angle between two points in a chart where the two points are close enough so that the energies join. Can be considered either harmonious or challenging, depending on the planets involved and their placement.

Cusp: A dividing line between signs or houses in a chart.

Degree: Degree of arc. One of 360 divisions of a circle. The circle of the zodiac is divided into twelve astrological signs of 30 degrees each. Each degree is made up of 60 minutes, and each minute is made up of 60 seconds of zodiacal longitude.

Earth: One of the four basic elements. The earth signs are Taurus, Virgo, and Capricorn.

Eclipse: A Solar Eclipse is the full or partial covering of the Sun by the Moon (as viewed from the earth), and a Lunar Eclipse is the full or partial covering of the Moon by the earth's own shadow.

Ecliptic: The Sun's apparent path around the earth, which is actually the plane of the earth's orbit extended out into space. The ecliptic forms the center of the zodiac.

Electional Astrology: A branch of astrology concerned with choosing the best time to initiate an activity.

Elements: The signs of the zodiac are divided into four groups of three zodiacal signs, each symbolized by one of the four elements of the ancients: fire, earth, air, and water. The element of a sign is said to express its essential nature.

Ephemeris: A listing of the Sun, Moon, and planets' positions and related information for astrological purposes.

Equinox: Equal night. The point in the earth's orbit around the Sun at which the day and night are equal in length.

Feminine Signs: Each zodiac sign is either "masculine" or "feminine." Earth signs (Taurus, Virgo, and Capricorn) and water signs (Cancer, Scorpio, and Pisces) are feminine.

Fire: One of the four basic elements. The fire signs are Aries, Leo, and Sagittarius.

Fixed Signs: Fixed is one of the three qualities, or categories, that describe how a sign expresses itself. The fixed signs are Taurus, Leo, Scorpio, and Aquarius. Fixed signs are said to be predisposed to existing patterns and somewhat resistant to change.

Hard Aspects: Hard aspects are those aspects in a chart that astrologers believe to represent difficulty or challenges. Among the hard aspects are the square, the opposition, and the conjunction (depending on which planets are conjunct).

Horizon: The word *horizon* is used in astrology in a manner similar to its common usage, except that only the eastern and western horizons are considered useful. The eastern horizon at the point of birth is the

Ascendant, or first house cusp, of a natal chart, and the western horizon at the point of birth is the Descendant, or seventh house cusp.

Houses: Division of the horoscope into twelve segments, beginning with the Ascendant. The dividing line between two houses is called a house cusp. Each house corresponds to certain aspects of daily living, and is ruled by the astrological sign that governs the cusp, or dividing line between the house and the one previous.

Ingress: The point of entry of a planet into a sign.

Lagna: A term used in Hindu or Vedic astrology for Ascendant, the degree of the zodiac on the eastern horizon at the time of birth.

Masculine Signs: Each of the twelve signs of the zodiac is either "masculine" or "feminine." The fire signs (Aries, Leo, and Sagittarius) and the air signs (Gemini, Libra, and Aquarius) are masculine.

Midheaven: The highest point on the ecliptic, where it intersects the meridian that passes directly above the place for which the horoscope is cast; the southern point of the horoscope.

Midpoint: A point equally distant to two planets or house cusps. Midpoints are considered by some astrologers to be sensitive points in a person's chart.

Mundane Astrology: Mundane astrology is the branch of astrology generally concerned with political and economic events, and the nations involved in these events.

Mutable Signs: Mutable is one of the three qualities, or categories, that describe how a sign expresses itself. Mutable signs are Gemini, Virgo, Sagittarius, and Pisces. Mutable signs are said to be very adaptable and sometimes changeable.

Natal Chart: A person's birth chart. A natal chart is essentially a "snapshot" showing the placement of each of the planets at the exact time of a person's birth.

Node: The point where the planets cross the ecliptic, or the earth's apparent path around the Sun. The North Node is the point where a planet moves northward, from the earth's perspective, as it crosses the ecliptic; the South Node is where it moves south.

Opposition: Two points in a chart that are 180 degrees apart.

Orb: A small degree of margin used when calculating aspects in a chart. For example, although 180 degrees form an exact opposition, an astrologer might consider an aspect within 3 or 4 degrees on either side of 180 degrees to be an opposition, as the impact of the aspect can still be felt within this range. The less orb on an aspect, the stronger the aspect. Astrologers' opinions vary on how many degrees of orb to allow for each aspect.

Outer Planet: Uranus, Neptune, and Pluto are known as the outer planets. Because of their distance from the Sun, they take a long time to complete a single rotation. Everyone born within a few years on either side of a given date will have similar placements of these planets.

Planet: The planets used in astrology are Mercury, Venus, Mars, Jupiter, Saturn, Uranus, Neptune, and Pluto. For astrological purposes, the Sun and Moon are also considered planets. A natal chart, or birth chart, lists planetary placements at the moment of birth.

Planetary Rulership: The sign in which a planet is most harmoniously placed. Examples are the Sun in Leo, Jupiter in Sagittarius, and the Moon in Cancer.

Precession of Equinoxes: The gradual movement of the point of the spring equinox, located at 0 degrees Aries. This point marks the beginning of the tropical zodiac. The point moves slowly backward through the constellations of the zodiac, so that about every 2,000 years the equinox begins in an earlier constellation.

Qualities: In addition to categorizing the signs by element, astrologers place the twelve signs of the zodiac into three additional categories, or qualities: cardinal, mutable, or fixed. Each sign is considered to be a combination of its element and quality. Where the element of a sign describes its basic nature, the quality describes its mode of expression.

Retrograde Motion: The apparent backward motion of a planet. This is an illusion caused by the relative motion of the earth and other planets in their elliptical orbits.

Sextile: Two points in a chart that are 60 degrees apart.

Sidereal Zodiac: Generally used by Hindu or Vedic astrologers. The sidereal zodiac is located where the constellations are actually positioned in the sky.

Soft Aspects: Soft aspects indicate good fortune or an easy relationship in the chart. Among the soft aspects are the trine, the sextile, and the conjunction (depending on which planets are conjunct each other).

Square: Two points in a chart that are 90 degrees apart.

Sun Sign: The sign of the zodiac in which the Sun is located at any given time.

Synodic Cycle: The time between conjunctions of two planets.

Trine: Two points in a chart that are 120 degrees apart.

Tropical Zodiac: The tropical zodiac begins at 0 degrees Aries, where the Sun is located during the spring equinox. This system is used by most Western astrologers and throughout this book.

Void-of-Course: A planet is void-of-course after it has made its last aspect within a sign but before it has entered a new sign.

Water: One of the four basic elements. The water signs are Cancer, Scorpio, and Pisces.

Using This Book

This book contains what is called Sun sign astrology; that is, astrology based on the sign that your Sun was in at the time of your birth. The technique has its foundation in ancient Greek astrology, in which the Sun was one of five points in the chart that were used as focal points for delineation.

The most effective way to use astrology, however, is through one-on-one work with a professional astrologer, who can integrate the eight or so other astrological bodies into the interpretation to provide you with guidance. There are factors related to the year and time of day you were born that are highly significant in the way you approach life and vital to making wise choices. In addition, there are ways of using astrology that aren't addressed here, such as compatibility between two specific individuals, discovering family patterns, or picking a day for a wedding or grand opening.

To best use the information in the monthly forecasts, you'll want to determine your Ascendant, or rising sign. If you don't know your Ascendant, the tables following this description will help you determine your rising sign. They are most accurate for those born in the continental United States. They provide only an approximation, but can be used as a good rule of thumb. Your exact Ascendant may vary from the tables according to your time and place of birth. Once you've approximated your ascending sign using the tables or determined your Ascendant by having your chart calculated, you'll know two significant factors in your chart. Read the monthly forecast sections for both your Sun and Ascendant to gain the most useful information. In addition, you can read the section about the sign your Moon is in. The Sun is the true, inner you; the Ascendant is your shell or appearance and the person you are becoming; the Moon is the person you were—or still are based on habits and memories.

Also included in the monthly forecasts is information about the planets' retrogrades. Most people have heard of "Mercury retrograde." In fact, all the planets except the Sun and Moon appear to travel backward (retrograde) in their path periodically. This appears to happen only because we on the earth are not seeing the other planets from the middle of the solar system. Rather, we are watching them from our own moving object. We are like a train that moves past cars on the freeway that are going at a slower speed. To us on the train, the cars look like they're going backward. Mercury turns retrograde about every four months for three weeks; Venus every eighteen months for six weeks; Mars every two years for two to three months. The rest of the planets each retrograde once a year for four to five months. During each retrograde, we have the opportunity to try something new, something we conceived of at the beginning of the planet's yearly cycle. The times when the planets change direction are significant, as are the beginning and midpoint (peak or culmination) of each cycle. These are noted in your forecast each month.

The "Rewarding Days" and "Challenging Days" sections indicate times when you'll feel either more centered or more out of balance. The rewarding days are not the only times you can perform well, but the times you're likely to feel better integrated! During challenging days, take extra time to center yourself by meditating or using other techniques that help you feel more objective.

The Action Table found at the end of each sign's section offers general guidelines for the best times to take particular actions. Please note, however, that your whole chart will provide more accurate guidelines for the best time to do something. Therefore, use this table with a grain of salt, and never let it stop you from taking an action you feel compelled to take.

You can use this information to gain an objective awareness about the way the current cycles are affecting you. Realize that the power of astrology is even more useful when you have a complete chart and professional guidance.

Ascendant Table

Your Sun Sign	Your Time of Birth					
	6–8 am	8–10 am	10 am–Noon	Noon–2 pm	2–4 pm	4–6 pm
Aries	Taurus	Gemini	Cancer	Leo	Virgo	Libra
Taurus	Gemini	Cancer	Leo	Virgo	Libra	Scorpio
Gemini	Cancer	Leo	Virgo	Libra	Scorpio	Sagittarius
Cancer	Leo	Virgo	Libra	Scorpio	Sagittarius	Capricorn
Leo	Virgo	Libra	Scorpio	Sagittarius	Capricorn	Aquarius
Virgo	Libra	Scorpio	Sagittarius	Capricorn	Aquarius	Pisces
Libra	Scorpio	Sagittarius	Capricorn	Aquarius	Pisces	Aries
Scorpio	Sagittarius	Capricorn	Aquarius	Pisces	Aries	Taurus
Sagittarius	Capricorn	Aquarius	Pisces	Aries	Taurus	Gemini
Capricorn	Aquarius	Pisces	Aries	Taurus	Gemini	Cancer
Aquarius	Pisces	Aries	Taurus	Gemini	Cancer	Leo
Pisces	Aries	Taurus	Gemini	Cancer	Leo	Virgo

Your Sun Sign	Your Time of Birth					
	6–8 pm	8–10 pm	10 pm–Midnight	Midnight–2 am	2–4 am	4–6 am
Aries	Scorpio	Sagittarius	Capricorn	Aquarius	Pisces	Aries
Taurus	Sagittarius	Capricorn	Aquarius	Pisces	Aries	Taurus
Gemini	Capricorn	Aquarius	Pisces	Aries	Taurus	Gemini
Cancer	Aquarius	Pisces	Aries	Taurus	Gemini	Cancer
Leo	Pisces	Aries	Taurus	Gemini	Cancer	Leo
Virgo	Aries	Taurus	Gemini	Cancer	Leo	Virgo
Libra	Taurus	Gemini	Cancer	Leo	Virgo	Libra
Scorpio	Gemini	Cancer	Leo	Virgo	Libra	Scorpio
Sagittarius	Cancer	Leo	Virgo	Libra	Scorpio	Sagittarius
Capricorn	Leo	Virgo	Libra	Scorpio	Sagittarius	Capricorn
Aquarius	Virgo	Libra	Scorpio	Sagittarius	Capricorn	Aquarius
Pisces	Libra	Scorpio	Sagittarius	Capricorn	Aquarius	Pisces

How to use this table: 1. Find your Sun sign in the left column.

2. Find your approximate birth time in a vertical column.

3. Line up your Sun sign and birth time to find your Ascendant.

This table will give you an approximation of your Ascendant. If you feel that the sign listed as your Ascendant is incorrect, try the one either before or after the listed sign. It is difficult to determine your exact Ascendant without a complete natal chart.

2017 at a Glance

Ever since Saturn's trek through Sagittarius began in December of 2014, our collective attention has been trained on the big picture—that is, the rules, regulations, and accepted social mores by which we live our lives. The thing is, as recent events have proven, those rules and regulations—especially as they pertain to politics, religion, and education—seem to be badly in need of an update. Fortunately, if anyone is qualified to inspire us to rewrite anything official, it's Saturn, and in the sign of Sagittarius, he tends to have a far broader perspective than usual. As Saturn passes into his own sign of Capricorn in December of this year, we'll all finally begin to put together a plan and realistically decide exactly what needs to happen so that we can all get along, regardless of race, religion, sexuality, gender, or educational level. No, it won't be easy, and yes, there will be struggles, but with Saturn operating so powerfully in his own sign, there's no doubt it will happen.

And then there's Uranus—Mr. Unpredictable himself. Technically he's moved past the irritating squares that he and Pluto formed and just wouldn't release over the past few years, but that doesn't mean their feud has been settled. In fact, it's at this moment—during the separating square, that is, between Uranus in impulsive, impatient Aries and relentless Pluto in no-nonsense Capricorn—that we'll finally get to see exactly which point they were working so hard to drive home. It's not over yet, but we'll continue to witness the marriage of unadulterated freedom and respect for the rules.

Now, as for Neptune, the ultimate Water Goddess—well, she'll be just about halfway through Pisces by the end of the year, but even afterward, she'll continue on through Pisces for years, which is her very own sign, by the way. This planet rules liquids—like water, gas, and oil, for example—so it's really not hard to imagine the distribution of those resources becoming more and more Neptunianly confusing over the next decade—and maybe even sooner. Neptune breaks down boundaries and barriers and insists that we all get along and share—but with these three liquids, she has her work cut out for her. The good news is that Neptune's fondness for wireless communication will continue, bringing all kinds of imaginative, ultra-portable electronic accessories into our eager little paws. Just you wait and see what's coming up! This is the stuff that even the makers of *Star Trek* and *Star Wars* might have had trouble predicting.

When it comes to Pluto—well, his specialty involves the underground, but he doesn't just bury things. He's also a master at digging things up—secrets of a collective nature, for example—but he lets them lie there stewing until the time is right. He'll continue along on his path through Capricorn this year, exposing the follies and foibles of politicians and other authority figures, demanding answers and passing out consequences, even to—no, most especially to—those short-sighted and narrow-minded members of the rich and famous.

2017 SUN SIGN BOOK

Forecasts by
Kim Rogers-Gallagher

Aries

The Ram
March 21 to April 20

♈

Element: Fire	Glyph: Ram's head
Quality: Cardinal	Anatomy: Head, face, throat
Polarity: Yang/masculine	Colors: Red, white
Planetary Ruler: Mars	Animal: Ram
Meditation: I build on my strengths	Myths/Legends: Artemis, Jason and the Golden Fleece
Gemstone: Diamond	House: First
Power Stones: Bloodstone, carnelian, ruby	Opposite Sign: Libra
	Flower: Geranium
Key Phrase: I am	Keyword: Initiative

The Aries Personality

Your Strengths, Gifts, and Challenges

Yours is the first of the twelve signs, Aries, which certainly explains a lot. You love being the first to arrive and you're usually the first to leave, too. Being first means avoiding a line, and since waiting is tantamount to torture in your book, showing up early is the thing to do. Okay, so you're not exactly world-famous for being the very soul of patience. There's more to it than that. Being first takes a certain amount of bravery, one of your sign's most famous qualities. Aries is under the planetary rulership of Mars, the ancient Roman god of war, so adrenaline is like a drug for you, and dashing in where angels fear to tread certainly will spur production of that hormone. You probably also have a bit of a temper, but unlike many of us, once you've expressed your anger, you're able to forget the whole thing and move on. Besides, who has time to hang on to a grudge? You're assertive and fast-moving by nature, so your next goal is far more fascinating than anything in the past.

Speaking of goals, once you set your mind to something, there's only one way to go after it: in point A to point B fashion. When roadblocks get in your way, you pay very little attention to them. Obstacles of any kind are to be charged over and through—never around. Of course, all that red-hot energy is perfect for beginning new ventures but is not always ideal for finishing up. You'll feel best about yourself if you tackle that pile of unfinished projects in the corner with as much energy as you put into starting them. Clearing the decks of what's no longer useful makes room for pursuing something new—which just so happens to be your specialty.

Romance, Friendships, and Casual Relationships

Be fair. Warn anyone who decides to join you for a weekend adventure to expect to learn what truly being alive feels like! That goes for friends, acquaintances, and lovers alike. Anyone who wants to be with you had better have a taste for fire and passion, because you're the human equivalent of a spark plug. Keeping company with you requires a willingness to act spontaneously and switch gears quickly, so in friendships you tend to surround yourself with other fiery, adventuresome types, like Leo and Sagittarius, who'll also make terrific life partners—provided you two can settle down long enough to put down roots, that is. Your fire-sign partner comes with an added perk, however. They'll be more than happy to give you a run for your money in an argument, and since you're usually looking for someone who's equal parts lover and worthy opponent, these two signs seldom disappoint. Life with the air signs—Libra, Gemini, and Aquarius—can be fun, too, since the one thing fire loves more than more fire is being fanned higher by air. Expect these signs to excite and stimulate you, not just physically but also intellectually.

Career and Work

Beginnings are your business, Aries. Finishing? Not so much. For this reason, it's best for you to take on a profession that will allow you to switch gears fast, because once you're bored, you lose interest, and losing interest in your work won't ensure a long-lasting career of any kind. Of course, you might also be quite happy with the idea of changing careers to suit your current passion. That's just fine if it makes you happy and keeps food on the table and a roof over your head, but if you're after the kind of job security that it takes years to earn, it would be better to consider professions like exercise training, welding and mechanics, or firefighting. Think of words that growl, via those R sounds—such as adrenaline, fire, exercise, assertion—and bring those things into your life on a daily basis.

Money and Possessions

You're so impulsive and fast-moving in all areas of life that it's tough to imagine you slowing down long enough to balance your checkbook or tend to your possessions, Aries. But once you've learned that accumulating and keeping track of a certain amount of money is necessary for you to have the things you want and makes it possible to pursue the activities you love, you'll work it out. And while you can definitely be an impulse shopper at times, you're just as likely to employ your love of the hunt to find exactly what you're after. The truth is, you don't mind heading off in search of toys that appeal to you or activities that are new and exciting. In fact, you probably think of it as a challenge—to find what you want in record time for a remarkable price, that is—so you're really more of a power shopper. Still, once you know where your prey is housed, you'll employ your standard m.o. to capture it: Point A to point B. Race to the mall, park at the entrance closest to your target, enter and attack—and heaven help that slow-moving sales clerk.

Your Lighter Side

Let's go back to that love of adrenaline we talked about earlier—because when it comes to having fun, that really only happens when your blood pressure jumps up a couple of notches. Movement, excitement, and at least a touch of unpredictability are absolutely necessary in some way for you to consider anything fun, but honestly, taking chances really does turn you on. Does this mean you might decide to stand up on one foot on your motorcycle as you speed down the highway toward your skydiving lesson? It sure might. In fact, I know an Aries who often does just that. But even if your taste for entertainment is a tad less risky, you'll still be drawn toward danger—like bungee jumping or rollercoasters, for example. At the very least, feed your adrenaline craving an action movie with lots of car chases, preferably interspersed with an equal amount of dramatic, fiery explosions. Needless to say, you're at the top of the list of signs who just can't tolerate being bored. Keep busy and you won't get cranky.

Aries Celebrities

Talk about being in good company! Check out this list of feisty, fun-loving, impatient, assertive, and totally unique people born under your sign: Russell Crowe, Kourtney Kardashian, Quentin Tarantino, Steven Seagal, Kate Hudson, Lady Gaga, Heath Ledger, Robert Downey Jr., Keira Knightley, Ewan McGregor, Pharrell Williams, Eddie Murphy, David Letterman, Maya Angelou, Rosie O'Donnell, The Undertaker. Not a quitter in the bunch. Aren't you proud to be an Aries?

Words to Live By for 2017

Being true to yourself is what really counts. This year, aim for that goal first.

The Year Ahead for Aries

Venus is in charge of matters of the heart and the pocketbook. Ordinarily, she zips through a sign from as little as three weeks to as much as two months, but this year, she's decided to spend more than three months in your very own sign, Aries. Now, this will put the Goddess of Love in your solar first house of personality and appearance, so obviously she'll be turning up the volume on your already irresistible fiery charm and adding heat and passion to all your relationships. That goes without saying. But she'll also be intent on coaxing you into a whole lot of impulse shopping, so be warned. In fact, from February 3 to April 2 and again from April 28 to June 6, you might want to bring a chaperone along on shopping trips to prevent you from whipping out your plastic without just a few seconds of considered thought. Make sure you choose someone who won't be afraid to pry those cards out of your hand for safekeeping, too, because you won't exactly be a font of willpower. Of course, if you've been on the prowl for a big-ticket item for some time, you might just find it, but try to stay away from March 4 through April 15, when Venus will be moving retrograde.

The good news for your loved ones is that you'll be willing to spoil them in a very big way—and not only in terms of gift giving. Keep in mind that outgoing, generous Jupiter will be holding court in your solar seventh house of one-to-one relationships straight through October 10, all done up in partner-oriented Libra, so overindulging dear ones will come easily for you. Big changes might also be afoot with regard to your closest relationships, à la Jupiter's fondness for taking everything to the limit—and well past it, too.

If you're involved and thinking of settling down, bet you'll make your feelings known during Venus's stay in your sign. Likewise, if you're no longer feeling satisfied, the combination of freedom-loving Jupiter in your seventh solar house and Venus in your own restless sign will probably be the straw that breaks the camel's back. If you're attached and happy about it, during this time frame you might also want to keep that chaperone we talked about on retainer—and close by your side when you're socializing without your sweetheart. Venus and Jupiter are Mr. and Ms. Feelgood, the heavens' two most pleasantly indulgent planets, and when they're working together, resisting anything or anyone delicious can be tough, to say the least. And when Jupiter moves into sexy, possessive Scorpio on October 10, he'll be setting up shop in your solar eighth house of shared finances and intense experiences, which could mean the results of your decisions will hit home—big time. Aim toward making those results positive by making sensible choices.

Saturn

Serious Saturn will continue on his trek through your solar ninth house of long-distance travel, advanced education, and opinions, Aries, urging you to get involved and take a stance with regard to a topic or cause you firmly believe in. It's time to put your money where your mouth is—or your energy, at least. Your natural courage will be a big help and may impress someone with a large degree of political or social influence—possibly even enough to change their mind on an important issue. If you need advice or counsel from a higher-up, elder, or other authority figure, you'll likely find them more than willing to go out of their way for you, especially if you're trying to make a name for yourself in your chosen field. Listen carefully to their suggestions and recommendations. When Saturn sets off for Capricorn and your solar tenth house of career, professional matters, and higher-ups on December 19, you might find yourself in a position of authority, due in no small part to the wisdom and guidance of your mentor. It's important to remember that while Saturn doesn't pass out goodies like generous Jupiter does—just because you're such a good kid, that is—he most definitely does give credit where it's due. Rewards, too. Preparation is the key, and hard work is necessary to reap these Saturnian pats on the back. But if you apply yourself, follow the rules, and pay attention, before too long you'll be in a position to become a mentor yourself.

Uranus

Uranus is hands down the most unpredictable energy in the heavens. That's one of the very few things all astrologers agree upon. And here's another: when he's in the neighborhood of one of our planets, there's really no telling what might happen—only that it will be the very last thing on Earth—or anywhere else, for that matter—that you'd ever have expected. But I don't have to tell you all that, do I? You've been dealing with this guy in your very own sign since 2010, so at this point, you've probably gotten used to living with a degree of uncertainty—to say the very least! This year, however, as he storms through the last third of your sign, those of you who were born between April 8 and 19 will feel his effects quite...well, let's just say "dramatically." The good news is that your natural love of adrenaline will make this transit much easier for you than many of us. Uranus's visit to the Sun feels like a nonstop earthquake, complete with aftershocks that roll in just when you thought it was safe to come out. The good news is that although lots and lots of things will change—and suddenly, too—once this transit is over, you'll look back on it as one of the most liberating periods in your life. Whatever is holding you back from becoming your truest self is about to make a quick exit. Cooperation is your best bet. Never mind just letting go of what's no longer working, be it relationships, jobs, possessions—whatever. Take charge! Fling it all away, wipe your hands on your jeans, and go have a look in the mirror at a whole new you.

Neptune

If you were born between March 27 and April 3 and you've been feeling a bit confused lately by circumstances and events beyond your control—not to mention the extremely odd behavior of a certain someone you thought you knew—you really shouldn't beat yourself up about it. It seems that the lovely lady Neptune is making a semisextile aspect to your Sun as she passes through Pisces, which just so happens to be the sign she considers her home turf and the place where her charms and illusions are most potent. The thing is, semisextiles aren't famous for being especially dramatic, so as I said, feeling a bit confused—as opposed to totally befuddled—will probably be the worst of it. But let's not forget that Neptune's specialty is subtlety, so it may be that little things you never really noticed before will begin to bother you now. For example, it may be much easier than usual for you to feel bruised by an unintended offense, and it's far more likely that you'll recoil from harsh words, bright lights, and unpleasant sounds or odors. That's okay. Yes, you're an Aries, and yes, you're tough, but this transit is all about listening to the whispers of your subconscious. In some way, you're beginning to mellow, so if your skin is a bit thinner than usual, so be it. Back away from what's hurtful, offensive, or bewildering. Not everything has to be a battle.

Pluto

Pluto's transits by square aspect often usher in power struggles, Aries, and he's been forming that aspect to your Sun sign for nine-ish years now. He's also been passing through Capricorn and your solar tenth house of authority figures, so it's not hard to imagine you having a few spats here and there with the powers that be, especially if a certain elder or higher-up seems to be unduly pressuring you. If you were born between April 4 and 11, you're probably feeling that pressure right around now and are jee-ust about ready to initiate a serious confrontation—if for no other reason than to alleviate the pressure. The thing is, Pluto's visits are meant to inspire us to either take control of situations that make us feel powerless or, if that's not possible, to at least put some distance between ourselves and all that unpleasantness. It's probably time for you to make a decision along those lines, and although career matters and issues having to do with your public profile are most likely on the front burner, your closest personal relationships will likely come into play as well. It's time to evaluate your priorities and adjust the weight of your responsibilities so they're actually bearable. If you're feeling manipulated or controlled, remember, only you can change that. Life is short. Get yourself free.

How Will This Year's Eclipses Affect You?

Eclipses are celestial exclamation points. They amp up the volume on ordinary life whenever they occur, but the signs and degrees they activate also bring along events and circumstances that are quite intense. Eclipses occur in pairs, six months apart. Solar Eclipses are super-charged New Moons. They bring the Sun and Moon together, marking peak times for planting spiritual seeds and announcing intentions of all kinds known to the Universe. Lunar Eclipses are high-energy Full Moons, and like these monthly oppositions between the Sun and the Moon, they signal times of dramatic culmination and fulfillment. Here's where and how 2017's eclipses will affect you most.

In 2017, the first set of eclipses will arrive in February. On February 10, a super-emotional Full Moon will form a Lunar Eclipse in the sign of Leo, which just so happens to be your solar fifth house of playtime. Now, Leo just loves to love and be loved, so affairs, casual relationships, recreational pursuits, and fun times with playmates and kids are all on the agenda for you. Oh, and if ever there was a perfect time to launch a creative project, this is it. Put your talents to work for you. You might be able to turn a much-loved hobby into a source of income this year.

On February 26, the first Solar Eclipse will occur, all done up in woozy, dreamy, highly intuitive Pisces. This lunation will bring the Sun and Moon together in your solar twelfth house of secrets, and since new beginnings are the specialty of New Moons, you might want to think twice before you engage in anything that's not quite fit for public consumption. What may seem like a one-time indiscretion could turn into a habit or addiction before you realize it. Keep your wits about you, and consult with someone you trust unconditionally, especially if your intuition tells you you're treading in dangerous waters.

The second set of eclipses will occur in August. On August 7, a Lunar Eclipse will arrive in the sign of Aquarius, turning on a bright light in your solar eleventh house of groups. You'll probably receive some rather startling news about a friend or learn something surprising about a group you are part of or are thinking of joining, but not to worry. As fond as you are of change—especially now, with unpredictable Uranus still in your sign—you'll be up for whatever the Universe tosses your way. This is a terrific time to pursue spiritual or metaphysical goals with kindred spirits.

The final eclipse of the year will be a Solar Eclipse. It will occur on August 21, and like the Lunar Eclipse of early February, Leo and your solar fifth house will be its location. If you set plans in motion with the Solar Eclipse in late February, you'll see the results now. That goes double for anything of a creative nature—which includes procreation, by the way. The arrival of a new family member could be announced or a child may present you with some terrific news. If you're attached, be careful not to stray!

Aries | January

Relaxation and Recreation

Playtime will be hard to come by from January 18 through January 24, thanks to a testy square between hardworking, responsible Saturn and your ruling planet, energetic Mars. Just this once, try to be patient. Put in your time and get your chores done like a good little ram. You can grab a quick break on January 28 and 29.

Lovers and Friends

A pack of planets in dreamy Pisces will make their way through your dimly lit solar twelfth house of Privacy, Please this month, Aries, asking that you spend some time behind the scenes with those you completely trust and that you find yourself a confidant. Apologies will be easily accepted or extended on January 1, 12, 15, or 16.

Money and Success

The temptation to walk away from your current position or tell an authority figure what's what will be especially strong around January 10 and 11, especially with the Full Moon in emotional Cancer set to turn up the volume on your feelings on January 12. If the time is right and you know it, waiting will be out of the question. Just say it.

Tricky Transits

Navigating financial waters with a partner, be they romantic or professional, will be especially tricky around January 26. Your first impulse will be to spend or invest more, possibly to regain recent losses, but that really isn't the way to go. Be sure you have your facts straight before you reach for your checkbook or plastic.

Rewarding Days

3, 4, 5, 8, 20

Challenging Days

10, 11, 15, 17, 19, 31

Aries | February

Relaxation and Recreation

Don't count on getting much rest this month, Aries. Venus and Mars will join Uranus in your sign to amp up your energy level, big time—especially when it comes to flirtations, romance, and passion of the one-to-one variety. New friends who'll be around forever are waiting in the wings. Don't rule anyone out because their appearance is a tad odd.

Lovers and Friends

Love at first sight. Does it really exist? Well, if it does, Aries, you'll be able to tell us all about it—and soon, too. With both magnetic Venus and your passionate ruler, Mars, in your sign, there's no romantic time to waste. If you're already in love, you two may have a few spats, but provided it's nothing serious—well, what fun making up will be!

Money and Success

If you're ready to talk turkey with a higher-up about that raise, bonus, or promotion—or about giving you more freedom on the job—schedule the meeting as close to February 23 as possible. Authority figures will be open to even the most outrageous ideas. Do you want to work hours that are comfortable for you or work from home? Now's the time to make your case.

Tricky Transits

The emotional Moon will jump into a testy situation with expansive Jupiter, shocking Uranus, and no-nonsense Pluto on February 8, Aries, activating your solar chart in a very big way. If you've been mulling over a major decision, especially if it involves a career issue, this may well be the time you stop thinking and start acting.

Rewarding Days

9, 11, 13, 16, 20, 23

Challenging Days

7, 8, 10, 15, 21

Aries | March

Relaxation and Recreation

Five of the ten planets will spend at least some of March in your energetic, assertive sign, Aries, so once again, rest won't be easy to come by. The good news is that you'll feel like Super Aries—able to leap tall buildings, soar higher than any plane, etc. Superpowers aren't bestowed very often, you know. Your mission is to channel these temporary gifts in positive directions. Help someone.

Lovers and Friends

Well, Aries, loving Venus has decided to spend another month in your sign and your solar first house. Yes, your sex appeal will be running on high. The tough part is—well, could be—that Venus will turn retrograde on March 4, and issues involving old loves will rear up, demanding to be solved. That goes double if you were born close to April 3

Money and Success

The Full Moon on March 12 will shine her bright light into your solar sixth house of work-oriented matters. She's all done up in hardworking, humble Virgo, so if you've been quietly doing your job, not expecting any kudos—but maybe kinda wishing someone would notice what you've done—well, this is the time you'll make those headlines.

Tricky Transits

Mercury and the Sun will take turns squaring serious Saturn on March 12 and March 17, Aries, bringing up power struggles with authority figures and squabbles with higher-ups. Sit tight and behave yourself. The better you can hold your tongue and keep your patience, the more permanent your rewards will be. Think long-term goodies and smile pretty.

Rewarding Days
5, 18, 20, 25, 26, 27

Challenging Days
2, 11, 12, 17, 23

Aries | April

Relaxation and Recreation

Venus will spend most of the month in woozy, dreamy, and oh-so-sentimental Pisces, Aries, which just so happens to be your solar twelfth house of retreat and recuperation. You'll feel the need to break away from the madding crowds quite often this month, at times simply to recharge your batteries through a little quality time alone with yourself— or one delicious companion you trust above all others.

Lovers and Friends

Speaking of delicious companions, Aries, look to the Full Moon in Libra and your solar seventh house on April 10 to bring along yet another applicant for the much-envied honor of being your one and only. Does this mean you will, in fact, settle down? Maybe. Maybe not. But with expansive, excessive Jupiter on board, if you do sign up, you'll jump in with both feet.

Money and Success

If you've been working with a partner to create and maintain a business, you two can make leaps and bounds together on April 10. The Full Moon in your solar seventh house will get together with generous, outgoing Jupiter to provide you with all the tools you need to succeed. If you're looking for a partner, regardless of why, get out there and mingle.

Tricky Transits

On April 8, you may have the feeling that what you have and what you love are being challenged—so much so that even if no one has said or done anything directly, you'll want to take steps to protect you and yours. Honestly? That's not a bad idea. Your antennae will be running on high. Listen to the voice of your subconscious.

Rewarding Days

1, 6, 7, 10, 17, 24, 28

Challenging Days

3, 4, 8, 21

Aries | May

Relaxation and Recreation

Relaxation could be tough to come by this month, Aries—but for only the most delightful of reasons. It seems that charming Venus will spend the month in your sign and your solar first house of personality and appearance, making you quite the hot commodity. If you're single, better double up on those vitamins and catch a nap whenever you can.

Lovers and Friends

Loving Venus is set to meet up with outgoing, excessive Jupiter on May 19. You'll find yourself staring at your current partner for no reason other than how happy they make your eyes—not to mention your heart. If you've been thinking about taking the plunge and becoming monogamous—well, it's happened with far less astrological inspiration, so prepare yourself for that conversation.

Money and Success

The Sun will stay on duty in your solar second house of personal finances until May 20, Aries. He's all done up in quality-conscious Taurus, so you'll definitely insist on quality, no matter where you're shopping or what you're after. Fortunately, thanks to loving Venus in your sign and Jupiter in Libra, you'll be able to charm just about any salesperson into just about anything.

Tricky Transits

Mercury will turn direct on May 3, Aries, and as per usual, you'll be quite ready to get moving again. The thing is, on May 9—the day before the Full Moon—Mercury will collide with shocking Uranus in your already impulsive sign and your solar first house of personality and appearance. Yes, moving forward is a good thing, but just this once, don't leap before you look.

Rewarding Days

2, 3, 4, 18, 19, 20

Challenging Days

5, 14, 27, 28

Aries | June

Relaxation and Recreation

The Sun will move into your solar fourth house of home and domestic matters on June 20, Aries, just three days before the New Moon in that same sign plants a seed of new beginnings in this tender, family-oriented place. Ready or not, a new arrival could be along shortly—which might not bode well for relaxation in the near future. Better kick back while you can.

Lovers and Friends

Venus will leave your fiery sign behind on June 6, Aries, but not to worry—the romantic fun is far from over. In fact, since Venus will be taking up residence in sensual, touch-loving Taurus—oh, and making contact with your fiery, passionate ruling planet, Mars, on June 9—you might find that a certain relationship that was on the casual side suddenly becomes a lot more intimate.

Money and Success

Venus will stay on duty in earthy, practical Taurus from June 6 through July 4, Aries. Now, she's the Goddess of Love, but she's also pretty handy with finances and possessions, and she'll hold court in your very own solar house of personal stuff for the duration. It might be a tad tougher to please you, but you'll stick to your guns until you have exactly what you want.

Tricky Transits

Getting your family members to agree with a recent decision you and your partner have announced might not be easy around June 24 or 25, Aries, especially if your family sees the situation as a case of you giving in to keep the peace. Of course, that whole "giving in" thing isn't something ordinarily associated with your sign, but it does happen. At least consider their arguments.

Rewarding Days

1, 2, 3, 9, 10

Challenging Days

4, 5, 15, 24, 25

Aries | July

Relaxation and Recreation

It's playtime, Aries! Venus sets off for fun-loving Gemini and your solar third house on July 4, just in time for a fabulous Fourth of July with friends and neighbors. But wait—there's more! Your ruling planet, Mars himself, will enter fiery, playful Leo on July 20, and the Sun will catch up with him just two days later. Variety will most definitely be the spice of your life—enjoy!

Lovers and Friends

The emotional Moon in team-oriented Aquarius and your solar eleventh house will get together with charming Venus and chatty Mercury on July 10, Aries, urging you to mingle, meet new friends, and catch up with anyone you regret having lost track of. You'll have two days to accomplish these aims, but no one says you can't do it by scheduling a whole lot of lunches over the coming weeks.

Money and Success

Well, Aries, that ship you've been waiting for is about to actually come in. On July 7, you'll receive some terrific news about a project you've been invested in for some time now. Before you make any decision based on this good fortune, however, keep in mind that even better news could come along on July 18 or 19. Don't be hasty. Sit back and enjoy your success.

Tricky Transits

On July 24, you may have to go back on a promise you've made to a loved one, and if so, it will break your fiery little heart. The thing is, in the long run it will be best for them if you do withdraw your support, so before you cave due to a case of the guilts, consider all the facts. You can't be all things to all people.

Rewarding Days

4, 5, 7, 10, 11, 19, 20

Challenging Days

8, 9, 23, 24, 25

Aries | August

Relaxation and Recreation

Your ruling planet, Mars, will spend the month in Leo, your dramatic fire-sign cousin, which will put this impossible-to-ignore energy in your solar fifth house of lovers, playmates, and fun times. Needless to say, if you're single, Aries, you might not be much longer. Don't scare them away by pursuing too hard, too soon. Take some time out from wooing for other adventures.

Lovers and Friends

Mysteriously fascinated with someone you've only thought of platonically in the past, Aries? Or is a current relationship not turning out to be what you'd expected? Well, if it's August 7 or 21, prepare yourself. You're being influence by a pair of eclipses, and these astrological teams refuse to be ignored. Prepare to take action. It's time to redefine your relationship.

Money and Success

Loving Venus has taken up residence in home and family-loving Cancer and your solar fourth house, Aries, and since she's in charge of not just love but also money, expect financial issues related to your domestic situation to keep you busy. No cause for concern, though. Could be you're finally able to invest in your own place, move to a larger home, or welcome a new arrival.

Tricky Transits

Two astrological Titans will square off on August 4, Aries, putting your relationship matters and your career at odds. Yes, you may need to tell a certain someone that your availability will temporarily be limited, but not to worry. Even if they're not happy about the situation initially, once you show up with tickets, presents, or news of a raise over the coming weeks, all will be forgiven.

Rewarding Days

2, 3, 13, 20, 22, 27

Challenging Days

4, 5, 7, 21, 23, 24

Aries | September

Relaxation and Recreation

The Sun, Mercury, Venus, and your ruling planet, Mars, will take turns passing through Virgo and your solar sixth house of work and daily duties this month, Aries, so days off won't be easy to come by. They're available, though, so if you've done your chores—to perfection, mind you—and you have personal days on tap, you'll probably be able to manage at least one day. Aim for the weekend of September 15.

Lovers and Friends

You're probably too busy to make any major plans, Aries, but that doesn't mean someone else won't do it for you—and insist that you enjoy yourself, at least for a little while. One of those someones might actually catch your attention in a very nice way, too—especially if you can tell they really took the time to pay attention to what was going on in your life.

Money and Success

Whether you're taking on overtime to pay off some bills in advance or just to clear up old debts that have been hanging over your head for far too long, keep at it and stay focused on your goal. By the end of the month, you'll be very proud of yourself, Aries. In fact, while you're at it, you might want to put away just a bit of cash for playtime next month.

Tricky Transits

Jupiter will make the trek into Scorpio on October 10, Aries, which will put him right smack dab in the middle of your solar eighth house of intimacy and shared finances for the entire coming year. Intensity will be the name of the game for you in this department. For a preview of coming attractions, pay attention to incidents that tweak your antennae on September 23 and 24.

Rewarding Days

11, 12, 14, 17

Challenging Days

13, 15, 16, 24, 25, 28

Aries | October

Relaxation and Recreation

You've been pushing yourself for over a month now, Aries, and it's most definitely time to take a breather—as soon as October 1, in fact. Just be sure all your bases are covered on October 5, 8, and 11. Higher-ups and authority figures will be doing some especially diligent inspections. If you're ready and all is well, this could mean a nice fat raise, bonus, or promotion.

Lovers and Friends

The Sun and Mercury will join up with Jupiter late this month, Aries, in your solar eighth house of shared resources, inheritances, and joint finances. If you've been out to impress the powers that be, this team will be happy to help. The thing is, you might also be fighting a mad attraction to a coworker. Force yourself to consider the consequences before you do anything rash.

Money and Success

If you don't have a five-year financial plan in place yet, Aries, it's a terrific month to get that show on the road. Jupiter will oversee the planning stages as of October 10, and the Sun and Mercury will join him in determined Scorpio by month's end. Your mission now is to lay the groundwork for financial security and stay on track—and with this team on board, it couldn't be easier.

Tricky Transits

You'll be more than ready to have some serious fun on October 31, Aries. The emotional Moon will remain on duty in Pisces right through the witching hour, and since Pisces just loves disguises and costumes, it won't take much for you to be just about invisible. Just be sure you're not hiding out because you're about to get yourself into some trouble—even if it's delicious trouble.

Rewarding Days
12, 13, 14, 19, 28, 29

Challenging Days
4, 5, 6, 9, 23, 27

Aries | November

Relaxation and Recreation

With Mars dashing through Libra, you won't be bored, Aries. Or lonely. Everything will be more fun with a partner, and partners will be easy to come by. Whether they be lover, spouse, or BFF won't matter on the fun scale, but do be careful. A casual flirtation with someone new and fascinating at a wedding or other large social gathering could end up being more than you bargained for.

Lovers and Friends

Your ruling planet, Mars, is currently storming through your solar seventh house of one-to-one relationships, Aries, demanding fire and passion from all your relationships. Now, this could mean there'll be some arguments, but you've never been one to walk away from that sort of thing, so no worries—but here's a thought. Why not channel all that red-hot energy into other activities? You'll still be tired, but much happier, I'll bet.

Money and Success

The Full Moon and the New Moon will trigger your solar money houses this month, Aries, so finances will be very much on your mind. You'll probably be ready to resume work on that five-year plan we talked about last month. If you can't manage five years, by the way, how about five months? Start now. Yes, really. If you can budget during the holidays, you can budget forever.

Tricky Transits

On October 16, Venus, the queen of feelin' good, will get together with dreamy, hypnotic Neptune to convince you that everything is already exactly the way you want it to be. The truly tricky part is that with these two in cahoots, believing is easy—even if it's not so. On the other hand, everything might actually be perfect. Keep an earthy, practical friend nearby to fan away the pink smoke.

Rewarding Days

10, 11, 12, 21, 25

Challenging Days

13, 14, 19, 30

Aries | December

Relaxation and Recreation

With Venus, Mercury, and the Sun dashing merrily through Sagittarius, laughter and lightheartedness will be easy to come by. You might end up laughing with someone with a delightful accent who has a part to play in your life, too, so if you hear a drawl, twang, or brogue that tickles your brain, introduce yourself. That goes double for December 9, 10, and 11.

Lovers and Friends

There's going to be an awful lot of playful, adventurous Sagittarius energy circulating in the heavens this month, Aries, so let's not even pretend it will be easy for you to muster up anything even remotely resembling willpower. Fortunately, Saturn will have your back on December 6, 7, and 8, when a good dose of self-restraint could actually put an end to a rift that's gone on too long. Think about what really matters.

Money and Success

Saturn will set off for Capricorn on December 19, putting him squarely in your solar tenth house of career and professional matters for the next two and a half years. This doesn't just *sound* serious, it *is* serious—and while Saturn's presence here bodes quite well for your odds at success, you'll need to settle down and maybe even deprive yourself of playtime every now and then. Before Saturn really gets going next month, go play. Seriously.

Tricky Transits

Mercury will start his thrice-yearly retrograde on December 3, Aries. He'll be tugging on your shirttail in the department of far-off family members, friends, and lovers for three full weeks, during which time you will experience a barrage of images, memories, and dopplegangers—until you finally take the hint and call that certain someone. Don't bother fighting it. 'Tis the season. Resisting sentimentality is futile. Just do it.

Rewarding Days

6, 7, 9, 10, 11, 20

Challenging Days

2, 5

Aries Action Table

These dates reflect the best—but not the only—times for success and ease in these activities, according to your Sun sign.

	JAN	FEB	MAR	APR	MAY	JUN	JUL	AUG	SEP	OCT	NOV	DEC
Move	12, 27					23					3, 18	
Start a class	12			24	4		4, 6, 7	7, 8		12, 13		3
Join a club		13, 23		21		13, 14		7, 8				
Ask for a raise			5, 7				6, 19, 24		5		27	
Get professional advice	27, 29	8	29, 30		18		19	22, 26, 27		12		
Get a loan		8	18, 19		9, 10	1			12	1, 3		
New romance		14, 20		28, 29	19					14	3	1, 17
Vacation		16, 27				8		20	27			31

Taurus

The Bull
April 21 to May 21

☉

Element: Earth

Quality: Fixed

Polarity: Yin/feminine

Planetary Ruler: Venus

Meditation: I trust myself and others

Gemstone: Emerald

Power Stones: Diamond, blue lace agate, rose quartz

Key Phrase: I have

Glyph: Bull's head

Anatomy: Throat, neck

Color: Green

Animal: Cattle

Myths/Legends: Isis and Osiris, Ceridwen, Bull of Minos

House: Second

Opposite Sign: Scorpio

Flower: Violet

Keyword: Conservation

The Taurus Personality

Your Strengths, Gifts, and Challenges

Okay, so your symbol is the Bull, and no, bulls aren't famous for backing off or being taken off course by anything less than an act of nature. So maybe that's where this whole "stubborn" thing came from? Well, yes, that's certainly a part of it, but you're also a fixed sign, and fixed signs aren't easily dissuaded from following the paths they've chosen. You're an earth sign, too—so let's think for a moment about what it might be like to move a pile of heavy, solid earth. Yep. That would be you when you've made up your mind, and no amount of heavy earth-moving machinery will get you to change your mind until you've decided that's the thing to do. In the meantime, any project you've begun will take up absolutely every ounce of your attention and effort—which is the sort of trait that makes for a person who's reliable, thorough, and practical—not to mention determined.

It's that determination to succeed, achieve, and become prosperous that keeps you doggedly on your path—and there's absolutely no one or nothing that can pull you aside unless you go along willingly. That determination to stick with the plan doesn't always work in your favor, though. Watch out for a tendency to fall into comfy routines that can turn into ruts without you realizing it, and do spoil yourself with wonderful treats on a regular basis. Your ruling planet, Venus, just loves the richest and most luscious of sensory delights—nothing but the best, that is—and she's passed this down to you, along with the ability to sniff out quality. Oh, and you're a money magnet, too.

Romance, Friendships, and Casual Relationships

Well, Taurus, if no one's ever told you, let me be the first: you're delicious. Your opposite sign, Scorpio, is usually given sole astrological rights to the word "sexy," but...well, truth be told, you're every bit as magnetic, and just as focused on having and keeping the partner who pleases your senses, too. Your talent in the department of dimly lit romance is also quite legendary, so it's no wonder that you're seldom alone—and only when you want to be. Venus, the Goddess of Love, is your ruling planet, so it's easy to see how you might already be packing some serious magnetism. But you're also an earth sign, and earth signs certainly do know how to enjoy all the sensory goodies life on this delightful planet provides—which, of course, includes charming, sensual partners. So once you find someone who fits the bill, you'll invest everything you've got to make it work—and the longer you've been together, the more effort you'll put into keeping it going. The other earth signs, Virgo and Capricorn, can be comfortable matches for you, and both they and home-loving Cancer could make excellent choices for long-term, sturdy, practical relationships—in other words, if you're looking to put down roots, be they personal or professional. If you're craving excitement, however, find yourself a Scorpio with a twinkle in their eye.

Career and Work

Fine music. Money. Art. "Real" art, that is—the kind you find in a museum or gallery. Gourmet food. Glamour and beauty. If you can find a way to pursue even one of these and be successful, you'll be a very happy little Taurus. If you can combine two or more, so much the better. Your specialty is knowing what brings pleasure to the five senses and finding a practical way to provide it for others. Of course, the aesthetic side of you would ideally like to be in pleasing surroundings while you're working on the project, so make it a practice to keep your work area not just practically arranged but also physically appealing. You'll always be far more creative in a pretty place than in a plain gray cubicle.

Money and Possessions

Let's go back for a second to Venus, your patron ruling planet who wants you to have nothing less than all the absolute best that life has to offer—in all physical departments. She's the reason you so love nice stuff—like cutting-edge electronics that just came out yesterday, designer clothes, and artwork that obviously didn't come from a department store. You take pride in choosing quality over quantity every time. This materialistic fondness came to practical little you along with a realization, however—that you'd have to work for the money to have all those wonderful things. Now, working does tend to interfere with one's social schedule, as you also came to realize early on, I'm betting. But, fine. Your attitude is that if you have to work hard to play hard, well, then, that's what's got to be done. For that reason, you tend to tackle work by thinking of it as a way to accumulate resources. This thorough, no-nonsense approach means you're a terrific worker who just won't quit, whether you're working for yourself or someone else. Your mission is to keep your priorities in order—which will often mean putting someone else's needs right up there with your own.

Your Lighter Side

Pleasure means different things to different people, Taurus, and many of us aren't really sure how to go about pursuing it. You, however, have no such problem. You're an expert at finding physical delights and comforts, like quality music venues, mom and pop restaurants that are just unbeatable—and, closer to home, that sweet-smelling spot just behind your sweetheart's ear. When you're out for fun, then, it absolutely must involve having at least one of your senses absolutely tickled with delight. Don't forget, however, that the best things in life really are free. Make time to take in the aesthetic beauty of a sunrise or sunset, and in spring, go outside after it rains. That deep, rich scent is Taurus. Take it in.

Taurus Celebrities

Speaking of sensual, sexy artists and mega-talented music makers, take a gander at this list of celebs who were born under the sign of Taurus: Stevie Wonder, Penelope Cruz, Adele, Barbra Streisand, Dwayne "The Rock" Johnson, Ella Fitzgerald, Al Pacino, Uma Thurman, Billy Joel, Cher, and Bono. Oh, and speaking of being a money magnet—like, we're talking *serious* money—did I mention Mark Zuckerberg? Or George Clooney? Or Wayne Dyer?

Words to Live By for 2017

I stand by all my decisions and only make promises I can keep.

The Year Ahead for Taurus

Back in September of 2016, Jupiter set off for your solar sixth house of work and health, Taurus, where he'll continue holding court straight through October 10 of 2017. Now, ever since Jupiter arrived—because, after all, this guy is famous for his knack for inspiring excess—you've either been overdoing it at work (in which case, somebody who loves you is probably none too pleased with this whole missing-in-action situation) or overdoing it physically in one way or another. It could be you've completely forgotten about watching your weight and exercising because you really haven't had much free time. Or you might be grabbing all the overtime you can handle, which would make perfect sense, since you always strike while the iron is hot when there's money to be made. Still, the state of your health and the time it takes to nurture your relationships with family and other loved ones is an energy investment that's equally worthy of your time. Your mission this year is to learn to juggle it all, and with Jupiter in Libra, the sign that's mastered restoring balance, you have an excellent shot at the title. In addition, you might want to keep in mind that once Jupiter heads off into Scorpio in October, he'll be in your solar seventh house of one-to-one relationships, so you'll be every bit as into your relationships with dear ones as you are into your work at the moment. Anyway, the point is that whatever you can do now to keep things on an even keel will most certainly count for brownie points next year, so store 'em up.

Now, let's talk about the lovely lady Venus, the head of the department of love, money, and stuff. She'll be in quite the impulsive mood for three months this year, thanks to the fact that she'll be passing through Aries, a sign that's never been especially famous for waiting, pausing, or hanging on for just a second. No, Aries planets are red-hot bullets, packed with energy that goes from point A to point B, and Venus is all about feeling good. You see what I'm getting at here? She's your ruling planet and she's infused you with her fondness for feeling fabulous in all sensory departments. Basically, from February 3 through April 2 and again from April 28 through June 6, despite your well-earned reputation for evenhandedness, practicality, and even thrift, you'll be a lot more likely to throw caution to the wind, both financially and romantically. No one's saying that either of those urges would be a bad idea, especially since if anyone has killer intuition in both those areas, it's you. The thing is, with Jupiter encouraging you to work hard and play superperson on the job and Venus (your astrological commanding officer) telling you to actively pursue and obtain whatever you want that feels good, you might need to be reminded to rest every now and then. Well, this is that. Work hard. Play hard. But please don't leave your king-sized pillow-top mattress with the huge-numbered Egyptian cotton sheets and the ultra-dreamy pillows unused. (I know. That was sneaky. But I really do want you to rest.)

Saturn

Saturn will remain in Sagittarius and your solar eighth house until December 19, Taurus, which still gives him just about an entire year to wrap things up and be sure all is settled here. Now, this house is where the side of you that specializes in intimate matters lives, but issues related to joint finances and shared resources are most definitely a big part of it, too. With Saturn making his presence known, you may have had to take on more money-oriented responsibilities over the past two-ish years, such as managing the finances of a group you're a part of or tending to the needs of a dear one who's no longer capable of handling things on their own. Fortunately, managing money just happens to be one of your specialties, so even if that situation continues throughout this year, you're more than qualified to handle it. The amount of time it takes may cut into your social and recreational life, however. But let's get back to your relationships—the closest ones, that is. If things have been strained between you and your partner and you haven't yet addressed it, better get right on that. Even if things are terrific, it's a great time to lay down some ground rules for the future. Who's responsible for what? Make sure you're clear about what you expect from each other and that you're on the same page as far as where this thing is going, long term. If you're single, you might run into someone delicious who's quite a bit older or younger than you. Don't bother doing the math. Focus on what you have in common, not what sets you apart. More than one May-December relationship has turned out just fine.

Uranus

Startling Uranus has been storming through impulsive Aries and your solar twelfth house of secrets since 2010, Taurus, causing quite a ruckus in this ordinarily very quiet place. Needless to say, you've probably come to understand that most, if not all, secrets don't always stay that way forever. Now, whether you learned this the hard way or it just suddenly came to you as a flash of insight—one of Uranus's specialties, by the way—doesn't really matter. The thing is, you've no doubt discovered by now that if you have something you'd like to keep to yourself, the only way to do that is not to share it at all—or, if necessary, to share it only on a need-to-know basis. The thing is, Venus is set to keep company with Uranus in Aries for three months, and where the Goddess of Love and Money goes, attention follows—which goes double because she's your astrological ruler. You might, then, either hear some gossip that's totally delicious or be the subject of a rumor. Your mission is to be anonymous whenever possible and not get yourself in trouble even when you believe you absolutely can't be seen. If you were born between May 9 and 20,

Uranus will be forming a semisextile aspect to your Sun, so all this goes double for you—but you'll need to pay attention to very subtle clues the Universe tosses your way. Oh, and since Uranus loves computers, be especially vigilant about online friendships, especially if you can tell that they're moving toward actual human contact.

Neptune

Your solar eleventh house of friendships and group affiliations has been playing host to spiritual, woozy Neptune since 2011, Taurus, so spiritual and metaphysical groups have probably been a very big part of your world of late. You're very well rooted on the material level, but Neptune encourages us to shuffle quietly away from anything physical when she's in the neighborhood, so you may have gotten yourself involved lately with a spiritual, religious, or mystical group. Oh, and right about now, you may be having doubts about the whole thing. Well, relax. If you're involved because you share a belief system with a current peer group, it's all well and good—and to be honest, it might be that they'll lead you along a path toward a very spiritual and successful future. On the other hand, when Neptune is on duty, just about everything sounds like a good idea. If that little tiny voice in the back of your head tells you to jump ship, then doing just that—even if it seems crazy—might not be such a crazy thing. Listen up. If your intuition tells you all is well, then go ahead and jump. Confidently. Oh, and Neptune loves romance, by the way, and she's an expert at conjuring it, too. If you were born between April 29 and May 5 and you think you're in love, even though you may be extra-sure, you should probably wait just a bit to determine whether or not it's true. You may have selected a reasonable facsimile of what you really want because you want to be in love. Don't do that. Patience now will mean being truly contented down the road.

Pluto

Well, Taurus, you've been dealing with the nonstop, relentless energy of all-or-nothing Pluto in your solar ninth house of long-distance travel, education, and higher beliefs ever since he set off for career-oriented Capricorn in early 2008. Now, this guy doesn't fool around when it comes to professional matters, and you don't either, so if you haven't become professionally qualified in your chosen field as of yet, you really should get yourself started on that path. It's time to think about long-term, big-picture goals, not just how to fund your next wonderfully hedonistic extravaganza. That goes double over the coming year for all of you born between May 5 and May 11, but not to worry. Pluto will form an easy trine to your Sun, and trines are notoriously good at producing a big payoff for very little effort. The thing is, they're also notoriously lazy, and while you're not—as a rule—you might feel pretty comfy right around now. Don't forget about your five-year plan. In fact, come up with a ten-year plan and get started. Whatever you have to do to become officially qualified to do what you love to do, get out there and do it. Get your class hours or internship done, then get your official papers signed and stamped. Be prepared to work, though. No matter what certificate or official document you're after, if Pluto's involved, you really can't cut corners.

How Will This Year's Eclipses Affect You?

Eclipses are celestial exclamation points. They amp up the volume on ordinary life whenever they occur, but the signs and degrees they activate also bring along events and circumstances that are quite intense. Eclipses occur in pairs, six months apart. Solar Eclipses are supercharged New Moons. They bring the Sun and Moon together, marking peak times for planting spiritual seeds and announcing our intentions to the Universe. Lunar Eclipses are high-energy Full Moons, and just like these monthly oppositions between the Sun and the Moon, they signal times of dramatic culmination and fulfillment.

The first Lunar Eclipse of the year will occur on February 10 via the Full Moon in dramatic Leo and your solar fourth house of home and family. Now, this is the ultimate recipe for Drama with a capital D in your home, and you really don't care for that sort of thing—but nobody's saying it has to be unpleasant. If you've just finished a home-oriented project, you'll be wearing a big smile and enjoying the fruits of your labor. If you're just now considering redoing or rearranging something or even making major renovations—both on the physical and emotional realms—this is a terrific time to do your homework.

The first Solar Eclipse of the year will arrive on February 26, all done up in woozy, dreamy Pisces. This lunation will plant a supercharged seed in your solar eleventh house of group affiliations and kindred spirits, urging you to get busy, get out there and find your people. When Pisces energy is on duty, we often feel that we're rather isolated, but that doesn't have to be the case. Don't just sit around wishing you could share yourself with like-minded others. Every now and then, the

Universe opens a door—or sometimes a window—and allows us full, easy access to those folks. This is one of those times. All you have to do is mingle. Suffer through it.

On August 7, the second Lunar Eclipse will come along, wearing ultra-rebellious Aquarius. This lunation will activate your solar tenth house of career matters and dealings with authority figures, but it could also bring about a power struggle between your professional and personal life, especially if you've been pulling a whole lot of overtime and your loved ones are beginning to forget what you look like. On the other hand, you may have become a bit complacent lately and lost sight of what you really want for you and yours, long term—in which case, you can expect a conversation with a dear one to be quite the wakeup call.

On August 21, a Solar Eclipse will arrive in your solar fourth house—which, you'll remember, was the site of the Lunar Eclipse on February 10. Whatever plans you set in motion at that time regarding home, family matters, or your own emotional health will come to a close now, and you'll be given a chance to finish things up, wipe the slate clean, and start all over. Rest assured that whatever is ending really had to go. Bless it and dismiss it. Whatever is starting will need your careful hand to ensure that it reaches its full creative potential.

Taurus | January

Relaxation and Recreation

With loving Venus in dreamy, woozy Pisces this month, your solar eleventh house of friendships and group relationships will be a very spiritual and possibly very confusing place, Taurus. If you're already part of a metaphysical or religious group, circumstances may push you into rethinking your position, if not the reason for your connection to them. If you like what you see, you'll stay on. If not, don't feel guilty about withdrawing.

Lovers and Friends

Outgoing Jupiter will stay on duty in your solar sixth house of work-oriented relationships, all done up in sociable, partner-oriented Libra. Keep an eye out for a new coworker who's absolutely delicious. This house is all about playtime, so you really should make arrangements January 22, when the emotional Moon in playful Sagittarius will fire things up and provide an opportunity for adventure.

Money and Success

You're an earth sign, Taurus, so your material instincts are pretty much right on and you don't often need any advice about when to take financial action. Still, though, if you're negotiating a big contract or trying to land a major position you've been training for, it wouldn't hurt to plan your meetings and interviews around January 6, or better still, around the Full Moon of January 12.

Tricky Transits

Mercury will spend the first week of the month retrograde, Taurus, backing up through your solar eighth house of shared resources and intimate matters—all done up in excessive Sagittarius, by the way. Whether you're negotiating responsibilities related to your home situation with regard to your primary partner or ironing things out with your business partner, wait until after January 12 or 13 to sign on the dotted line.

Rewarding Days
1, 2, 3, 6, 12, 14, 20

Challenging Days
7, 8, 9, 19, 26, 31

Taurus | February

Relaxation and Recreation

The Moon in partner-loving Libra will be on duty in your solar sixth house of work on Valentine's Day, Taurus, so if you're done flirting with that delicious new workmate, this would be the perfect time to put your money where your mouth is. Invest in a card at least—or better still, have lunch. You won't know what's really there until you get away from the office.

Lovers and Friends

Your ruling planet, loving Venus, will set off for fiery Aries on February 3, joining passionate Mars and startling Uranus in that same sign. Now, this trio will hold court in your solar twelfth house all month, a place where Privacy, Please is the order of the day. You might spend a bit more time than usual behind the scenes, but it's likely going to be for delightful reasons.

Money and Success

With Venus in impulsive Aries, this might not be the best time for you to make any long-term investments, and major impulse purchases will be tough to resist. You're usually pretty darn practical and always out for nothing but the best, but with this team on duty, you might be short on willpower. Take a friend along on shopping trips to provide a voice of reason.

Tricky Transits

On February 8, the emotional Moon in Cancer and your solar third house of conversations and communications will form a testy grand square with three planetary heavy hitters. Prepare for an eye-opening chat with a loved one, possibly regarding children or changes to your home base—but don't worry. The Sun will team up with change-loving Uranus the next day to help you adapt, adjust, and move forward.

Rewarding Days
3, 4, 14, 15, 16, 19

Challenging Days
7, 8, 10, 21, 26

Taurus | March

Relaxation and Recreation

Your ruling planet, Venus, will stop in her fiery little Aries tracks on March 4, Taurus, and old friends could cross your path—even if they currently live in another state or on another coast. The same goes for old lovers. In fact, you might suddenly have the urge to reach out to the one who got away. Why not? Maybe they're not quite as gone as you'd imagined.

Lovers and Friends

Fiery, passionate Mars will set off for your sign on March 9, Taurus, turning up the thermostat in your solar first house of personality and appearance. Prepare for some fireworks, even if you're generally quite tough to rile up, and watch your temper as best you can. Your mission is to count to ten. Or maybe twenty, depending on the situation.

Money and Success

Venus will make her way retrograde through impulsive Aries all month, Taurus, so if you somehow resisted the urge last month to spend money on a whim without doing your homework first—well, that battle will continue. The good news, however, is that now that Venus is retrograde, if you did buy something and you're not happy with it, you can return it now. You did save the receipt, right?

Tricky Transits

A testy square between chatty Mercury and no-nonsense Saturn will combine forces with the Full Moon on March 12 to raise your blood pressure a notch or two, Taurus. If you've been simmering about something a friend said that seemed deliberately hurtful, try to have a rational conversation about it before things get out of hand. You could be wrong. Remember, Saturn plays for keeps.

Rewarding Days

5, 6, 7, 15, 16, 29

Challenging Days

9, 11, 12, 17, 18, 23

Taurus | April

Relaxation and Recreation

Your solar eleventh house of peer groups and like-minded others will be inhabited by lovely Venus for most of the month, all done up in woozy, dreamy, and oh-so spiritually inclined Pisces. Thanks to that legendary charm, if you're involved with a metaphysical or philosophical group, you might be called upon to take the wheel in the absence of the person who's usually at the helm.

Lovers and Friends

There are all kinds of ways to tell someone you love them, Taurus, and you're particularly good at every single one. So with Venus—your affectionate ruling planet—currently on duty in creative, romantic Pisces for the month, it's not hard to imagine you finding a wonderfully creative way to let a new admirer know that you care. Just don't forget to do the same for your tried and true friends.

Money and Success

On April 6, career-oriented Saturn will turn retrograde, Taurus, ready to help you take stock of your recent work performance. Fiery Mars in your very own sign will also form an easy trine aspect with intense Pluto that day, so if you really want to get noticed, update your resumé, with a professional if possible. It's time to think about recreating your professional image.

Tricky Transits

A day before Mercury stops dead in his tracks on April 9 to turn retrograde, two extremely testy squares will inject some tension into your primary relationships. You'll feel compelled to act immediately, but don't. You may not have all the info you need to make a sound decision. Cross your arms and sit tight. When has anyone ever been able to rush you?

Rewarding Days

6, 7, 16, 17, 26, 27

Challenging Days

8, 9, 10, 20, 21

Taurus | May

Relaxation and Recreation

This is your month, Taurus. With the Sun passing through your sign and your solar first house, you're the star of the show, at the top of everyone's guest list. As such, a full night's sleep will be tough to come by, but you'll be enjoying yourself too much to worry about it. No whining. Make yourself a cup of gourmet coffee and get yourself to your next social engagement.

Lovers and Friends

Around May 19, a new coworker could make quite an impression on you, Taurus—in a strictly nonprofessional way. Now ordinarily, you'd be able to resist the urge to get too close, too soon, but with your ruling planet, Venus—the Goddess of Love herself—all done up in impulsive Aries, your chances don't look all that good. Ah, well. If neither of you are involved, why worry?

Money and Success

Terrific news, Taurus. If you're looking to schedule an interview for a raise, bonus, or promotion, look no further than May 17, when the emotional Moon in inventive, one-of-a-kind Aquarius will trine lucky Jupiter in your solar sixth house of work. Be bold—and be sure everyone can see just how uniquely qualified you are for the job. That's it. You're pretty much golden.

Tricky Transits

On May 25, the New Moon in chatty Gemini will arrive, Taurus. She'll join forces with an edgy square between Venus in Aries and intense Pluto—and this is quite often the stuff that relationship-oriented rumors are made of. Keep your nose clean and your actions aboveboard. Avoid suspicion of any kind. Regardless of whether they're true or false, rumors are tough to kill.

Rewarding Days

2, 9, 23, 24, 31

Challenging Days

3, 5, 16, 27

Taurus | June

Relaxation and Recreation

Your ruling planet, Venus, will set off for your sign and your solar first house of personality and appearance on June 6, Taurus, and smooth sailing will become the order of the day. But with the Sun and Mercury in lively Gemini, you won't want to just float around on a raft. Adventure awaits you—and lots of fun conversations, too!

Lovers and Friends

After months of fun, impulsive encounters—both romantic and platonic—you're ready for a bit of stability in your life, Taurus, and it's recently occurred to you that weeding out a few unproductive relationships might be a good place to start. Well, you're absolutely right—and not to worry. Your tried and true friends will never be far.

Money and Success

On June 24, your ruling planet, Venus, will get into an easy trine aspect with Pluto—who just so happens to be wearing career-oriented Capricorn. If you've been waiting for the right time to oh-so-casually cross paths with a higher-up or authority figure, wait no longer. This is it. You can make terrific progress toward reaching your goals now. Be sociable, friendly, and genuine.

Tricky Transits

If you suddenly get the feeling that the powers that be are watching you at work, Taurus—well, you might be right, especially if it's June 15 or 19. The good news is that if you dot those i's and cross those t's, your rewards could be right around the corner.

Rewarding Days

1, 5, 6, 9, 24, 25

Challenging Days

4, 15, 19, 27, 28

Taurus | July

Relaxation and Recreation

One of your very favorite places to be is at home, Taurus, surrounded by all your dear ones and all your special things. You'll have plenty of time to enjoy them all this month, thanks to the Sun, Mercury, and, yes, even Mars, all of which will pass through home and family-loving Cancer. Your attention will definitely be drawn to your home turf. Take that vacation next month.

Lovers and Friends

And speaking of Mars in Cancer, let's talk about your solar third house of conversation and communications—and the fact that Mars is a pretty darn passionate fellow. If there's someone you've been eyeing for some time now and you still haven't let your feelings out, you won't be shy much longer. Mars isn't famous for inspiring patience—and it's been long enough, hasn't it?

Money and Success

You'll be in the mood to be entertained this month, Taurus, but you'll also want to stay as close to home base as possible. If you do spend any money to speak of, it will probably be on an entertainment center or on another electronic creature to add to your family's sizable entertainment inventory. Venus is in communicative Gemini, urging you to upgrade and not settle for anything less than the very best.

Tricky Transits

Don't even bother getting into an argument over religion, sports, or politics with a dear one this month, Taurus, especially around July 16. First off, you'll need to agree to disagree—and then to accept your dear ones as they are, even if you're mystified by their choices and beliefs. Relax. Let it slide. You have bigger fish to fry.

Rewarding Days
6, 7, 11, 14, 18, 19

Challenging Days
2, 9, 16, 17, 29

Taurus | August

Relaxation and Recreation

On August 27, outgoing Jupiter and cautious Saturn will come together in an easy, stimulating sextile aspect, the stuff that lucky encounters and fortunate occurrences are made of. In your case, their knack for putting us in the right place at the right time might mean you're about to meet someone who'll make both your brain and your soul happy.

Lovers and Friends

Mercury will spend the entire month in your solar fifth house of fun times and playmates, Taurus. While half of the month will feature Mercury moving retrograde, that doesn't mean you won't still have fabulous fun with someone you haven't seen in quite some time, regardless of exactly how long it's been since last you tripped the lights fantastic.

Money and Success

Mercury will turn retrograde in work-oriented Virgo on August 12, and since he tends to call our attention to what needs to be redone and he just so happens to be on duty in your solar sixth house, you may need to redo a project you thought was finished. No fair pouting. Just be sure it's done right this time around.

Tricky Transits

There will be two eclipses this month, Taurus, and since they'll be in stubborn fixed signs like your own, you may find it a bit tougher than usual to deal with changes that come your way via the outside world. No, you may not have arranged these changes, but yes, you will probably have to abide by them. Cooperation is your best bet.

Rewarding Days

1, 2, 3, 10, 13, 19, 27

Challenging Days

4, 5, 9, 15, 16, 18

Taurus | September

Relaxation and Recreation

Four planets will pass through your solar fifth house of playmates and lovers this month, Taurus. Obviously, you won't have a whole lot of time to relax, but for reasons as delicious as these, you won't mind a bit being just a tad tired—but extremely happy—as you toddle into work just a tad late. Don't make a habit of it. The late part, I mean.

Lovers and Friends

All that activity in your solar fifth house—including red-hot Mars, by the way—means that if you're inclined to socialize this month, your schedule will be on fire, Taurus. If you're more in the mood to hang out with your sweetheart at your place, however, that can work out just fine, too. There are all kinds of ways to use fiery energy.

Money and Success

You've gotten used to having solid Saturn in your solar eighth house of joint finances, so you probably haven't noticed all of the responsibilities you've accumulated over the past few years—only that you definitely have more now. In less than three months, Saturn will move on. So what can you do now to begin the process of lightening your financial load?

Tricky Transits

We all breathe a sigh of relief when we hear that Mercury has turned direct, especially if the previous three weeks have been tough. That's exactly how you'll feel on September 5, when Mercury finally does an about-face in your solar fourth house of emotions. Don't get too comfy just yet, though. Venus and startling Uranus have surprises in store for you on the home front on September 17.

Rewarding Days

2, 8, 9, 10, 12, 22

Challenging Days

3, 4, 5, 13, 16, 25

Taurus | October

Relaxation and Recreation

Venus and Mars will see to it that you continue to be busy for most of October, Taurus, but it will probably be because you're showing off a hobby or talent rather than just socializing for the sake of having fun. That's not to say you won't enjoy yourself, but there'll be chances to get out there and shine. Jump on them!

Lovers and Friends

With loving Venus on duty in your solar fifth house of lovers until October 14, you'll have plenty of company, Taurus—maybe even more than you're up for. Don't hesitate to refuse an offer if you're just not in the mood to go out. Silence—or good music played on a state-of-the-art system like yours—well, it's good for the soul.

Money and Success

It's time to tend to paperwork and official documents, Taurus, with an eye toward paring back your responsibilities and making things simpler and less expensive for you and yours. You'll need to cut back a bit in a month or so. Why wait for the Universe to insist? Take matters into your own hands. Bet there's at least one plastic card in your wallet you can live without.

Tricky Transits

Jupiter will slip off into Scorpio on October 10 after a year in sociable Libra and your solar sixth house of work. This could mean you'll soon need to go back to working alone, as opposed to having a partner to rely on. On the other hand, it may be that only the financial arrangements need to change. Just be sure they do.

Rewarding Days

1, 3, 12, 16, 18, 26

Challenging Days

4, 5, 6, 9, 10, 11, 23

Taurus | November

Relaxation and Recreation

Three planets will make their presence known in sexy Scorpio and your solar seventh house of one-to-one relationships, Taurus, so if you've been trying to keep your feelings for a certain delicious someone under wraps, that's probably not going to be possible much longer. In fact, the person may actually demand to know what's going on with the two of you. Confess!

Lovers and Friends

Mercury will dash off into funny, friendly Sagittarius on November 5, urging you to pull out all the stops and have some serious fun, Taurus. If someone invites you—yet again—to come out and play after work, why not go? Might be fun—and you might find that you're surrounded on a daily basis by many more kindred spirits than you'd realized.

Money and Success

Here's your two-minute warning, Taurus: if you have financial matters to put in order—especially if they involve a whole lot of paperwork—better get the wheels in motion now. Serious Saturn will leave your solar eighth house of shared finances behind next month, so you'll have to be ready to operate without that safety net you've had on hand for the last two to three years.

Tricky Transits

The New Moon on November 18 will activate your solar seventh house of intimate partnerships, Taurus, urging you to either take a certain relationship a step further or let it go. One way or the other, it's time to make a decision—and you know it. Make it as easy on yourself—not to mention others—as you possibly can.

Rewarding Days

3, 4, 9, 10, 11, 16

Challenging Days

7, 8, 13, 14, 19

Taurus | December

Relaxation and Recreation

Mercury will spend much of the month retrograde, so your holiday plans may or may not turn out as you'd imagined, Taurus. But since this chatty, friendly fellow is in funny, generous Sagittarius, even if you aren't where you thought you'd be, you'll enjoy the company you've found. Spontaneity is the order of the day.

Lovers and Friends

Your ruling planet, Venus, has set you up for a lovely month, Taurus. She'll be on duty in fiery, funny Sagittarius until December 25, urging you to make the most of the holiday season by surrounding yourself with outgoing, loving people—and there'll be no shortage for you to choose from. You may have more invitations than you can manage, but hey—it sure could be worse!

Money and Success

Table all matters that have anything to do with money until as late as possible this month, Taurus—and in fact, if you can manage to stall until next month, that would really be your best bet. You may not have all the information you need just yet to make the best decisions for you and yours.

Tricky Transits

Saturn will set off for earthy Capricorn on December 19, and even though you're also an earth sign and therefore quite quality-conscious, Taurus, this energy will turn up the volume on even your own choosy, practical tastes. The thing is, you may be trying to cut back on your expenses. The good news is that you'll learn how to cut corners without feeling even the teeniest bit deprived.

Rewarding Days

6, 7, 8, 10, 16, 20, 27

Challenging Days

2, 3, 13, 14, 21, 22

Taurus Action Table

These dates reflect the best—but not the only—times for success and ease in these activities, according to your Sun sign.

	JAN	FEB	MAR	APR	MAY	JUN	JUL	AUG	SEP	OCT	NOV	DEC
Move	12, 15			26	9	22, 23, 24	23					
Start a class	3	5, 6					7, 8		27		25, 27	2
Join a club			2, 27		12						1, 26, 29	
Ask for a raise	6, 20				10, 11			7		16		
Get professional advice	29	25		17		1, 3		27		8		
Get a loan		23	29		24		24	27				
New romance		3, 10		7, 10					15, 17	28, 29	3, 9	29
Vacation	1, 2		24, 25, 26				30					7, 8, 10

Gemini

The Twins
May 22 to June 21

Ⅱ

Element: Air

Quality: Mutable

Polarity: Yang/masculine

Planetary Ruler: Mercury

Meditation: I explore my
inner worlds

Gemstone: Tourmaline

Power Stones: Ametrine, citrine,
emerald, spectrolite, agate

Key Phrase: I think

Glyph: Pillars of duality,
the Twins

Anatomy: Shoulders, arms,
hands, lungs, nervous system

Colors: Bright colors, orange,
yellow, magenta

Animals: Monkeys, talking birds,
flying insects

Myths/Legends: Peter Pan,
Castor and Pollux

House: Third

Opposite Sign: Sagittarius

Flower: Lily of the valley

Keyword: Versatility

The Gemini Personality

Your Strengths, Gifts, and Challenges

Your astrological ruler is Mercury, the fastest-moving of all the planets. He's the guy who's often depicted with wings on his head and feet—which certainly explains a lot about your nature, Gemini. You're an air sign, for starters, so if you could, you'd probably spend your days soaring through the skies with the birds. As it is, you crave change and movement, both physically and intellectually, and when you don't get it—well, let's just say there's a whole lot of fidgeting, fiddling, and tapping goin' on. The only thing worse than boredom in your book is waiting, which is absolute torture for you, especially since you do tend to be rather short on patience in general. Obviously, biding your time and pacing yourself are two practices you've never seen the need to cultivate.

You're happiest when your mind is well fed and your body is in motion, hopefully at the same time, which makes you the ultimate multitasker. The funny thing is, while your ability to switch tasks midstream often makes you appear scattered to the average bear, you have no problem coming full circle to finish what you've started—eventually. Okay, so you can be pretty easily distracted at times—*Look! Kittens!*—and no, it's not hard to get you sidetracked. Still, it's this mental flexibility that allows you to notice even the tiniest of details, so pulling the wool over your eyes isn't usually an easy thing to do. Of course, since Mercury is also well known for being the Trickster, you don't have any trouble at all pulling a prank when you want to. You can tell a story better than most, learn quickly and easily, and have no problem passing along the information you've gathered to others. This makes you an expert communicator, teacher, wordsmith, and intellectual gymnast, and one of the most entertaining and flexible signs out there. Your mission is to keep your curious mind fed with only positive, productive information.

Romance, Friendships, and Casual Relationships

"Variety is the spice of life" was written just for you, Gemini, and it certainly does apply to your attitude about relationships. That's not to say that you can't be quite loyal and devoted when you're attached, but only that no one person will ever be able to satisfy your need for an extremely diverse collection of companions. You're the original social butterfly, always game to meet someone new and different. Needless to say, being your friend is easy and lots of fun, but anyone who wants to call you their own will have to enjoy flitting from group to group and person to person. Your brain needs a constant supply of new information and interesting conversation, and while you wouldn't be with anyone who bored you, keeping you occupied definitely isn't a one-person job. That said, freedom-loving Sagittarius and unconventional Aquarius often make excellent partners, especially because they also love to mingle and socialize. Of course, Libra is a fellow air sign and is definitely no slouch in the department of chatting, but they may tend to be a bit too possessive of your time and attention—at least, until they realize that holding on to you can only be done with an open hand.

Career and Work

Any task that lasts too long or keeps you from moving around simply won't do, Gemini. That sort of thing falls under the heading of Tedious, which is very close to Boring, and we all know how you feel about being bored. At any rate, there aren't too many of you who enjoy working in a carpeted cubicle, but that's not to say you can't pull it off if you have to. If your work is interesting—or better still, *fascinating*—you'll manage, especially if it involves being attached to a computer, phone, or other electronic gadget. In youth, you're often drawn toward jobs that require constant movement and conversation with a host of unique, constantly changing customers, like driving a bus—or better still, a cab, where your knack for finding shortcuts really comes in handy. Throughout your life, your gift for communication will also make you the perfect candidate for teaching and lecturing. You're personable and chatty—a natural for the hospitality field—so food service, customer service, and reception can also be fun. If you're in charge, your employees will adore you. Who else could make the daily grind so much fun?

Money and Possessions

Although you do tend to be impulsive in most areas of life, Gemini, when it comes to money, things can go either way. You'll be either extremely precise and meticulous—or extremely not. The thing is, you tend to view money as a necessary evil. You'd much rather be out and about enjoying the myriad experiences our lovely planet has to offer—but then, you can't do much of that if you don't have currency. You're quite resourceful, however, so if you don't have the cash you need to conjure up the gadgets you want and activities you're after, you'll find a way to get it. Might be teaching a class or doing some side work on computers, but you'll make it happen.

Your Lighter Side

Life is a celebration of the five senses in your opinion, Gemini, full of sights, sounds, colors, and activity, so just about anything can be fun for you, provided you haven't tried it before or it's something that changes enough to keep you fascinated. That includes games, puzzles, lively conversations, and unusual people with interesting backgrounds, of course, but you love to look at things, too—especially collections of things—so museums and galleries are at the top of your list. Carnivals, parades, and boardwalks will do the trick, too, since they're always jam-packed with humans of every shape and size, and again, you do appreciate variety above all else. Truthfully, however, you're happiest when you're learning or teaching—even if you don't realize you're doing it. You love to hear a good story, and you're pretty darn good at weaving one yourself. Be sure to choose playmates who are spontaneous and open-minded.

Gemini Celebrities

Their styles and specialties are vastly different, but none of these celebrities have a problem expressing themselves—and it's impossible not to pay attention when they clear their throat. These are your kindred spirits, Gemini, a multifaceted collection of expert communicators: Kanye West, Angelina Jolie, Clint Eastwood, Joan Rivers, Russell Brand, Morgan Freeman, Anne Frank, Anderson Cooper, Venus Williams. Oh, and Donald Trump. Did I mention the part about speaking your mind?

Words to Live By for 2017

Balancing work, play, and relationships is my priority.

The Year Ahead for Gemini

Generous Jupiter set off for charming, partner-oriented Libra and your solar fifth house last September, Gemini, marking the beginning of a year's worth of love, luck, and lollipops, delivered to you courtesy of playmates, children, and lovers. Yes, it's probably been quite delightful, and yes, you've had more than your share of wonderful experiences. Well, it's not going to change anytime soon—not until October, in fact—so relax and continue enjoying yourself. No matter what else happens to be going on in your life, you can count on these folks to warm your heart, show you how much you're loved, and, in the process, restore your faith in the Universe. That goes double for those of you who were born around June 4 or 14, since Jupiter will spend a bit longer in your corner of the neighborhood this year, forming an easy, cooperative trine aspect with your Sun. All kinds of delicious experiences will come your way, and opportunities to turn your hobby into a part-time job (at the very least) will abound.

The thing is, trines are lazy aspects, so if you don't take action, very little will happen. If you do take action, however, expect for things to go your way very, very easily. This applies to romance, by the way, so if you're drawn to someone, stop staring and make your move. If you're seeing someone and deliriously happy, you two might decide to take advantage of Jupiter's expansive nature and take your relationship to a whole new level—in which case, congratulations! The same applies if you're attached and welcoming a new family member or enjoying a brand-new home. Oh, and lest I forget, this house also has quite a bit to do with speculation and Jupiter just so happens to be Mr. Lucky, so if you're so inclined, pick up a lottery ticket around February 6 or June 9. Don't get crazy, though. It only takes one to win. Now, loving Venus will spend three months in fiery, impulsive Aries this year, which will put her in your solar eleventh house of groups—along with startling Uranus, by the way—so if you've been searching for a new group of friends, a casual (and possibly quite appealing) acquaintance could introduce you to your new peer group, especially during February, March, and May. Get out there and mingle!

Saturn

Saturn will continue on his path through your solar seventh house of one-to-one relationships straight through December 19, Gemini, so you're probably at the tail end of a very important life lesson regarding what you want—and, more importantly, what you don't want. That goes for all kinds of relationships, be they personal or professional. The positive bonds you've created and nurtured with others will become even more constant, steady, and stable, and you'll be pleased and contented with the commitments you've made. The thing is, this is the end of a two-and-a-half-year trek, and this serious fellow is famous for stubbornly driving his point home, no matter what it takes, so anyone who's had a negative influence on you will probably have to go, if they haven't already. At this point, however, even if you've been sorely disappointed, you should be able to see the reasons that others may have acted the way they did. Are you beginning to understand the signals you're sending out that tell others you'll allow yourself to be treated this way? If you checked the "yes" box, you're seeing the reality of the situation, which is Saturn's true mission. His methods often leave something to be desired, but Saturn isn't really such a bad guy. He's just determined to get you to wake up, smell the coffee, and apply the brakes when you see this sort of thing starting to happen again.

Uranus

If you were born between June 9 and June 21, Uranus will spend the year dashing in and out of a fun, energizing, and exciting sextile to your Sun. With Uranus in your solar eleventh house of friendships and group connections—and due to the fact that he's wearing feisty, impetuous Aries—this points to yet another busy year for you in the company of lively, fiery friends. Yes, it does sound like fun, doesn't it? The thing is, the eleventh house also has a lot to do with our goals for the future, and it's quite true that we are who we associate with. If you were born before or after those dates, your mission is the same—to resist the inclination to have such a good time that you don't pay attention to the path your peer group is leading you along. If it's exactly where you want to be at this point in time, wonderful! Go forth. Be totally spontaneous. Share laughter, thoughts, and opinions with your kindred spirits and enjoy this delightful time. If you're not so sure your current peers are a good influence on you, then use the energy of this rebellious, electric fellow and make some changes. Big ones. Either way, be sure to pay attention to "coincidental" encounters with others who more closely share your ambitions. Uranus has a habit of sending along inspiring messengers. Oftentimes they arrive with a seriously unusual appearance, personality, or story, but even if they're dressed and coiffed conservatively, their mission is to motivate you by showing you just how easy it is to be true to yourself—even if it means shaking things up a bit!

Neptune

If you were born between May 30 and June 5, the lovely lady Neptune will spend 2017 forming a testy, energetic square to your Sun from her spot in your solar tenth house of career matters, reputation, and authority figures, Gemini. Now, Neptune's visits are often tough to notice, much less understand, because she operates almost invisibly. In your case, she may be silently pushing you toward a profession that more closely reflects your belief system. If you're currently involved with work that doesn't sit very well with your conscience, let it go. Chances are good it's already dissolving anyway, so holding on won't help. Likewise, if you're carrying on a relationship that isn't quite fit for public consumption, keep in mind that secrets don't usually stay secret forever, so if your reputation could be damaged by continuing on, it might be time to begin withdrawing yourself from the situation. Pay attention to your dreams. Matter of fact, if you haven't already, start a journal. You'll be amazed at how aptly the symbols in your dreams reflect the truth of the matter, even if you're not yet ready to see it. Needless to say, you'll also have to tap into your intuition during daylight hours to help you see the point of all this, so pay attention to that little voice in the back of your head, even if it doesn't seem practical. Neptune's visits have nothing to do with being practical, following the rules, or acting as you "should." Her mission is to subtly enlighten you, oftentimes by quietly and gradually removing structures in your life that you've come to depend on—so that you'll have to actually trust your gut.

Pluto

Pluto is quite the intense fellow, Gemini, and wherever he happens to be transiting is quite an intense area of life. In your case, he's spending yet another year in sturdy, practical Capricorn and your solar eighth house of intimate partners and joint resources. Pluto is fond of creating urgent, inevitable situations, which often surface via power struggles, so it's not hard to imagine you dealing with less-than-pleasant circumstances regarding inheritances, joint finances, loans, and legacies. Dealing with financial disputes with family members and other loved ones may be quite disappointing and frustrating, and their behavior could be causing you to question how well you really know them. It might also be that you've begun to examine the role others are playing in your life with regard to shared responsibilities, be they financial or personal.

Regardless of the issue, ask yourself: are others pulling their own weight or have you been shouldering most of the responsibilities yourself? It may take a huge amount of willpower to separate yourself from any negative influences, especially if you're financially tied to someone. Don't let that stop you. It's time to use Pluto's no-nonsense energy to ditch anyone or anything that's draining your resources or taxing you emotionally. Remember, Pluto replaces what's lost with something brand-new and positive, but he can't work his magic until you clear the decks and make room for it. If you were born between June 6 and June 12, Pluto's message will be doubly strong due to the fact that he'll be forming an inconjunct aspect to your Sun, so you may also be dealing with someone who insists on using control and manipulation to keep you where they want you. Enough. If you've been waiting to get yourself free, there's no time like the present. Cut them loose and move on.

How Will This Year's Eclipses Affect You?

Eclipses are celestial exclamation points. They amp up the volume on ordinary life whenever they occur, but the signs and degrees they activate bring along events and circumstances that are especially intense. Eclipses occur in pairs, two weeks apart, every six months. Solar Eclipses are supercharged New Moons that bring the Sun and Moon together, marking peak times for planting spiritual seeds and announcing our intentions to the Universe. Lunar Eclipses are high-energy Full Moons, and like these monthly oppositions between the Sun and Moon, they signal times of dramatic culmination and fulfillment. Here's where and how 2017's eclipses will affect you most.

On February 10, the first Lunar Eclipse of the year will occur, all done up in playful, amorous Leo. This lunation will activate your solar third house of communications and conversations, so if you've been trying to catch someone's attention, romantically speaking, you won't hesitate to pull out all the stops. This is a great time to show off your creative talents, especially if you've been toying with the idea of turning the hobby or pastime you love into a source of income. Since Leo has a lot to do with children, you might be spending more time than usual with them. If a crisis comes along, you'll be right there, every step of the way, and if the news is joyous, they'll want you to share every bit of it.

On February 26, the first Solar Eclipse of 2017 will flip a switch in your solar tenth house, signaling a terrific time to get the attention of a higher-up or authority figure you've been out to impress for some time now. It may not be obvious immediately, but your efforts on the job will be noticed. If you've been waiting for news about a raise, bonus, or promotion, this may be the time when word arrives. On the other hand, if you're feeling any dissatisfaction with your current position, get out there and shake some hands. An offer to work in a field that far better reflects your personal beliefs could be right around the corner.

The second Lunar Eclipse will arrive on August 7, set to liven things up in a big way in your solar ninth house of education and long-distance travel. Eclipses tend to act suddenly, and this one will be in startling Aquarius, so expect sudden opportunities to hit the road for parts unknown or visit loved ones you haven't seen in far too long. If you've been thinking of returning to school, a loan or scholarship you've been waiting to hear about could finally be granted to you. You could also have an aha moment and suddenly realize that the path you're on isn't the one you want to follow—in which case, it's back to classes for you!

The last Solar Eclipse of the year will occur on August 21, bringing the Sun and Moon together in Leo and your solar third house. Anything you put into motion back in February that's of a creative nature will be very much on your mind, most likely because you've discovered a way to actually make it happen. Don't turn down any chances to exhibit your work. A new lover could be along, and if so, they'll be quite impossible to miss. Leo specializes in fire and passion and loves being in love, so don't expect to get much rest!

Gemini | January

Relaxation and Recreation

With loving Venus and passionate Mars in woozy, dreamy Pisces, you may not get much rest, but you'll certainly have plenty of opportunities for behind-the-scenes recreation in dimly lit places, Gemini. Just be sure you're not stepping on any toes before you get involved with that delicious new someone.

Lovers and Friends

Secrets don't always stay that way forever, Gemini, so if you've been carrying on behind closed doors with a certain someone who just so happens to be a business acquaintance, you might want to dial it back a bit toward the end of the month or end it entirely. Consider the outcome of continuing with anything your conscience isn't happy about.

Money and Success

If you've been mixing business with pleasure, it could affect your reputation and your wallet, Gemini, so taking the high road is your best bet. No one is saying you have to deny your feelings. Just be sure they're real and you're willing to deal with the financial and personal consequences of staying on your current path.

Tricky Transits

Your ruling planet, Mercury, will turn direct on January 8, Gemini, in your solar seventh house. If you have unfinished business with regard to a partnership, be it personal or professional, you'll be able to clear it up by the Full Moon of January 12. In the meantime, prepare to deal with joint finances and shared responsibilities.

Rewarding Days

3, 4, 21, 22

Challenging Days

1, 10, 11, 18, 19, 31

Gemini | February

Relaxation and Recreation

Your ruling planet, Mercury himself, will set off for spontaneous, brilliant Aquarius on February 7, Gemini. Talk about a good time! Together with Venus and Mars in Aries, he'll arrange all kinds of surprise encounters, some of which will really and truly leave you speechless—no easy feat. The best part? Someone you meet under extremely odd circumstances will help you along your career path.

Lovers and Friends

You're in luck, Gemini—big time. Just in time for a wonderfully romantic Valentine's Day, the emotional Moon will set off for your solar fifth house of lovers, all done up in partner-loving Libra. If you aren't already attached, not to worry. You may be soon—in fact, if you're interested in someone new, this would be the perfect day to let the truth be known.

Money and Success

There's going to be a Solar Eclipse in your tenth solar house of career on February 26, Gemini, which could most definitely mean that you're in the mood to change not just your job, but your actual profession. Sure, it's a major shift, but you've probably been thinking about it for months. Talk things over with a trusted elder or a higher-up who understands you.

Tricky Transits

On February 8, the Moon in your solar second house of personal finances will form what's known as a Grand Cardinal Cross with startling Uranus, intense Pluto, and exaggerating Jupiter, Gemini—so if you've been teetering on the brink, money-wise, this could be a make-it-or-break-it kind of day. Now that you know what's coming, have plan B ready—just in case.

Rewarding Days

5, 6, 11, 13, 16, 21, 23

Challenging Days

7, 8, 9, 26

Gemini | March

Relaxation and Recreation

Venus will stay on duty in Aries all month, Gemini, and by March 20, Mercury and the Sun will be there with her in your solar eleventh house. Now, this place is all about the crowd you hang out with. Be they bankers, bikers, or fellow PTA members—or all three—you'll feel the urge to let them know you're ready to branch out.

Lovers and Friends

The New Moon on March 27 will fire up already fiery Aries and your solar eleventh house of group activities and friendships, Gemini, urging you to boldly go forward, possibly barging down the doors of a group you've been trying to become part of for some time now. Oh, go ahead. At worst, you'll be proud of yourself for showing up, despite your feelings. At best, you'll end up with a bold new accomplice.

Money and Success

Venus isn't just the Goddess of Love, Gemini. She's also in charge of money matters. So when she stations to turn retrograde on March 4—and basically begins backing up for the next six weeks—she'll be giving you a second chance to straighten out two very pressing issues, one romantic and one monetary. Don't let this blow by you.

Tricky Transits

On March 20, the Sun will set off for Aries and spring will arrive, a time period that's all about new beginnings. You're always eager to move forward, Gemini, but with the Moon in dutiful, cautious Capricorn for the next day or so, you might have to wait to get the show on the road. Yes, I know you hate this, but yes, you really should do it anyway.

Rewarding Days

2, 3, 18, 19, 22, 29

Challenging Days

10, 11, 12, 16, 17, 30

Gemini | April

Relaxation and Recreation

You do love surprises and you're definitely a prankster, Gemini, but this particular April Fool's Day, you should be careful not to push the envelope too far—at least, not with people who won't see you coming. The Moon in your clever, quick-witted sign will be on duty, so your humor will be especially keen. Be sure not to overdo it.

Lovers and Friends

On April 2, loving Venus will back up into ultra-sentimental Pisces, leaving fiery Aries behind just long enough to give us all another chance to find the right partner and/or the right work. In your case, finding a profession that more closely matches your belief system could be quite possible—provided you pay attention to the words of someone new who seems to know an awful lot about it.

Money and Success

Taurus is the sign that's known for being a money magnet, Gemini, so when your ruling planet, Mercury, stops in his tracks to turn retrograde in that very sign on April 9, it's a given that you, of all people, should be watchful and cautious in all money-oriented situations. Be especially careful to keep an eye on your wallet over the following three weeks.

Tricky Transits

On April 21, red-hot, passionate Mars will set off for your sign and your solar first house of personality, Gemini, so you should probably warn your dear ones that for the next couple of months...well, you might be just a tad confrontational. Of course, you're never shy about expressing your opinions, but let's just say that for the duration, you'll be using a lot more exclamation points when you express yourself.

Rewarding Days

1, 10, 11, 23, 24, 25

Challenging Days

4, 20, 21, 22, 30

Gemini | May

Relaxation and Recreation

Your ruling planet, Mercury, has spent roughly six weeks in fast-moving Aries, Gemini, so finding time to kick back hasn't been easy. Well, you'll be happy to hear that as of May 16, when Mercury passes into solid, sensual Taurus, all that will change. As an added bonus, this touch-loving energy will spend three weeks in your dimly lit solar twelfth house. Yes, delightful indeed—or restful, at the very least!

Lovers and Friends

Loving Venus will spend the month in impatient Aries and your solar eleventh house of groups, Gemini, so if a friend suddenly appeals to you on far more than a platonic level, you'll want to tell them all about it—right away. If you can be patient, you may not have to say a single word. Toss them a meaningful glance on May 23 or 24. That ought to do it.

Money and Success

With the Sun on duty in solid, comfort-loving Taurus until May 20 and Mercury set to join him there on May 16, you probably won't be in the mood to do a whole lot of running around, Gemini, so your social tab will most likely be less than usual. Even takeout gets costly after a while, though. How long has it been since you actually cooked?

Tricky Transits

A pile-up of cardinal energies on May 22 could make for a rough start to the workweek, Gemini. If you're barraged by added duties as soon as you walk through the office door, that urge to walk right back out could resurface. Just be sure you have plan B ready to go before you literally quit your day job.

Rewarding Days

7, 12, 15, 17, 25, 26, 30

Challenging Days

5, 6, 10, 11, 16, 27

Gemini | June

Relaxation and Recreation

At least half of the planets will be in fire and air signs at any given time this month, Gemini, which means that momentary lull in your social schedule will come to a rapid-fire end. Look to June 6, 7, and 8 for the return of an old lover or friend or for a brand-new someone who's oddly familiar to storm into your life.

Lovers and Friends

Your current sweetheart may need to step aside and give you some time to iron out some family issues this month, Gemini—and you really shouldn't be afraid to ask for all the time you need, especially around June 28 or 29. A loved one could come to you with a problem that seems—to them, anyway—impossible to solve, when all they really need is a bit of loving advice.

Money and Success

By month's end, three planets will be on duty in home-oriented Cancer and your solar second house of personal money matters, Gemini—so yes, you should probably expect a family member or one of the kids to ask for some monetary help. If this is the first time, you'll be more than willing. If not, you may need to think before you bail them out again.

Tricky Transits

The emotional Moon will be on duty in your sign from June 21 through June 23, Gemini, so absolutely everything you feel will be written all over your face. If you're happy, of course, this will be delightful—but if you're not and you're trying to keep the peace between family and your sweetheart, you could have your work cut out for you.

Rewarding Days

3, 6, 7, 8, 13, 14

Challenging Days

4, 15, 16, 27, 28, 29

Gemini | July

Relaxation and Recreation

Life is like a carnival for you, Gemini, and this month, thanks to your ruling planet, Mercury, you'll be right in the middle of it all. Mercury will spend just about three weeks in fiery, dramatic Leo, and in this sign, he'll make sure that you steal the show, especially with regard to those folks you see every day who may have foolishly forgotten just how wonderful and witty you really are.

Lovers and Friends

Jupiter in partner-loving Libra and your solar fifth house of lovers will be dancing with the lovely lady Venus all month, Gemini, and since she's in your sign and your solar first house of personality and appearance, it's easy to see how you'll probably be spending very little time alone. In fact, if you're looking for privacy—regardless of why—you may need to play sick.

Money and Success

Mars has never been known for his patience, Gemini, much less his self-restraint, and he's currently on duty in your solar second house of personal finances and money matters. Obviously, if you have shopping to do, a chaperone is in order. Choose someone with a strong disposition who knows you well enough to risk irritating you if it means saving your credit rating.

Tricky Transits

On July 17, loving Venus—who just so happens to be on duty in your sign, by the way—will form an active square with dreamy Neptune. Now, this is the stuff that love at first sight is made of—but only time will tell if that's what you've found. In the meantime, enjoy the pink cloud under your feet, but don't hop on a plane to Vegas. Wait and see. Please.

Rewarding Days
4, 6, 7, 18, 19, 28

Challenging Days
13, 16, 17, 23, 24, 25

Gemini | August

Relaxation and Recreation

Mercury is in your solar fourth house of home and family matters, all done up in detail-oriented Virgo. He'll stay on duty here all month, urging you to clean up, get organized, and tend to the mundane details of daily life. He'll turn retrograde on August 12, so if you need to revisit a project or huddle up with your loved ones to get closure, you'll be well equipped for the job.

Lovers and Friends

Generous Jupiter has been doling out goodies to you from his spot in your solar fifth house of lovers and playmates for just about a year now, Gemini, but he'll be moving on in October. This means you have about two months to ensure that whatever is at the top of your current wish list happens. Travel, maybe? Or do you just really need to tell someone you think they're amazing?

Money and Success

Loving Venus in family-loving Cancer will spend most of this month in your solar second house of finances, Gemini. Once again, you may need to unexpectedly raid your piggy bank to fund the needs of a child or to take care of a domestic issue that has surfaced again and is absolutely demanding your attention this time around.

Tricky Transits

There will be two eclipses this month, Gemini, on August 7 and 21. They're challenging you to change your mind about a subject you've been quite adamant about for a very long time—which means it definitely won't be easy. Your mission is to resist the urge to hang on to your former beliefs just because they're comfortable. How do you really feel?

Rewarding Days
3, 10, 13, 22, 23

Challenging Days
4, 11, 12, 15, 16, 17

Gemini | September

Relaxation and Recreation

That problem we talked about last month that was keeping you from enjoying your time at home with the family? Well, it might not be solved until after September 5, when fiery Mars storms onto the scene and helps you put your foot down, once and for all. Fortunately, if you step firmly, this might be the last time you'll have to.

Lovers and Friends

The clock is ticking, Gemini. Jupiter will leave your solar fifth house of lovers on October 10, so if you've been holding off on telling someone that you just adore them, there's no time like the present. Oh, and don't be surprised if that same someone beats you to the punch—finally! In any case, live it up now. Duty will be calling on you very shortly.

Money and Success

The Full Moon in ultra-sensitive Pisces will set up shop in your solar tenth house of career matters on September 6, Gemini, just a day after Mars sets off for hardworking Virgo. If you've been looking for a way to turn the hobby you love or the cause you live for into your actual occupation, there's no time like the present to get out there and shake some hands.

Tricky Transits

Just as the New Moon in precise, meticulous Virgo arrives on September 20, Gemini, the lovely lady Venus will set off for that same sign. Now, all this will occur in your solar fourth house of home, which has been a very busy place lately, but not to worry. It looks as if you'll just have to put the finishing touches on a pet project that's near and dear to your heart.

Rewarding Days

4, 5, 9, 12, 15

Challenging Days

1, 3, 16, 26, 27, 28

Gemini | October

Relaxation and Recreation

The New Moon on October 19 will occur in friendly, companionable Libra and your solar fifth house of lovers and playmates, Gemini, setting you up for some serious fun, at the very least. If you're attached, you two really should spend some quality time alone together, but if you're not…well, that's a different story. Go forth, circulate, and socialize. Someone new and delightful may be on the menu.

Lovers and Friends

And speaking of socializing, if you're thinking of taking off for a day or two in search of a new adventure, look to the weekend of October 28. Your mission will be to acquire some quality company and ignore your phone, tablet, and computer—and all electronic gadgets in general. Don't panic. We're not talking days—just long enough to enjoy what's right there in front of you.

Money and Success

On October 10, Jupiter will set off for Scorpio and your solar sixth house, Gemini, marking the start of a year's worth of intensity on the job for you. Might be that you land a long-term project that will take up a lot more of your time. Might be that you land a delicious coworker and you two end up spending every waking moment you can together.

Tricky Transits

Venus in detail-oriented Virgo will square off with Saturn in expansive Sagittarius on October 8, making it a bit too easy to be quite a bit dismissive of someone just because you disagree. Keep your mind open to new ideas. Oh, and be careful not to let something unimportant come between you and a loved one—even if it's an especially irritating habit. We've all got 'em.

Rewarding Days
12, 13, 14, 15, 16, 19

Challenging Days
7, 8, 9, 11, 18, 26, 27

Gemini | November

Relaxation and Recreation

Thanksgiving looks to be quite a time for you, Gemini. The emotional Moon in surprising Aquarius will be on duty in your solar ninth house of far-off places and long-distance loved ones, so you might be getting ready to visit someone you haven't seen in far too long. Lovely. And there's another option: a long-lost friend or family member could crash dinner at your mom's.

Lovers and Friends

Love at first sight will most definitely be a possibility on November 16, Gemini, when loving Venus and dreamy Neptune come together in an easy trine aspect. The thing is, Venus will be in sexy Scorpio, so lust will also most definitely be part of the equation. Keep that in mind before you start making wedding plans. Take your time. Drive it a while before you buy it.

Money and Success

An old financial dispute could come up once again around November 18 or 19, Gemini, and this time around, it won't be easy to ignore. The New Moon in intense, determined Scorpio will make it impossible to forget about, too. Do yourself a favor and tackle this thing head-on. It could be the only way your brain will give you any peace.

Tricky Transits

A testy pack of rather intoxicating energies will come together on November 13, Gemini, making this a prime time to manipulate or be manipulated. If your gut tells you that someone—a coworker, perhaps—is trying to brainwash or convert you to their way of thinking, don't question it. That could be exactly what's going on. Don't make any changes until you're ready.

Rewarding Days
5, 6, 11, 12, 22, 23, 24

Challenging Days
13, 16, 18, 19

Gemini | December

Relaxation and Recreation

The party's on, Gemini—and not a moment too soon, I'll bet. After all that intensity last month, you're ready to have some serious fun. Fortunately, Venus, Mercury, and the Sun are all very much on board with that idea, and since they're all done up in playful, excessive Sagittarius and in your solar seventh house of one-to-one relationships—well, just nap when you can.

Lovers and Friends

On December 25, loving Venus will get together with stable, responsible Saturn, combined energies that easily conjure a wonderful sense of contentment. You'll feel it most especially if you're looking around a table and seeing nothing but well-loved familiar faces, but if you've really been though it recently and come out on the other side, take just a moment to give yourself a well-deserved pat on the back.

Money and Success

Any serious conversations you've been putting off will go quite well if you have a sit-down around December 6 and 7, Gemini. Mercury, Saturn, and Mars will see to it that all parties concerned are willing to at least listen and possibly even negotiate. Your mission is to be even more open to compromise, especially if this dispute has been going on for a very long time.

Tricky Transits

Your ruling planet, Mercury, will retrograde through your solar seventh house from December 3 through December 22, Gemini, so you may find yourself dealing a whole lot with folks you know who haven't been around much lately—if at all. The good news is that most of them will make your holidays even happier, and anyone who's irritating will be easy to blow off.

Rewarding Days

6, 7, 8, 11, 12, 20, 26, 31

Challenging Days

4, 5, 19, 21, 22

Gemini Action Table

These dates reflect the best—but not the only—times for success and ease in these activities, according to your Sun sign.

	JAN	FEB	MAR	APR	MAY	JUN	JUL	AUG	SEP	OCT	NOV	DEC
Move	3, 11				1	23		20			18, 20	
Start a class		23, 27		20, 21			24, 30			9, 27, 28		
Join a club			2, 3						27			
Ask for a raise	20, 29		24		19	1, 24						
Get professional advice		11, 22		24				22, 27		16	9, 26, 27	
Get a loan			9				7	22, 27	19	18		
New romance	20		18, 19					24				10, 24
Vacation	23	16, 20		10, 17		16	6, 7				11	

Cancer

The Crab
June 22 to July 22

Element: Water

Glyph: Crab's claws

Quality: Cardinal

Anatomy: Stomach, breasts

Polarity: Yin/feminine

Colors: Silver, pearl white

Planetary Ruler: The Moon

Animals: Crustaceans, cows, chickens

Meditation: I have faith in the promptings of my heart

Myths/Legends: Hercules and the Crab, Asherah, Hecate

Gemstone: Pearl

House: Fourth

Power Stones: Moonstone, Chrysocolla

Opposite Sign: Capricorn

Flower: Larkspur

Key Phrase: I feel

Keyword: Receptivity

The Cancer Personality

Your Strengths, Gifts, and Challenges

Your astrological symbol is the Crab, Cancer—which certainly does explain a lot. To start with, crabs have very, very hard shells—that protect very, very vulnerable innards. So contrary to what you might think, but unbeknownst to absolutely no one who knows you, is the fact that even if you come off as a tad brusque at times, you're a serious marshmallow underneath it all. Now, when you're this vulnerable, armor of the emotional variety is absolutely necessary. The thing is, you can get so good at arming yourself with brusqueness that at times your manner will be a bit off-putting—especially if you're with people who aren't intuitive enough to understand what's motivating it. The other thing, however, is that it would break your heart to think that someone sweet and wonderful who might be in need of a hug, a good hot meal, or a foot rub was too intimidated to get close enough to ask. Yes, it's an emotional dilemma, but the good news is that it's easily remedied. Pay attention to the effect your mood swings have on others. You might need to hold back your feelings just a little every now and then—say, for example, when you're hungry. In other words, practice being nice to anyone who isn't responsible for your mood or your hunger. If you're prone to all-out displays of anger, counting to ten could be quite helpful, too. That goes for moments of petulance and snits in general, by the way. No, it's not easy to curtail your feelings with the emotional Moon as your patron planet, and yes, feelings are your job, but you can certainly make an effort to smooth out the rough edges and become more accessible. After all, unconditional love is your quest. Making yourself easy to love is in your best interests.

Romance, Friendships, and Casual Relationships

We've talked about the similarities between you and your sign's symbol, the Crab, but let's get back to that shell for a second, because when it comes to getting to know others, it's kind of mandatory that you either come out of there or let them come in. The thing is, that shell doubles as your home, and there's nothing more important to you than having a safe, secure place to return to after being out and about in that exhausting place known as the outside world. Needless to say, if you invite someone into your heart and your home to share your world, that's a very big compliment, and one can only hope they appreciate it. If they don't, however, you won't hesitate to show them the door. You have a big heart and you often tolerate a lot from others, but if you're hurt—whether the offense was real or imagined—you can fall into pouting and sulking, which might feel good initially but won't help you make your case in the long run. Ah, well. Surround yourself with other emotional water signs—like Scorpio and Pisces—and you stand a very good chance of being understood and appreciated, not to mention the fact that you'll also enjoy the company of someone who loves to hibernate as much as you do. If you're bored and restless, however, and looking for a change, seek out the company of airy Libra or fiery Leo, signs that love commitment and family as much as you do.

Career and Work

In an ideal world, each of us would spend every waking hour doing something we love to do, Cancer—which includes the hours we put in at work to earn our daily bread. In your case, working out of your home is obviously a goal to aim your energies toward—that is, if you haven't already found a way to pull it off. Being a stay-at-home dad or mom fits the bill nicely—and heaven help anyone who says that doesn't qualify as work, especially if they're foolish enough to say it in front of you. If you don't have a family of your own just yet, caring for other people's kids, homes, and/or animals will do just fine. You're built for taking care of homes, though, so selling, maintaining, or evaluating real estate will work nicely.

Money and Possessions

Security is priority number one in your book, Cancer, so having a cushy nest egg at the ready is important to your peace of mind. You're really, really good at keeping it not just secret but entirely unexpected and very well hidden, too. That said, if one of the kids needs something, you'll break into your stash just a bit to help them out, but until you replace it, you won't feel comfortable. Other than going for groceries—which is actually fun for you, since it allows you to spend money guilt-free—shopping expeditions are usually reserved for home or family-oriented needs. Every now and then, though, treat yourself—and not just to a pint of Ben and Jerry's.

Your Lighter Side

As much as you love your nest, your family, and your inner circle, Cancer, it's pretty darn obvious that the best of all worlds is having absolutely everyone you love over to your place—for a meal, at least, if not for an all-out day-long food fest. Yes, whether it's a reunion, a celebration, an anniversary, or a just-for-the-heck-of-it Sunday barbecue, it's what lights up your life—and the lives of those who've been invited, too! Oh, and did I mention the great love and affection you have for your kitchen, once you have it set up just right? I mean, honestly—could there be anything better than puttering around in there, listening to the voices of family and friends? In your book, Cancer, that's nirvana.

Cancer Celebrities

The emotional Moon is your patron planet, Cancer, and she's very fond of silver, which is quite the reflective element. So think mirrors and then impressionists—and then consider that you were born under the same sign as both Robin Williams and Meryl Streep, the master and mistress of ducking out of their own bodies and taking on another persona. But you folks also have a way of making your way into our hearts in a very big way. Like Tom Cruise, Ricky Gervais, Jessica Simpson, Princess Diana, Tom Hanks, Liv Tyler, Will Ferrell, and Malala Yousafzai, for example.

Words to Live By for 2017

My own needs must be met before I can meet the needs of others.

The Year Ahead for Cancer

Your solar tenth house will play host to the lovely lady Venus for a total of three months this year, Cancer—and wherever Venus goes, good things follow. Now, this house is where you handle matters pertaining to career, profession, and dealings with higher-ups, elders, and authority figures. Venus is a veritable magnet for all things sweet, pleasing, and satisfying, and in this spot—especially since she's all done up in Aries, a sign that's just about impossible not to notice—well, if you've been hoping to make your mark in your chosen field, you'll undoubtedly have the help of at least one influential person who'll take you under their wing. Of course, what goes around comes around, and you've taken many newbies under your own wing in the past, so think of this time period as the Universe's way of saying thank you for all your past efforts. In the department of romance, by the way—one of Venus's specialties—you might find that you're suddenly quite attracted to someone in a position of authority over you, and if that's the case, there may also be an age difference that causes you to worry. Don't. Focus on what you have in common, and let your relationship unfold as it will.

Professional partnerships are also spotlighted when Venus passes through the tenth house, especially if you're thinking of sharing financial responsibilities. The thing is, while Venus will spend her time here from February 3 through April 2 and again from April 28 through June 6, she'll be moving retrograde from March 4 through April 15, so if you've got anything official to sign, seal, and deliver, wait. You'll probably be quite busy with personal and domestic things, anyway, thanks to mighty Jupiter. He'll spend most of the year in your solar fourth house of home and family matters, so straight through October 10, even if you're working hard to advance your career, you can expect to be distracted by more tender matters. Jupiter is an expansive energy, so you'll probably need to make room for a new roommate at least, but you may also be moving in with someone yourself, marrying, or welcoming a new family member. News along those lines will arrive in early February or early June.

Saturn

Saturn is preparing to spend his last year in Sagittarius and your solar sixth house of work, relationships with coworkers, and health issues, Cancer. You've probably gotten super-organized—and as a result gotten a whole lot done—but I'll bet you still won't be sorry to see Saturn go. For one thing, this planet is extremely fond of structure and schedules, and as a rule, you water signs aren't. You'd rather go with the flow and allow your emotions to guide your activities throughout your day. Put another way, you folks just like to do your own thing. Period. Still, you've been dealing with this cranky taskmaster for two years now, so you've definitely learned to accommodate him, most likely due to added responsibilities that forced you to prioritize your time. The good news is that if these added duties were given to you on the job, you've probably outdone yourself, which puts you in a far better position—professionally speaking—than you were in a year or two ago. The even better news is that if you haven't already made room in your day for exercise, yoga, or meditation, you'll have the entire coming year to make it happen.

You're on such a regimented schedule right now that it would be easy
for you to forget about your health. Don't do that. Tend to yourself with
the same type of love and attention you give to others. Get thee to a gym
or start daily walks with friends. And watch your sugar intake!

Uranus

Where Uranus goes, change of the most sudden variety follows, Cancer.
Now, back in 2010, Mr. Unpredictable stormed off into fiery Aries and
your solar tenth house of authority figures, higher-ups, and career matters—which certainly does explain a lot, doesn't it? Ever since then, this
wired, twitchy energy has had you thinking about ditching it all and flee-
ing from your current profession and into the arms of the field you've
always wanted to pursue, maybe even from as early on as childhood.
This type of longing that Uranus inspires—to be yourself even while
you're at work, that is— is impossible to ignore. Plus, he's an insistent
kind of guy. At some point, then, you'll really have no choice but to give
in and follow your bliss—so what's the holdup? Why not get the show
on the road right now? That internal tension you're feeling is your first
clue that it's time to stop living up to the expectations of others at the
expense of truly being you, 100 percent of the time. If you feel stifled,
repressed, or restless and you haven't yet rebelled, prepare yourself,
because it's coming. Whoever or whatever is causing you to feel as if
you're in a straightjacket will simply have to leave your life—very soon.
Buckle up. All this goes double for those of you born between July 11
and July 23, because Uranus is also currently squaring your Sun. Uranus demands change. Aries planets demand speed. Squares demand
action. Any questions?

Neptune

You're a water sign, Cancer, aptly ruled by the Moon, the Queen of
Emotions. As such, you feel quite at home with other emotionally
inclined water energies—like Neptune, the Queen of the Oceans, for
example. Dreamy, sentimental Neptune has been moving comfortably
through equally watery Pisces for the past six-ish years, making it especially easy for you to snuggle up inside a comfy, cozy cocoon and take
a nice long nap whenever reality doesn't suit you. The thing is, if you
sleepwalk through this lovely transit, you'll be cheating yourself out of
an opportunity for serious spiritual growth—so please do force yourself
to get up off the couch, turn off the television, and find your tribe.

You've been longing for spiritual fulfillment, and there's really nothing like being in the presence of kindred spirits. If you were born between June 30 and July 7, Neptune will also be forming an easy trine aspect to your Sun, so finding these folks will be a piece of cake—again, provided you get up, get dressed, and get out there. Don't miss out on this chance to find new members of your spiritual family. Oh, and if you have the feeling that you're able to pretty much read other people's minds—well, don't question your sanity. Your instincts have always been right on, and now they're being heightened by Neptune—who erases boundaries and temporarily endows us with superpowers. Just don't let on to others that you know exactly what they're thinking. It's intimidating.

Pluto

Back in 2008, intense Pluto set off for your solar seventh house of one-to-one relationships, Cancer, all done up in serious, practical Capricorn. Now, this energy was tailor-made for commitment. After all these years in this house, there's no question that you've either made, broken, or seriously questioned a commitment to someone—unless, of course, you were born between July 7 and July 13, in which case, you're probably going through that right now. Whether that someone is important to you personally or professionally doesn't matter. The point is that you're going through a kind of molting period now in the department of relationships, and some of the people in your life will necessarily have to go. That goes double for anyone who only functions on a surface level or anyone who isn't having a positive influence on you. Now, this culling of the herd doesn't mean you'll be alone afterward—in fact, since Pluto replaces what's gone with something new and more positive, you might end up being less alone than you have been in a very long time. This isn't an overnight process, and no one's saying it's going to be a walk in the park, but you can count on feeling like a whole new person when it's done. In the meantime, resist the urge to hang on by bulldozing or manipulating. If you're over it, just go.

How Will This Year's Eclipses Affect You?

Eclipses are celestial exclamation points. They amp up the volume on ordinary life whenever they occur, but the signs and degrees they activate also bring along events and circumstances that are quite intense. Eclipses occur in pairs, six months apart. Solar Eclipses are supercharged New Moons. They bring the Sun and Moon together, marking peak times for planting spiritual seeds and announcing our intentions to the Universe. Lunar Eclipses are high-energy Full Moons, and just like these monthly oppositions between the Sun and the Moon, they signal times of dramatic culmination and fulfillment.

The first Lunar Eclipse of the year will arrive on February 10 in fiery Leo and your solar second house of possessions, money matters, and values, Cancer. If you've been thinking of making a major move—and actually, even if you haven't—this is a great time to begin the process of going through your things with an eye toward keeping what's important and letting go of what's not. Now, you usually attach emotions to possessions, especially gifts, but you can't move forward if you're still surrounded by the past, so be brave. You don't have to destroy anything—just see to it that it finds a good home where it will continue to be appreciated.

On February 26, you'll feel the effects of a Solar Eclipse in Pisces and your solar ninth house, Cancer. Now, this lunation will be working hand in hand with mystical, magical Neptune to open your eyes to new ideas—and possibly even a whole new belief system. If you've been searching for something more from the Universe, make it a point to check out other spiritual paths. Your kindred spirits are waiting. Metaphysical subjects will also fascinate you, and your already keen psychic abilities will be running on high. Remember to trust your gut above all else! If you were born around the first of July, a whole new vocation may be calling out to you.

The second Lunar Eclipse of the year will occur on August 7, all done up in startling Aquarius and set to make its presence known in your solar eighth house of joint finances and shared resources. Now, Aquarius is a big fan of sudden change, so if you've been angling to refinance your debts, thinking about a new investment, or preparing to bankroll someone else's business plans, something unexpected could be on the horizon. Prepare yourself so that even if you're surprised by what happens, you won't be at a loss. Oh, and this house also has a lot to do with intimate relationships, so if you're not already involved—well, that could change, suddenly and soon.

On August 21, a Solar Eclipse will bring the Sun and Moon together in Leo and your solar second house—which is exactly where February's Lunar Eclipse was. Whatever you ended way back then—and not just financially speaking—will now be replaced by something you probably didn't see coming that's bigger, better, or just plain old refreshingly different. Might be a new job, an entirely new profession, or a whole new set of higher-ups who actually appreciate your work. Regardless, you have a chance now to make a name for yourself in your field simply by doing your job to the very best of your creative abilities. Take advantage of it!

Cancer | January

Relaxation and Recreation

Venus will take off for woozy, dreamy Pisces on January 3, urging you to kick back, relax, and binge-watch at least one series you've been dying to see. If you have the right company and you're financially equipped, this wouldn't be a bad idea—provided you don't do it 24/7 for the entire month, which will be tempting.

Lovers and Friends

With Venus in Pisces, falling in love with love is always a possibility, but in your case, as sensitive and emotional as you are, you'll have to be doubly cautious. If you cross paths with someone who seems to be just perfect for you, you may indeed have found your soulmate, but just in case, don't propose until at least next month.

Money and Success

"Everything in moderation" is an old adage that rings true even now, and it applies especially well to the use of escape hatches when times get tough. If you're going through something tough and ducking out whenever possible, be sure you're not damaging your chances for a solid future. No one's saying you can't give yourself some breathing space. Just be sure you're also dealing with reality.

Tricky Transits

The New Moon on January 27 will join forces with fiery Mars to put you in the mood to rebel, Cancer, in a very big, very noticeable way. If you're taking up arms because you're just plain old done with someone's non-sense, don't hesitate to get them gone. Just be sure not to go into battle simply because you're in the mood for it.

Rewarding Days
1, 2, 3, 13, 15, 20, 23

Challenging Days
5, 6, 9, 11, 19, 27

Cancer | February

Relaxation and Recreation

With three planets in impulsive Aries and two in startling Aquarius and two eclipses scheduled, you probably won't have much time to yourself this month, Cancer, but you'll have some serious fun with unusual, interesting others who'll want nothing more from you than your company. What a refreshing change! Just for the heck of it, let one of them talk you into trying something new and exciting.

Lovers and Friends

Mars and Venus are the astrological equivalent of Antony and Cleopatra—one of the best-matched, most passionate, and most powerful teams. Venus attracts and Mars pursues—and they'll both spend the month in fiery Aries and your solar tenth house. If you find yourself attracted to someone older, younger, or in a position of authority, it's a given that the feelings will be mutual. Now what? Be careful!

Money and Success

The Lunar Eclipse of February 10 will occur in your solar second house, Cancer, which is where possessions and money matters are handled. This lunation will be in fiery, dramatic Leo, so if you've been having financial problems with one particular person, there's just no way they won't come to a head. Ready or not, it may be time to go to battle for what's yours.

Tricky Transits

Your ruling planet, the Moon herself, will form a Grand Square with Uranus, Pluto, and Jupiter on February 8, Cancer. She'll be initiating change of all kinds, but in your case, especially since you're so susceptible to her moods, you should prepare to question just about everything and everyone. Let your instincts guide you, especially with regard to conflicts and disputes. When have they ever let you down?

Rewarding Days

1, 4, 6, 17, 18, 25

Challenging Days

7, 8, 10, 21, 26

Cancer | March

Relaxation and Recreation

With so much Aries energy currently on duty in the heavens above you, Cancer, you probably won't get much rest. In fact, when the New Moon occurs on March 27, you might even be unable to sleep, no matter how hard you try. If this happens more than a night or two, sit down for a chat with someone who knows you and figure out what's really keeping you awake.

Lovers and Friends

Loving Venus will turn retrograde on March 4, and for the next six weeks she'll be inspiring you to review your past relationships, both long ago and recent. You may feel the urge to reach out and find the one who got away, and with social media, it probably won't be all that tough. Gather what info you can, but keep in mind that people really do change—well, every now and then, anyway.

Money and Success

Five planets will take turns passing through red-hot, ultra-impatient Aries this month, Cancer, which will put them on a stormy path through your solar tenth house of higher-ups and authority figures. Obviously, if you've got a work-oriented goal to accomplish, this crew will provide you with all the energy anyone could ever want to get the job done fast. Just be sure you also do it right.

Tricky Transits

On March 2, startling Uranus will be opposed by Jupiter, who expands and enlarges the energy of any planet he touches. This cosmic face-off will activate your solar fourth and tenth houses, which just might cause a conflict between your personal life and your professional activities. Hang tough. By March 6, you'll have it all worked out.

Rewarding Days

1, 6, 7, 9, 29

Challenging Days

2, 3, 4, 11, 12, 17, 30

Cancer | April

Relaxation and Recreation

The Sun, Mercury, and Mars will take turns passing through earthy Taurus and your solar eleventh house of friendships and group affiliations this month, Cancer. This practical, quality-conscious gathering of energies will introduce you to people you'll feel quite closely connected to just about immediately. If you've been searching for new friends, you'll most certainly find them.

Lovers and Friends

The lovely lady Venus is moving retrograde at the moment, Cancer. On April 2, she'll tiptoe back into Pisces to inspire you to review and reevaluate the relationships you've had with folks who are now a long distance from you, either time-wise or geographically. You'll want to reach out, and if you're fairly sure they've grown as much as you have—well, why not?

Money and Success

If you suddenly become aware that the kids need something fancy around April 6, even if you're not sure you can afford it, you'll want to get it for them. And it's not just the kids. You'll do the same for anyone you love, especially if you're still in the throes of infatuation. Don't put yourself in a bad financial place. Do what you can—and no more.

Tricky Transits

Mars will set off for Gemini on April 21, putting this impatient planet in an extremely communicative sign. Yes, this could mean you'll be a bit less able to react with your usual patience when someone comes to you for a favor—especially if it's a favor you've done for them many, many times. It might be time to take a deep breath and just say no.

Rewarding Days
6, 12, 16, 17, 18, 19

Challenging Days
4, 5, 20, 21, 28

Cancer | May

Relaxation and Recreation

Taurus has always been one of your favorite signs, Cancer—with good reason. It's solid and grounded, as firmly rooted to Mother Earth as you are. So this month, with both the Sun and Mercury passing through that sign, you'll probably find that going out when you don't have to will be just too much effort for too little pleasure. Pull on some sweats and kick back at your place.

Lovers and Friends

Your ruling planet is the emotional Moon, so when she reaches her full stage on May 10 in ultra-intense Scorpio, your feelings will be running on high, Cancer—to say the least. You might, in fact, want to step back from any especially emotional "discussions" if you get the feeling you're about to say something you'll wish you hadn't.

Money and Success

Thoughtful Mercury will take off for quality-conscious Taurus on May 16, urging you to resist buying anything that really isn't worth the ticket price. Of course, you still might do a bit of haggling, and you could end up with a number you're far more comfortable with. Well, go ahead—but set yourself a ceiling price and stick to it.

Tricky Transits

On May 3, after three long weeks in retrograde motion, Mercury will turn direct—which should mean that everything you've been waiting for career-wise is finally going to happen. Not so fast, though. You could be on the verge of getting the deal you've been after, but a few details will need to be worked out first. Sit tight just a bit longer.

Rewarding Days
8, 9, 15, 16, 23, 24, 31

Challenging Days
5, 10, 11, 25

Cancer | June

Relaxation and Recreation
The Sun, Mars, and Mercury will dash through your solar twelfth house of secrets this month, Cancer, wearing fast-moving, cerebral Gemini. This crew will urge you to do a whole lot of communicating in private—which could turn out to be as delightful as it sounds. Just be sure not to let a confidence slip out in casual conversation. Shh!

Lovers and Friends
Venus will leave impulsive Aries behind on June 6, when she strolls off into earthy, practical Taurus. Now, this might mean your social life will slow down quite a bit, but not to worry. You won't be bored, not by any means. You'll simply be focusing on quality rather than quantity—and one particular someone could take up a particularly special place in your heart.

Money and Success
On June 24, an easy trine between intense Pluto and Venus, Goddess of Love and Money, will make it all too easy for you to become obsessive about finances or possessions—especially with the Moon in your very own sign. Don't allow yourself to become attached to anything material for sentimental reasons. Ask a practical friend to advise you—and listen up!

Tricky Transits
The New Moon on June 23 will be in your sign, Cancer, urging you toward a whole new emotional beginning. The thing is, before anything new can make an appearance, everything that's not working has to go—just to make room. Your mission is to clear the decks and make room for whatever is coming next.

Rewarding Days
1, 2, 6, 9, 20, 21

Challenging Days
3, 11, 19, 26, 28, 29

Cancer | July

Relaxation and Recreation

It's playtime, Cancer! The Sun, Mars, and Mercury will all pass through fiery, fun-loving Leo this month, and you'll be in the mood to find at least one new way to keep your brain nourished and amused. Your best bet is to find classes or other regular get-togethers where curious minds meet. You might meet someone who fascinates you for many reasons.

Lovers and Friends

Venus will set off for witty, chatty Gemini on July 4, Cancer—which might ordinarily mean that you'd be doing a whole lot of socializing with little time for intimate encounters. Not so. Venus will be in your solar twelfth house of clandestine encounters until the end of the month, urging you to be very particular about the company you keep.

Money and Success

Impulsive Mars will storm off into your solar second house on July 20 just as an equally impulsive square arrives between startling Uranus and the Sun in your sign. Leave your checkbook and plastic at home—just in case you suddenly decide to bet the ranch on what you see as a guaranteed win. This is a most unpredictable day. No major moves, please.

Tricky Transits

On July 22, just two days after Mars sets off for Leo, the Sun will follow suit, and suddenly, the heavens' two fireballs will be looking for an audience. Yes, drama may be on your agenda that weekend, so if you're not in the mood for it, make plans that don't include being in the presence of anyone who knows exactly how to push your buttons.

Rewarding Days

10, 11, 14, 19, 25

Challenging Days

2, 3, 4, 5, 8, 20

Cancer | August

Relaxation and Recreation

This is going to be an extremely intense month, Cancer, so if you're thinking of taking off for some much-needed downtime, try your best to set it up for the weekend of August 25. Mercury will be retrograde, so you'll have to do some serious troubleshooting, but Venus will be in fiery, playful Leo, so even if you're stalled or delayed, you'll find a way to make it fun.

Lovers and Friends

Venus will spend most of the month in your very own sign, Cancer, and since she's so magnetic and you're so comfortable to be around, you should probably expect at least one new someone to come along in search of advice that only you can offer. Be careful not to get overly involved. This too shall pass—and quickly.

Money and Success

There will be two eclipses this month, Cancer, both of which will activate your money houses. The financial changes you've been expecting are due to occur, along with one or two you might not have foreseen. Stay calm. It's simply time to prioritize. What's important and what's not? Think of this as molting. If you don't need it, why burden yourself?

Tricky Transits

On August 4, expansive Jupiter will square off with intense Pluto, creating the potential for what often astrologically adds up to a god complex. Now, not everyone will be affected, but if you notice that someone dear to you suddenly seems quite full of themselves, at least you'll know the inspiration behind it. That doesn't mean you have to be cooperative, however, especially if they're being unreasonable.

Rewarding Days
1, 10, 11, 20, 22, 27, 28

Challenging Days
3, 4, 5, 7, 12, 18, 21

Cancer | September

Relaxation and Recreation

Four planets will make their way through your solar third house of short trips and communications during September, Cancer, all of them wearing detail-loving, meticulous Virgo. In a nutshell, it's time to get organized. Big time. ASAP. It might be your physical home that's begging for attention, but it might also be your spiritual self. Either way, meditation can't hurt.

Lovers and Friends

In the department of romance, you'll still be dealing with a bit of drama, Cancer, thanks to the lovely lady Venus, who'll continue kicking up a storm on her way through Leo. Arguments over money are entirely possible, but if either of you plays the "if you loved me, you would" card, consider the relationship to be in a bit of trouble.

Money and Success

That whole money thing you've been going through for months now, on and off? As of September 9 or so, it will be done for good. Signed, sealed, and delivered. Yes, that's a relief, and yes, you'll be able to take a breather from work, but don't get comfy just yet. The Universe has big plans for you, career-wise, set to arrive with the Full Moon next month. In the meantime, relax.

Tricky Transits

About that pack of planets moving through Virgo? If you have a detail-oriented hobby that you'd like to turn into a part-time source of income, they're prepared to help. Before you get too caught up in perfecting your craft, however, remember that this type of focus can put a bit of a wedge between you and yours. Take a break every now and then and be your own sweet self.

Rewarding Days
1, 2, 9, 10, 12

Challenging Days
5, 6, 13, 14, 16, 19

Cancer | October

Relaxation and Recreation

Jupiter will move into your solar fifth house of playmates and recreation on October 10, Cancer, marking the start of a very social and very lucky year for you. New and unusual friends who'll support you on your current path will be popping up the entire time, so prepare for your social horizons to be widened—big time. It's time to mingle. Get out there and shake some hands.

Lovers and Friends

Well, speaking of expansion, Jupiter's presence in the house associated with love affairs means you single folks should probably nap now while you can. Chances are good that the coming year will be extremely intense—in a delightful way. You attached Cancers might want to line up reliable babysitters now, because you'll definitely want some quality time alone with your sweetheart.

Money and Success

Five planets will make their presence known in Libra during October, Cancer, all of them urging you to keep your domestic finances on an even keel. Now, this could be easier said than done around October 14, 15, and 19, but if you're determined not to touch your nest egg, don't let anyone who hasn't directly contributed to it make so much as a suggestion about how to spend it. Stand your ground.

Tricky Transits

Well, speaking of tricks, on Halloween, your ruling planet, the Moon, will be all done up in Pisces—the sign that most adores wearing costumes and just loves hiding out behind glamorous masks. As susceptible as you are to her moods, you'll definitely be in the mood for some mischief—most likely of the most romantic kind—but be sure you're not kidding yourself about the future.

Rewarding Days

1, 2, 3, 12, 16

Challenging Days

4, 5, 6, 8, 15, 19, 26

Cancer | November

Relaxation and Recreation

The New Moon on November 18 will set up shop in your solar fifth house of playtime, Cancer, urging you to find a new way to have fun and express yourself creatively—possibly involving a whole new cast of characters. Oh, and on November 21, Venus and Pluto might see fit to introduce you to someone delicious at a gathering of entirely new friends.

Lovers and Friends

With Venus in sexy, intense Scorpio for most of the month, it's not hard to imagine you being quite taken with someone, Cancer—possibly so much that it's really tough to leave them to go to work. Well, we've all been there, but trust me when I tell you that it's a lot easier to stay in love when you have enough cash for pizza, candles, and other treats. Embrace them fondly, but do go to work.

Money and Success

Right up until November 7, Venus will be on duty in your solar fourth house of home and family matters, and on November 3, you may receive an SOS from a family member or child who really needs a financial safety net. If you can manage to help without hurting yourself, you'll do it. If you can't, don't beat yourself up about it. Give what you can.

Tricky Transits

On November 19, powerful Pluto will square off with red-hot Mars, who just so happens to be on duty in your solar fourth house of home and family matters. Yes, this could certainly mean there'll be a display of anger in your home, but not to worry. You'll be perfectly equipped to handle it. Heaven help anyone who thinks they can manipulate you now!

Rewarding Days
1, 3, 7, 9, 11, 16, 17

Challenging Days
2, 8, 13, 14, 15, 19

Cancer | December

Relaxation and Recreation
A Full Moon will occur in lighthearted, fun-loving Gemini on December 3, a cerebral energy that can't help but inspire you to make the holidays at your place just perfect with creative meals and decorations. If you're off to visit instead, expect an amazing cast of characters to make the gatherings special. Someone new will make quite the impression on you.

Lovers and Friends
Mars—the most passionate planet of all—will slip silently into sexy Scorpio on December 9, Cancer, which will put this amorous energy in your solar fifth house of lovers—which is obviously a very amorous place. Yes, this does sound wonderful, and you really should enjoy it to the fullest, as you see fit. Just don't forget about family and friends. 'Tis the season, after all.

Money and Success
If work takes you away from your home, you probably don't always enjoy it. But this month, Cancer, several planets in funny, philosophical Sagittarius will pass through your solar sixth house of work, and no matter where you are, a good time will be had by all. Just don't get too crazy with take-out. You could gain a bit of weight even before the holidays arrive. Moderation!

Tricky Transits
After two and a half years, Saturn will change signs on December 19, Cancer. The thing is, he'll be setting off for your solar seventh house of one-to-one relationships, and he's a very serious, practical fellow. Your more lighthearted, casual relationships may fade away now, but not to worry—they'll be replaced with friendships and partnerships that will provide you with support and stability in the years to come.

Rewarding Days
4, 7, 9, 16, 20, 21, 24, 25

Challenging Days
2, 3, 5, 11, 13, 14

Cancer Action Table

These dates reflect the best—but not the only—times for success and ease in these activities, according to your Sun sign.

	JAN	FEB	MAR	APR	MAY	JUN	JUL	AUG	SEP	OCT	NOV	DEC
Move	12, 13			10		23		4			17	
Start a class		9, 10, 11			9				27, 28, 29			1, 6, 12
Join a club			5, 18		10		24, 26				11	
Ask for a raise	3, 20	13, 22				1, 24			15, 17			20
Get professional advice		22, 23		17, 24			19, 24	22	12, 13	16		19
Get a loan	20				12, 17		18, 19	20				
New romance				16, 17				21		14, 27	13	24
Vacation	23		24, 26		12	9					16, 25	

Leo

The Lion
July 23 to August 22

Element: Fire

Quality: Fixed

Polarity: Yang/masculine

Planetary Ruler: The Sun

Meditation: I trust in the strength of my soul

Gemstone: Ruby

Power Stones: Topaz, sardonyx

Key Phrase: I will

Glyph: Lion's tail

Anatomy: Heart, upper back

Colors: Gold, scarlet

Animals: Lions, large cats

Myths/Legends: Apollo, Isis, Helios

House: Fifth

Opposite Sign: Aquarius

Flowers: Marigold, sunflower

Keyword: Magnetic

The Leo Personality

Your Strengths, Gifts, and Challenges

Your astrological symbol is the Lion, which suits you well, Leo. You most certainly do prowl, and you purr—and maybe even knead—when you're happy. Like a lion, you really and truly are quite brave and amazingly loyal, and you're never afraid of attracting attention by standing up for you or yours, something that tends to blunt a good many well-meaning swords. You adore attention and applause, and if you have to roar to get it every now and then, that's just fine with you—especially if you happen to draw a bit of an admiring crowd in the process. You know exactly what to do to please most of the people most of the time, so when you're on stage, on your game, and feeling loved and appreciated, you rock, Leo. Period.

So now that I'm done praising you (and every word was quite heartfelt, I assure you), let's talk about your ego. Yes, you're fabulous—especially when you're performing for us. Everyone knows that. It's why you're always invited to all the really good parties. The thing is—and don't get mad—every now and then, you do tend to forget that not everyone is part of your audience and that the world doesn't always revolve around you. Now, in your defense, given that your ruling planet just so happens to be the Sun—around which the world does, indeed, revolve—it's easy to see why this might not be immediately evident to you. Learn to share the applause. You're terrific when you're entertaining us, but you're at your very best when you pave the way for others to enjoy their own center-stage bow.

Romance, Friendships, and Casual Relationships

When it comes to keeping company with you, Leo, it takes a lot of energy. You're the ultimate fire sign, an endlessly entertaining playmate and the most attentive partner anyone could ever wish for. Whether we're a friend, a lover, or a spouse, you can make us feel more special than any other sign. The other fire signs, Aries and Sagittarius, are often your choice for lovers or amorous playmates, since they're energetic enough to keep up and just as enthusiastic about adventure and new experiences. Libra tends to be a great match for you, too. Their unconditional devotion warms your heart and inspires you to return the favor—big time. But it's not just romantic partners who are so delightfully spoiled by you, Leo. In fact, anyone who enjoys the privilege of being loved by you will never have to worry—not about anything. Anyone who qualifies as a member of your pride is golden. You will always, always, have their back, and always be willing to do whatever you can to help—that is, as long as that help is accepted. If they happen to be going through a phase, however, and can't see their way toward allowing you and your loving support into their life, you won't take kindly to what you might read as rejection, even if it's not. Fortunately, that won't happen much. Far more often, it's the fact that you give too much that can be a tad problematic at times. Learn to support your dear ones without propping them up, and work on being just a bit less thin-skinned.

Career and Work

If anyone can inspire us, Leo, it's you. First off, no matter what you do to earn your daily bread, you're a great example of how it should be done. You won't bother with anything you don't do exceptionally well, and perfecting your professional reputation is something you tend to quite carefully, so obviously, you're a terrific coach, mentor, and advisor. After all, if anyone is an expert at gaining applause and attention, it's you, and passing down a few of your tried-and-true secret techniques can be invaluable to novices and youngsters. Then again, your ability to hold our attention in the most delightful fashion can also put you on the stage quite literally, via acting, art, fashion, or music, but chances are that no matter how you spend your day, you're onstage and in a starring role in one way or another for most of it. Whether you're in a classroom, a bar, or a leading role, be sure you're doing what you love.

Money and Possessions

Okay, so let's go back to that whole "pride" thing we talked about earlier. You're royalty and you know it, so you tend to surround yourself with fine things and treat yourself to the best experiences money can buy. The reality of what you have and the time you spent working to have it is not lost on you, however, so you tend to your possessions with TLC. You love to pick up the tab, buy gifts, and surprise others with show tickets, so you probably have a feast-or-famine relationship with the dollar bill, but with meticulous Virgo as ruler of your solar second house of earned income and money matters, you know exactly what you have to play with at any given time.

Your Lighter Side

Fierceness aside, lions do purr when they're happy, comfy, and well loved, so going home to the right family situation is what you look forward to most at the end of the day. But it's also important for you to do what you do best—cut loose and play! Since you're pretty much a big kid yourself, you enjoy children, and they enjoy you. Be sure to set a few hours aside regularly for adult pleasures too, and treat yourself often to art, music, and, of course, theater or movies. Trying out for the local improv group wouldn't be a bad idea either, just for kicks.

Leo Celebrities

Remember how we talked about your love of the spotlight and your inimitable ability to attract attention? Well, here's a short list of the celebrities your Sun keeps company with: DeNiro. Madonna. Lucy. Napoleon. Jagger. JLo. Hitchcock. Jackie O. YSL. Notice anything? Yep. Only one word, kids. Just the one. Of course, Dame Helen Mirren has worn a royal leonine crown many times in her career, and Daniel Radcliffe, Sean Penn, Sandra Bullock, Dustin Hoffman, and Antonio Banderas are impossible to miss. Regardless of the field they're in, Leo celebrities are easy to spot by the regal way they carry themselves.

Words to Live By for 2017

Prepare to take a bow. That long, hard task is almost done.

The Year Ahead for Leo

Well, first of all, Leo, you'll be happy to know that Venus, the Goddess of Love—and Money, by the way—has decided to spend no less than three full months in Aries, one of your equally impulsive fire-sign cousins. Now, this puts her charming, impulsive little energy right smack dab in your solar ninth house for an extended visit—and speaking of extended visits, this, friends, is the stuff that long-distance relationships are made of. If you're already happily involved with someone, better keep a careful distance from anyone new who shows up with a fascinating accent or a pack of exciting stories about life in their country or on their coastline—because with Venus in this impetuous sign, you might be short on willpower. If you're in the market for a playmate or lover, however, that accent and those stories are exactly what you should be keeping an ear out for. The good news is that even if your first thought is that long-distance relationships don't work, I'm here to tell you that you might not need to worry about that. People move long-distance all the time, for all kinds of reasons, and anyway, Aries planets aren't notorious for inspiring us to settle down. Think of this as an adventure and enjoy yourself to the fullest. (That goes double during late February and early March for any of you who were born around April 5.) Remember, though, that Venus is also in charge of possessions and money matters, so if you're tempted to make an impulsive financial move, whether it's a major purchase or a loan or investment, the very least you should do first is to consult with a friend who'll be able to pry the plastic out of your hands—with force if necessary.

But let's get back to relationships, because if all that red-hot Aries energy that Venus will be packing won't be enough astrological excuse to find you in the mood to partner up, there's Jupiter, who'll spend up until October 10 in charming Libra, a sign that's ruled by Venus. He'll be passing through your solar third house of thoughts and communications for the duration, so you'll have relationships on your mind—that's a given. This is also the house of short trips, so don't be surprised if you run into others in supposedly "circumstantial" situations. With lucky Jupiter and magnetic Venus in cahoots, being in the right place at the right time to meet the perfect person for you along the way will be easy, and once you've met whoever you were supposed to meet, you'll be golden. All you have to do is pay attention, especially if your schedule is suddenly torn asunder and you're not happy about it. Something that seems like a coincidence could make a major change in your life. It's up to you to recognize that nothing happens by accident. The Universe is trying to get your attention. Listen up!

Saturn

Saturn has just under a year to go on his trek through Sagittarius, and once again, he's going to spend it in your solar fifth house of fun times and love affairs—which, admittedly, doesn't sound like a really good time. Lest you forget, however, you've been dealing with this serious fellow for two years now, and I'm quite sure you've had a chance every now and then to have some serious fun—provided, of course that your chores and your homework have been done before you even think about heading out to join the pack at the usual spot. This house also describes the type of playmates who'll be waiting for you there, and since Saturn insists on some type of return on your time, your peer circles of late have probably been made up mostly of coworkers or others who are in your field or share your career and professional interests—folks who can either help you to advance or give you a push in the right direction, that is. Keep in mind that Saturn just loves it when we prepare ourselves for what's coming next, so surrounding yourself with others who enjoy what you do is a great idea. That goes double since Saturn will take off for your solar sixth house of work on December 19, at which time you'll begin a two-year period of intense focus on perfecting your chosen craft. Make the connections you'll need now.

Uranus

Startling Uranus has been on duty in fiery, spontaneous Aries since 2010, Leo, so you've probably gotten used to being quite spontaneous yourself, especially when it comes to traveling, taking classes, or even getting involved in local politics or community administrations. Well, it's not over yet. As he's made his way through impulsive Aries and your solar ninth house of higher beliefs, it's only natural that the big issues—that in, religion, politics, and education—have no doubt caught your attention in a very big way, and held on to it, too. Uranus is urging you to stretch, to expand your horizons in an equally large way, and in the process, to develop a belief system that's your own and no one else's—even if it clashes with that of your parents, friends, or spouse (and, à la Uranus, maybe even just because it clashes). Uranus inspires us to think about what we really want to be when we grow up, too, and to do some very intense intellectual explorations—soul-searching, that is. While he's in the neighborhood, we're a lot more willing to change, especially since all kinds of interesting people tend to make their way through our lives with this wild man on duty. You'll recognize them by the fact that they really don't care what anyone else thinks of them and by the unapologetic way they carry themselves. If you've been enjoying it—and I can't imagine how you wouldn't—then not to worry. The parade isn't going to stop any time soon.

Neptune

For yet another year, Neptune will continue on her path through your solar eighth house of intimate matters and shared resources, Leo. Now, this is an extremely private place where this woozy, dreamy planet can settle in and make herself extremely comfortable, and when she's relaxed, all of her most intoxicating charms are especially potent—from illusion to delusion to divine or spiritual inspiration. If you're happily attached, you two have probably arrived at a point in your relationship where you truly have moments of complete and total bonding—not just physically but also emotionally and spiritually. It's Neptune's job to dissolve boundaries and remind us that we are all part of The One, and passionate love is the best and sweetest way to drive that point home. Of course, when it comes to financial matters such as loans and inheritances, her woozy pink energy can be a bit problematic at times, especially if you're not paying attention to the signs and symbols the Universe is sending along. If you were born between July 30 and August 7, Neptune is also forming an uncomfortable inconjunct aspect to your Sun, so you've probably had your share of confusion along these lines lately, but not to worry. Be sure to keep a trustworthy, rational friend handy to help you sort fact from fantasy, and don't let anyone take advantage of you.

Pluto

Pluto's job is to help you to molt, to shed what's no longer useful or positive in your life and make way for new experiences, new inner growth, and new self-realization. This year, he'll once again spend his time in your solar sixth house of health, work, and work-oriented situations, the house that basically defines the rhythm of your day. That said, if you have a structured lifestyle, it could be that forces beyond your command are about to shake that up—say, via new management at work or a whole new position that's given to you during the early part of the year. It might also be that a health-related habit needs to change so you can rejuvenate and regenerate your lifestyle. The good news is that research shows that it takes only three weeks to reprogram ourselves by ditching old behaviors and creating newer, more positive routines. Regardless of how it comes about, letting go of some element of the past that was comfortable and constant is essential now. If you were born between August 8 and August 13, Leo, your Sun will also receive an inconjunct aspect from Pluto this year, so all this applies even more particularly to you. Just relax and loosen that white-knuckled grip on what's soon to be your past. Once you've let go and made some room, you'll be amazed at how quickly the Universe will fill in any voids with something that's much more productive for you.

How Will This Year's Eclipses Affect You?

Eclipses are celestial exclamation points. They amp up the volume on ordinary life whenever they occur, but the signs and degrees they acti-vate bring along events and circumstances that are especially intense. Eclipses occur in pairs, six months apart over a two-week period. Solar Eclipses are supercharged New Moons that bring the Sun and Moon together, marking peak times for planting spiritual seeds and announc-ing our intentions to the Universe. Lunar Eclipses are high-energy Full Moons, and like these monthly oppositions between the Sun and Moon, they signal times of dramatic culmination and fulfillment.

The first Lunar Eclipse of the year will arrive on February 10, right in your very own sign, Leo. If you were born on August 15, the Lunar Eclipse will directly activate your Sun. Whether it's a direct hit or not, you'll feel the effects of this high-energy Full Moon in all your relation-ships but most especially those of the romantic type. On February 26, the first Solar Eclipse of 2017 will arrive, all done up in dreamy, intuitive Pisces and your solar eighth house of shared resources, joint finances, and intimate matters. If you're about to sign papers for anything major, stall until after that date, and only after you've had a chance to confer with a professional. But remember, this house also has a whole lot to do with sexuality, so if a relationship starts now, you can count on it being life-changing in more ways than one in a long-term sense and extremely hot in the meantime.

On August 7, a Lunar Eclipse will set up shop in Aquarius and your solar seventh house of one-to-one relationships, and since Mercury will turn retrograde a few days later, you'll probably find that someone from the past has crossed your path "accidentally on purpose" or that you're suddenly in the mood to get together with someone you thought had left your life for good. Either way, be careful. Eclipses often show up in our lives as impulsive moves. Be sure you know what you're doing before taking any emotional risks. The last Solar Eclipse of the year will come along on August 21, Leo—and if you were born around that date, you're in for a wild ride. You'll enjoy a burst of energy that's primed and ready to help you initiate some new beginnings of the most dramatic and noticeable kind. Even if that's not your birthdate, don't be surprised if you have a sudden, overwhelming urge to do something different with your hair—sorry, I meant "mane"—or to change your look in some other equally striking way. The good news is that if you've been trying to get someone to notice you, regardless of why, this lunation will most certainly do the trick. You'll be even more impossible to miss than usual—and even more confident.

Leo | January

Relaxation and Recreation

The New Moon on January 27 will occur in your solar seventh house of one-to-one relationships, Leo, all done up in surprising Aquarius. That same day, red-hot Mars will head off into Aries, its astrological home turf, turning up the volume on your urge to take off for parts unknown—just for kicks. You won't have trouble finding a spontaneous companion for a weekend away. Have fun!

Lovers and Friends

With loving Venus set to spend the month in woozy, romantic Pisces and your solar eighth house of intimate relationships, Leo, it's easy to see you and a certain someone spending a whole lot of quality time alone together. Just be sure to let your friends, family, and fans know that all is well before you two disappear entirely.

Money and Success

The emotional Moon will spend the weekend of January 14 in your solar second house of personal money matters and financial dealings, Leo, and she'll be facing off with several ultra-emotional planets in Pisces. You may need to dig into your pocket to help a loved one who really has no one else to turn to.

Tricky Transits

On January 10 or 11, a conversation with an elder, authority figure, or higher-up on the job could turn pretty darn contentious quite suddenly, Leo. If the subject is money, that goes double. Your mission is to keep your wits about you, especially if a raise, bonus, or promotion is on the line. Don't step on any toes.

Rewarding Days

4, 8, 9, 13, 22

Challenging Days

10, 11, 12, 19, 27, 31

Leo | February

Relaxation and Recreation

Mercury will spend the first week of the month in hardworking, serious-minded Capricorn, so it might be tough to find time for playmates, but not to worry. As of February 7, when he takes off for spontaneous, impulsive Aquarius, loosening up your schedule to make time for fun will be a lot easier to do. Use this week to wrap up a project.

Lovers and Friends

Loving Venus is off for fiery, passionate Aries on February 3, Leo—which I guarantee will suit you just fine. She'll be holding court in your solar ninth house of long-distance friends and far-off loved ones, urging you to cut loose and maybe go on a trip you've been meaning to take for a very long time. If you can't get away, however, no one says they can't come to you instead.

Money and Success

The Solar Eclipse on February 26 could be a bit tricky for you, Leo—financially speaking. It will occur in your solar eighth house of shared resources and joint finances, all done up in Pisces, a sign that sometimes becomes confused about what's real and what's not. If you're gut tells you a deal is too good to be true, it probably is.

Tricky Transits

On February 8, the Moon in highly emotional Cancer will get into a testy Grand Square with Pluto, Uranus, and Jupiter—and this is the stuff that emotional drama is often made of. Now, you have no problem with drama, provided it's fun, but this particular bundle of energies could be tough to navigate—even for you. Stay calm.

Rewarding Days

3, 7, 9, 11, 20, 21

Challenging Days

8, 26, 27, 28

Leo | March

Relaxation and Recreation

With Mars, Venus, and Mercury taking turns visiting with unpredictable Uranus in your solar ninth house, Leo, you most definitely will not be bored this month. In fact, you might have more social engagements than you can actually get to. Now, that's nothing new for you, but this time around, be sure anyone who's expecting you knows in advance if you won't be able to make it.

Lovers and Friends

Loving Venus will turn retrograde on March 4, Leo, and since she'll be in your solar ninth house of far-off loved ones and long-distance relationships, you should expect to hear from someone you've been sorely missing for a very long time. The good news is that you two will have a full month to make plans to close the distance between you.

Money and Success

If you haven't been paying attention to your checking account balance or credit card statements, Leo, you could be due for a rather rude awakening around March 12. The Full Moon in your solar second house will focus a spotlight on your personal finances, calling your attention to something that's been left undone. Take care of it right away—or better still, well before this day arrives.

Tricky Transits

On March 30, mighty Jupiter and intense Pluto will get into an uneasy square aspect, and there's sure to be some tension in the air. In your case, it might be that a work situation has come to a head and you can no longer pretend there's nothing going on, or that a financial partnership isn't working out at all as you'd planned. Don't be afraid to end it—and be firm.

Rewarding Days

2, 3, 13, 18, 19, 29

Challenging Days

10, 11, 12, 17, 21, 30

Leo | April

Relaxation and Recreation

A playful Gemini Moon will be in the neighborhood on April Fools' Day, Leo, and since she'll be passing through your solar eleventh house of groups and friendships, you might be in the mood to play a prank on someone—or someone might go out of their way to play one on you. Not to worry. There's nothing mean-spirited about Gemini energy—and it will make for a great story.

Lovers and Friends

The lovely lady Venus has decided to back up into Pisces to finish up a few things, Leo, which will put her right smack dab in your solar eighth house of intimate relationships. In this oh-so-romantic sign, it's not hard to imagine you taking up with someone from the past for another shot at the title—but be sure you have new solutions to those old problems.

Money and Success

Venus is in charge of money as well as love, Leo, and since she'll be in woozy, dreamy Pisces for most of the month, you'll need to pay careful attention to your checkbook and plastic. Keep a watchful eye on your spending habits—and your actual physical wallet or purse, too. Pisces planets create very potent smoke screens and Venus is nothing if not intoxicating. Don't get distracted.

Tricky Transits

Mercury will stop in his tracks on April 9, Leo, preparing for a three-week retrograde trip through your solar tenth house of career matters. If you've been angling for a raise, bonus, or promotion—especially if this will be your second shot at it—this is the perfect time to update your resumé. Be sure that all your recent accomplishments don't go unnoticed.

Rewarding Days
1, 6, 7, 10, 17, 24, 27

Challenging Days
4, 8, 20, 21

Leo | May

Relaxation and Recreation

Mars is the most passionate, energetic guy in the heavens, Leo, and he's moving through your solar eleventh house of peer groups and friendships, all done up in chatty, sociable Gemini. Needless to say, you'll have another busy month, socially speaking, but with the Sun and Mercury on duty in your solar tenth house of career, you might also have to put in some serious overtime. Ah, well. You're a fire sign. You'll be fine.

Lovers and Friends

On May 28, you could easily end up in a testy situation with a friend, Leo, over an outstanding financial matter that you've both been pretty much trying to ignore for some time now. The thing is, you really can't do that any longer, but you also won't want to alienate your friend completely, so every word you utter will need to be carefully chosen.

Money and Success

The Sun and Mercury in Taurus will pass through your solar tenth house of career matters this month, Leo—and the good news is that Taurus planets are money magnets, so if you're looking to improve your situation financially, this is the time to do it. May 9 and 24 are the best days to schedule an appointment with a higher-up who can help you move up the ladder.

Tricky Transits

On May 11, impulsive Mars will square off with Neptune, and a friend may come to you in search of a loan. You'll want to help them out—as per usual—but before you grab your wallet, think. Is this the first time? Is the situation really as dire as they've let on? No one's saying you can't help. Just don't enable someone who's not trying to help themselves.

Rewarding Days
1, 2, 3, 17, 18, 19

Challenging Days
5, 10, 11, 16, 27, 28

Leo | June

Relaxation and Recreation

With the Sun and Mercury taking turns dashing through your solar eleventh house of groups and friendships—even if they weren't all done up in funny, fast-moving Gemini—it's easy to see how you'll probably be on the receiving end of far more invitations than you can accept. The thing is, someone is counting on you. Make a special effort to get to the important things.

Lovers and Friends

Once loving Venus tiptoes off seductively into sensual Taurus on June 6, we'll all be after only the richest, most delicious experiences. That goes double for you, Leo—first off because you already have a taste for the finer things in life, but mostly because you rightfully believe you deserve them. An equally delightful playmate will be necessary for the duration, of course. Bet you've got one handy.

Money and Success

Once Venus sets off for Taurus, you won't want to settle for anything less than what you really deserve, Leo, so if your efforts at work aren't appreciated, you won't want to hang around much longer. Chances are pretty good that you won't have that problem, though. In fact, a well-deserved pat on the back might actually be on the way.

Tricky Transits

Fiery Mars will spend most of the month in ultra-sensitive Cancer and your solar twelfth house, an extremely private energy in an extremely private place. Now, regardless of the sign he's in, Mars is the God of War. Needless to say, if anyone gets a bit too nosy or asks one too many questions, you won't take kindly to it.

Rewarding Days

1, 6, 8, 13, 14, 24, 25

Challenging Days

4, 15, 19, 27, 28

Leo | July

Relaxation and Recreation

The New Moon in your sign on July 23 will plant a very potent seed of new beginnings in your solar first house of personality and appearance, Leo—which obviously means it's probably high time for a new wardrobe and/or hairstyle, due to a whole new attitude. If you're not quite ready to do anything drastic, not to worry. The summer is young. You'll get there.

Lovers and Friends

Both fiery Mars and the Sun himself will storm off into your sign late this month, Leo, so don't be surprised if the ones who love you are a tad surprised at how especially feisty you are. Just be sure you're not overreacting to what might turn out to be imaginary offenses, especially around July 17 and 20.

Money and Success

Venus will square off with woozy Neptune on July 17, making it all too easy for you to be taken advantage of, financially speaking, but also for you to lose your cash, plastic, or checkbook. If you really don't need to have it all with you, leave your important stuff at home. Keep a twenty in your shoe, though just in case.

Tricky Transits

The Sun, Mercury, and Mars will all spend time in Cancer this month, the sign that belongs to the emotional Moon. Now, this puts them in your solar twelfth house of Privacy, Please, so while you don't usually have a problem expressing your feelings, circumstances beyond your control might force you to suffer in silence. It won't be for long.

Rewarding Days

1, 4, 7, 11

Challenging Days

13, 16, 17, 20

Leo | August

Relaxation and Recreation

When the Sun is in your sign—your home turf, by the way—you lions tend to be especially fiery and even more wildly entertaining. And now that Mars is set to spend the month in your sign and your solar first house of personality and appearance—well, let's just say that relaxation will be tough to come by, but you'll be smiling far too much to care.

Lovers and Friends

Jupiter is the King of Expansion, and he's all done up in partner-oriented Libra at the moment, Leo. On August 4, he'll square off with powerful Pluto, making intense and maybe even manipulative encounters the order of the day. If you're set to do something unusual with someone and you don't feel quite right about it, don't hesitate to back out—with no apologies.

Money and Success

Mercury will turn retrograde on August 12 in your solar second house of money matters, giving you a second chance to negotiate any recent financial matters that haven't worked out quite as well as you'd hoped. With what you've learned since then, a new shot at the title might be all it takes to wrap things up positively. Gather up your information.

Tricky Transits

There'll be two eclipses this month, Leo, both set to activate your solar relationship axis in a very big way. If you're deliriously happy, you might decide to make it official and move in, get engaged, or become monogamous. If you're not a happy camper and you've been thinking about making a break for it, you can make your escape now—but it's going to happen fast.

Rewarding Days

1, 2, 10, 13, 20, 22

Challenging Days

3, 4, 5, 16, 18, 24

Leo | September

Relaxation and Recreation

With so many planets making their way through dutiful Virgo, taking care of business will keep you pretty darn busy during September, Leo, but not to worry. You'll see the end result of all your hard work and attention to detail much sooner than you might have imagined if you tend to your responsibilities with special care around September 9, 12, and 22.

Lovers and Friends

You might be a tad more prone to be critical of the little things that drive you nuts about your sweetheart, Leo, but even close friends won't be entirely safe. Before you go off about these little things in a very big and dramatic way, keep in mind that we all have irritating habits. Yes, even you.

Money and Success

Four planets will pass through your solar second house this month, Leo, all done up in precise, meticulous Virgo. Now, you can probably guess what I'm going to say next, but stop rolling your eyes. Yes, it's time to tend to paperwork, and yes, I'm aware that you didn't want to hear that. Too bad. You'll thank me next month when you need accurate balance info and you actually have it.

Tricky Transits

On September 5, Mercury will turn direct. This would seem to indicate that all those irritating hindrances and annoying roadblocks that have gotten in your way for the past three weeks would suddenly dissolve. You'd think. The thing is, it takes a few days for this to actually happen. It's a gradual process, so you'll need to be patient.

Rewarding Days
9, 12, 17, 18, 22, 26

Challenging Days
1, 5, 6, 16, 20, 28

Leo | October

Relaxation and Recreation

On October 10, expansive Jupiter will set off for Scorpio and your solar fourth house of home and family matters, Leo, marking the beginning of a year of intensity on your home turf. Now, lest you worry for no reason, do remember that there are all kinds of intense feelings out there, and extreme happiness is on that list. Do what you can to feel it.

Lovers and Friends

On October 14, Venus—the Goddess of Relationships herself—will take off for one of her favorite signs, partner-oriented Libra. In a nutshell, Leo, since she'll be holding court in your solar third house of conversations and communications, this basically means that you'll be even more devastatingly charming this month than usual. Heaven help us all.

Money and Success

The Full Moon on October 5 will combine forces with the collision of Venus and Mars in your second solar house of finances to draw your attention to what could turn out to be an extremely pressing financial matter you weren't aware of. You'll notice it now for certain and be awfully glad you got your paperwork together last month.

Tricky Transits

On October 4, the Sun in partner-oriented Libra will get into a confusing inconjunct aspect with woozy Neptune, who's currently holding court in your solar eighth house of intimate relationships—and Mercury will follow suit on October 6. Needless to say, trying to determine exactly what *they* meant by *that* could become all-consuming. Don't let that happen. It really could be nothing at all.

Rewarding Days
1, 3, 12, 14, 24, 25

Challenging Days
4, 5, 6, 8, 9, 26

Leo | November

Relaxation and Recreation

Mercury—the most playful planet, by the way—will dash off into your solar fifth house of playmates and recreational activities on November 5, all done up in Sagittarius, a fire-sign cousin that never fails to amuse you. Yes, you'll have interesting mates, and no, you won't want to sleep unless it's necessary. Fine. Just don't forget your vitamins.

Lovers and Friends

You single folks should keep your ears open for the distinct sound of an interesting story being told in an entertaining fashion by someone with a wonderful accent. You need a change of pace and a mental challenge, and this could most definitely be someone who'll provide it. Hey, if worse comes to worst, at the very least you'll have a fascinating new friend.

Money and Success

Venus is in charge of money as well as love, Leo, and she's set to spend most of the month in intensely private Scorpio, so it might be that you're reluctant to disclose any financial details to anyone who's too eager to hear them. Obviously, from your perspective, you're not being paranoid, but if you're also hiding Benjamins under your mattress, you might want to ask yourself why.

Tricky Transits

Serious Saturn will move into an easy, cooperative trine aspect with startling Uranus on November 11, which will make it very, very easy for you to have what you want—maybe even without a whole lot of effort. If you feel that the Universe is gifting you, don't just sit there on the couch smiling. Take advantage of this energy to figure out what it will take to make your future happen.

Rewarding Days

5, 6, 10, 11, 17, 25

Challenging Days

8, 13, 14, 19

Leo | December

Relaxation and Recreation

A little bit of the exuberance and enthusiasm of Sagittarius goes a long way, Leo—unless you're a fellow fire sign and you just so happen to crave adrenaline. In that case, you're about to be a very happy little lion, and a very busy one as well. You usually have a busy social schedule, but this—well, this will be extraordinary. Make time for the events that are important to someone you adore.

Lovers and Friends

Venus in Sagittarius will keep your social schedule full all month, Leo. Once Venus marches off into Capricorn on December 25, you'll be able to stop worrying about whether or not you remembered a gift for everyone on your list and begin thinking about how important it is to give them each a really big hug. 'Tis the season.

Money and Success

With Venus in excessive Sagittarius until Christmas Day, you'll have plenty of astrological reasons to be quite extravagant when it comes to holiday gifts, Leo. Your mission is to please keep in mind that your total and complete attention for one entire afternoon might mean more to someone than anything you could possibly pick up at Macy's.

Tricky Transits

On December 19, Saturn will set off for a two-and-a-half-year stint in Capricorn, the sign he considers his home turf and the one he's strongest while wearing. This no-nonsense guy will be on duty in your solar sixth house of work, coworkers, and health-related issues and he just loves preparation, so going on a diet or quitting a bad habit would be a great way to keep him happy—and keep yourself healthy.

Rewarding Days

6, 7, 8, 10, 16, 17, 26

Challenging Days

1, 2, 3, 5, 21, 22

Leo Action Table

These dates reflect the best—but not the only—times for success and ease in these activities, according to your Sun sign.

	JAN	FEB	MAR	APR	MAY	JUN	JUL	AUG	SEP	OCT	NOV	DEC
Move			27		10			3, 4				13
Start a class		3, 19				7, 8	7				10, 11	
Join a club	1, 2, 3	16		13, 17	25				29	27		3
Ask for a raise			5, 7, 9, 29	17, 24		1	8, 9	13, 22			13, 14	
Get professional advice		23	7, 29				19, 20	27		1, 3, 16		
Get a loan	20			18, 27				27				
New romance	12		27, 29			6, 7	20, 22		15, 17			10, 12
Vacation		24			12, 13				7	22	5, 21	

Virgo

The Virgin
August 23 to September 22

Element: Earth	Glyph: Greek symbol for containment
Quality: Mutable	Anatomy: Abdomen, gallbladder, intestines
Polarity: Yin/feminine	Colors: Taupe, gray, navy blue
Planetary Ruler: Mercury	Animals: Domesticated animals
Meditation: I can allow time for myself	Myths/Legends: Demeter, Astraea, Hygeia
Gemstone: Sapphire	House: Sixth
Power Stones: Peridot, amazonite, rhodochrosite	Opposite Sign: Pisces
	Flower: Pansy
Key Phrase: I analyze	Keyword: Discriminating

The Virgo Personality

Your Strengths, Gifts, and Challenges

In at least one area of life, Virgo, you're a perfectionist who just won't stand for anything less than precision and exactness. It might be your physical appearance, your home, or your possessions that you strive to perfect, or maybe all three. Usually, though, you train your attention toward the minute inner workings of your work situation. On the plus side, this means that every job you take on will be done to the very best of your ability, with an eye toward tending carefully to the little things. It's that attention to detail that makes you an expert in your chosen field—provided, of course, that you're not just treading water for a paycheck until the job you're dying for comes along.

You can be equally focused on details when it comes to health issues, so you also tend to be a bit of a hypochondriac at times—usually when you're bored or when a recent encounter has left you feeling abandoned or neglected. Do yourself a favor. Resolve to stay away from WebMD or websites like it, and avoid friends or acquaintances who always seem to be suffering from some vague illness that keeps them from being their best. Most importantly, keep yourself so happily distracted you don't have time to fret. Life's too short to focus on what's wrong about it. Kick back and count your blessings every now and then.

Romance, Friendships, and Casual Relationships

You do love to fix things, Virgo. It's highly satisfying for you. The thing is, you're often tempted to take that fondness for remodeling, revamping, and restoring into your relationships with actual humans—who, at times, may not be in the mood to be fixed. It's true that you do attract others who are needy, broken, or almost-perfect-except-for, but if those relationships haven't worked out well for you, it's time to take the hint. Your quest is to find someone who's operating on an independent level—taking care of themselves physically, emotionally, and financially. From this day forward, feel free to ghost anyone your intuition tells you is hanging around in hopes of being repaired. Not your job. A functional, industrious partner is what you deserve. If you don't have them by your side just yet, Jupiter in partner-oriented Libra will be happy to send along some wonderful applicants for the position this year. Careful, though. You can be a tad critical of others at times, Virgo, especially if they don't know you well enough to understand that straightening their tie or tucking in a tag is nothing compared to how tough you can be on yourself. Look to earthy Taurus and Capricorn for easy, comfortable matches. Scorpios, however, are fascinating—and often provide just the right amount of intellectual competition to keep you interested in the long term.

Career and Work

Let's talk about details, Virgo, and your innate ability to spot them immediately and retain them indefinitely. The thing is, those little things may actually seem little—and/or unimportant—to others, but when you're focused, you're a human microscope, capable of spotting the tiniest flaws in the machinery that can cause huge problems from a mile away. This is an extraordinary skill that can most definitely be a blessing, especially if you channel it into positive, productive activities and outlets. It makes you the ideal employee and the ideal employer at the same time. Your fondness for being precise and exact often draws you toward service-oriented positions in hospitality and healthcare, but honestly, you can master any skill you set your mind to. As long as you spend your day troubleshooting, fixing, or providing meticulous care, you'll be fine. Oh, and numbers. You folks are usually very good with numbers, so accounting, data entry, and bookkeeping are also right up your alley.

Money and Possessions

In general, you tend to have a rather practical and even frugal attitude toward money and possessions, Virgo. You prefer to live on what you can afford—and you're extremely proud when you prove to yourself that you can maybe even whittle things down and live on a bit less. This year, however, with expansive Jupiter in your solar second house of finances, all bets are off. Anything is possible, from winning the lottery to declaring bankruptcy. Even if nothing drastic arises, though, pay attention to the big picture as it pertains to your financial situation. Do you have a five-year plan? If not, get busy. You know you can handle the paperwork, and you're good at keeping to a schedule. You're also usually pretty darn accurate with your bank and financial records and credit card statements, so you'll have no problem tracking your spending patterns. If you're one of the lucky few of us who know how to refinance debts for the best interest rates every few months, get on it. It's time to make the most of what you have. That goes for possessions, too. You love to fix things and you're quite crafty, so refurbished and repurposed items make you happy. With lucky Jupiter in this house, if you're a collector, keep your eyes open. You could be on the verge of finding the real deal at a yard or estate sale.

Your Lighter Side

Like your cerebral Gemini cousins, there's only one state of affairs that you really can't tolerate, Virgo—that is, being bored. You share your ruling planet with Gemini—none other than Mercury, the god with the wings on his feet and his head. Constant movement is a must for you both, but in your case, top-quality conversation is pretty darn important, too. That means having meaningful and maybe even challenging chats with others involving issues and events—rather than gossiping about other people or discussing the last episode of *The Bachelor* (which may actually be one of your favorite, highly secret guilty pleasures). When you're looking for solitary amusement, puzzles and games will work just fine, but whether you know it or not, it's putting things in order—regardless of the reason—that soothes your soul and makes you happy.

Virgo Celebrities

Are you Virgos really perfectionists? Well, let's see, there's Michael Jackson, arguably the most famous Virgo, who went through plastic surgeries on a regular basis to perfect his appearance. Then there's Dr. Phil, who helps fix broken relationships, and Mother Teresa, who spent her life trying to fix broken people. Your sign is also chock full of folks who have simply perfected their chosen paths, however—like Pink, Stephen King, Beyonce, Salma Hayek, James Gandolfini, and Cameron Diaz.

Words to Live By for 2017
I'm perfect just as I am.

The Year Ahead for Virgo

Generous and often quite excessive Jupiter made his way into your solar second house last fall, Virgo, where issues of personal finances and money matters are handled. Now, this guy is famous for overdoing it, so in this house, his presence can work out one of two ways. First off, and hopefully, his love for expansion and the lucky times his visits often accompany might mean that your financial situation is about to change for the better—in which case, you either are currently or will soon be enjoying a whole lot of extra income. If that's the case, congrats—but please, don't spend it all in one place. Seriously. The thing is, if you spend too much, even if it's just on paper, via big payments or long-term loans you're not sure you'll reasonably be able to keep up with—well, you'll be trapping yourself on the famine side of the feast-or-famine syndrome that transits from this extravagant guy often inspire. Keep a lid on your spending, don't abuse your plastic, and think hard before you cosign for someone with bad credit or agree to co-finance a project or business you're not really sure about.

Jupiter will spend his time in partner-oriented Libra, so partnering up for joint financial reasons might not be a bad idea—just be sure you know exactly what you're getting yourself into. And speaking of partnerships, let's talk about the lovely lady Venus, who'll spend three months in impulsive Aries and your solar eighth house of intimate partners over the course of the year. She'll enter this passionate place in this fiery sign on February 3 and stay put there until April 2, returning to finish up a few things from April 28 to June 6. During these periods, it will be all too easy for you to fall madly in love—or lust, anyway—with someone new and fascinating who doesn't seem to be afraid of or intimidated by anything. You two may start a love affair, but before you get too invested, keep in mind that some people aren't meant to have a permanent place in our scrapbooks. Some folks, in fact, are only in our lives temporarily, basically serving as messengers or as living how-to guides. If you've found a long-term soulmate, wonderful. If you haven't, allow yourself to enjoy the person just as they are.

Saturn

If you haven't yet gotten your domestic situation organized—and I really do find that hard to believe—you most certainly will this year, Virgo. Saturn has been hard at work in your solar fourth house of home, family, and living situations since the fall of 2015, busily providing you with events and circumstances specially designed to open your eyes to just how much easier life would be if everything were in order. Now, creating order is one of your sign's talents, but you don't always apply it to all areas of your life. In fact, you often keep it contained to one life department. Saturn, however, is just as good at noticing details as you are but is not as easily distracted. He won't be satisfied that your room is clean just because your underwear drawer is in perfect order. Force yourself to take a realistic look at the entire picture. At any rate, you'll have one last year with Saturn here to get it all worked out—and the sooner, the better. Of course, if you're one of those Virgos who does manage to keep absolutely everything in neat, orderly piles, you are probably enjoying Saturn's company and have taken advantage of his ultra-structured approach to alphabetize your DVDs. Seriously, though, if you've used Saturn's energy well, you're about to see some serious results. This structure-loving fellow may reward your efforts by making it possible for you to buy or build a home, make some major renovations, or put in a security system to keep your nest and your dear ones safe and secure.

Uranus

Back in 2010, your solar eighth house was invaded by an erratic and extremely exciting energy: Uranus himself, aka "Mr. Unpredictable." Now this is the slice of your solar personality that deals with intimate relationships, for one thing—and Uranus just loves raising eyebrows. Obviously, it's entirely possible that someone you were sure you knew very well has said or done something since then that has absolutely floored you—and if it hasn't happened yet, buckle up. On the other hand, it might just be you who's amazing and astounding the masses due to a major attitude shift or lifestyle change. You may suddenly be drawn to someone who's most definitely not your usual type. That goes double for those of you who were born between September 11 and September 23, since your Sun will be receiving an uncomfortable inconjunct aspect from Uranus this year. This is the stuff that rather awkward displays of rebellion are often made of—the kind that don't work out well for the doer in the long run. In short, if you're angry with the world, another person, or even yourself, try to resist the urge to show it in a rude or offensive way. If you feel that something is being taken from you, consider the fact that you may not need or want it anyway—and that you may have been sending out subconscious signals to that effect. Whatever leaves your life now was meant to go. Release it gracefully. Discovering the new you will be exhilarating—not to mention fun!

Neptune

Neptune will continue on her trek through your solar seventh house of one-to-one relationships throughout 2017, Virgo, where she's been on duty since 2011. Ever since then, you've probably developed a distinct tendency to either (A) see the best side of everyone or (B) be completely and totally disappointed by everyone. The thing is, Neptune dissolves boundaries, which makes it easy to blend and bond with others—but if you're blending and bonding with others who carry around negative energy, you're going to blend and bond with that energy, too. That would be where the disappointment might come in.

Since you'll be enjoying Neptune's company in your seventh house for several more years, learning to avoid negative energy and interactions with negative people is really not just the best course of action, it's the only one that will allow you to grow and prosper on a spiritual level, which is really what this transit is all about. This year, all of this will come home to those of you who were born between September 1 and September 7 in a very big way, since your Sun will also be receiving an opposition aspect from this dreamy, romantic, and often quite confusing energy. Your mission is to listen to your antennae, especially with regard to new relationships. If there's something that's just not right between the two of you or you're sure someone isn't who they say they are—well, you're probably right. Run. Once you've escaped, you'll be able to share your experiences with others who are being taken advantage of in similar ways but are not yet sure about how to break the pattern.

Pluto

If you were born between September 8 and September 14, life has probably been pretty darn good lately, Virgo—especially with regard to career matters, elders, and higher-ups. Pluto is in authoritative Capricorn and your solar fifth house, a very creative place—and he's currently forming an easy, cooperative trine aspect with your Sun. If you've had professional problems to solve, then coming up with a fresh approach probably hasn't been all that tough. And if any bumps in the road come up this year, rest assured you'll be able to handle them beautifully if you force yourself to think outside the box. Pluto is making it oh-so-easy for you to take charge of your life and everything in it—which also goes for relationships.

The fifth house also pertains to lovers, playmates, and dealings with kids—or basically, anything we consider fun. Pluto is a pretty darn intense guy and Capricorn planets aren't famous for cutting loose, so regardless of your birth date, you have probably not been able to kick back and relax much for years now, most likely because your natural organizational qualities often draw others to ask you to take charge— yes, maybe even while you're on vacation. That will continue this year, too—but hey, nobody says you can't refuse to get behind the wheel. Yes, you're hardworking and practical, and yes, you do love to serve, but you do deserve to have just a wee bit of fun every now and then. Insist on it.

How Will This Year's Eclipses Affect You?

Eclipses are celestial exclamation points. They amp up the volume on ordinary life whenever they occur, but the signs and degrees they activate also bring along events and circumstances that are quite intense. Eclipses occur in pairs, six months apart, over a two-week period. Solar Eclipses are supercharged New Moons. They bring the Sun and Moon together, marking peak times for planting spiritual seeds and announcing intentions of all kinds known to the Universe. Lunar Eclipses are high-energy Full Moons, and like these monthly oppositions between the Sun and the Moon, they signal times of dramatic culmination and fulfillment.

The first Lunar Eclipse of 2017 will occur on February 10 in dramatic, fiery Leo and your solar twelfth house of secrets. If you've been keeping something under wraps for a dear one, that may not be possible any longer—but there's really no reason to beat yourself up about it. Just be sure they understand your position and know what's coming before you open your mouth. Make sure anyone else who'll be affected by the news is also aware of the situation. Communication is your specialty and you're very good at it. Know that every word you utter will be especially potent now, and remember that words can be weapons.

On February 26, a Solar Eclipse will arrive, planting a tenderhearted Piscean seed in your solar seventh house of one-to-one relationships. The opportunity to make spiritual connections will come your way from every direction, from casual encounters with strangers that give you something to think about to intimate physical exchanges with tried-and-true loved ones. One way or the other, you'll know the feeling of being truly bonded with another human being. You may also be called upon by a dear one who needs your help to combat an addiction or change a bad living situation. If you yourself are indulging in something unhealthy or harmful, reach out and ask for a hand.

The second set of eclipses will occur in August, beginning with a Lunar Eclipse in Aquarius on August 7. This lunation will turn on a spotlight in your solar sixth house of health habits, work, and relationships with coworkers, forcing you to see exactly how what you do on a daily basis affects the state of your health and well-being. If you've been taking care of yourself for some time now, this eclipse will reinforce your determination to take care of the physical you and to see to it that your work reflects your ideals. If not, a diet or drastic change in your habits is in order. If you're not happy with the way you earn your daily bread and you just can't stand it a moment longer, you may need to cut back financially to start over in a new field—but it sure will be worth it.

On August 21, a Solar Eclipse will land in your solar twelfth house of secrets, giving you a chance to release any guilt you're carrying around with regard to the revelations you initiated back in February. By now, you should be able to understand why it was so important for you to get everything out in the open at that time—but if you haven't yet had an aha moment, just wait a while. The Universe will send one along shortly.

Virgo | January

Relaxation and Recreation

Venus and Mars will spend the month together in your solar seventh house of one-to-one relationships, Virgo, all done up in dreamy, woozy Pisces. This team inspires sighs and smiles but also passion. If you're happily attached, you two will be close to inseparable this month. If you're single, know that love at first sight is in the air. Just take your time deciding if you've really found it.

Lovers and Friends

The Full Moon in Cancer on January 12 will occur in your solar eleventh house of groups and friendships, Virgo, a warm and fuzzy energy that will bring your dear ones right to your door. Of course, you may need to extend an invitation to make it happen, and you'll probably have to throw in at least one home-cooked meal, but hey—what's better than feeding the ones you love?

Money and Success

Generous Jupiter is making his way through your solar second house of money and possessions, Virgo, passing out goodies as often as he can. If you've already been on the receiving end of his benevolence, sharing whatever else comes your way this month would be a lovely way to pay it forward. Bet you know exactly who to share with, too.

Tricky Transits

On January 15, the Moon in your practical, earthy sign will face off with Venus and Neptune in Pisces—a distinctly dreamy pair. If you're not in love at the moment, you may be soon. Whether you're with someone now or you run across a soulmate then, be sure to set your feet back on the ground every once in a while afterward—just to be sure you're not dreaming.

Rewarding Days

1, 3, 12, 13, 23, 29

Challenging Days

6, 7, 11, 19, 27, 31

Virgo | February

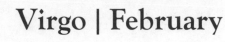

Relaxation and Recreation

An event you were really looking forward to might not turn out as you'd imagined around February 8, Virgo, especially if a volatile personality you weren't expecting to show decides to attend. You may have to step up and take action suddenly—perhaps even by asking them to leave. No fair feeling bad about it, either. Put your foot down firmly.

Lovers and Friends

The emotional Moon will be on duty in partner-loving Libra and your solar second house of money matters and possessions on Valentine's Day, inspiring you to pull out all the stops and make it a special day for your sweetheart. Excessive Jupiter is on duty here as well, so you're already in the mood to torture your plastic. Just don't get too crazy.

Money and Success

Power struggles on the job are possible around February 22, Virgo, and it will take everything you've got to resist the urge to get involved in them. Do yourself a favor, though. If you're not directly affected, remain impartial. You may not know the whole story, and as you well know, one tiny missing detail can change everything.

Tricky Transits

A cardinal T-square on February 8 will put tension in the air, Virgo, possibly accompanied by a sudden argument. Neptune has been tuning up your antennae for years now from her spot in your solar seventh house of one-to-one relationships, so even if the reasons behind it are vague or confusing to others, you'll be able to see the true motivations of all parties involved.

Rewarding Days

1, 6, 13, 16, 22, 23

Challenging Days

2, 3, 7, 8, 21, 26

Virgo | March

Relaxation and Recreation

You have been working very hard for a very long time, Virgo, and are definitely in line for a break. An unscheduled day off really isn't much to ask, especially since you probably have tons of personal days stored up. Use one (or maybe two) around March 21, and if you can manage it, talk a certain someone into playing hooky with you.

Lovers and Friends

If you've been seeing someone casually but thinking seriously about making this thing exclusive, have a chat with them about the situation around March 7 or 9. It may not sound very romantic, but if you two can be clear and honest about what you want from each other, there'll be plenty of time for music, candles, and bubble baths.

Money and Success

Jupiter is on duty in your solar second house of finances, Virgo, an excessive and sometimes overly optimistic kind of energy that's been inspiring you since last September to do a bit more spending than you know you should. You're pretty practical by nature, so you've probably resisted quite well up until now, but if times are tough, a bit of retail therapy may be in order.

Tricky Transits

Jupiter and Pluto will square off on March 30, Virgo, an astrological team that's often been accused of inspiring a god complex. This isn't to say that you'll be feeling omnipotent yourself, but only that someone else will be around that time, and you'll need to figure out how to handle them. Are they really insignificant in your life? If so, refuse to invest any energy in arguing.

Rewarding Days

1, 5, 7, 9, 27, 29

Challenging Days

2, 12, 17, 23, 24, 30

Virgo | April

Relaxation and Recreation

Sitting still has never been easy for you, Virgo, but with loving Venus moving retrograde into your solar seventh house of one-to-one relationships, someone you know and love may be able to talk you into a relaxing afternoon of catching up. Why resist? When was the last time you gave yourself permission to stop fixing, caretaking, and planning? It's official. You need a day off.

Lovers and Friends

After six weeks moving retrograde, the lovely lady Venus will turn direct on April 15, finally clearing the way for you to get in touch with someone you just seem to keep missing. Hopefully, you haven't taken these failed connections personally, because you're about to hear the true reason you two haven't been in contact—and it most certainly wasn't you.

Money and Success

If you've been abusing your plastic a bit too much lately and not considering the consequences, the Universe may be about to arrange a wake-up call in that department, Virgo. On April 10, the Full Moon will illuminate your solar second house of money matters, and a statement or unexpected bill will most definitely open your eyes. Relax. You can fix this.

Tricky Transits

Two testy squares will make it tough for you to resist getting into an argument around April 7 and 8, Virgo, but think before you do. Your words will carry more weight than they usually do, so if you're at all angry, you may say something that will have permanent repercussions. Put some distance between the two of you instead of tempting fate.

Rewarding Days
12, 16, 17, 24, 26, 27

Challenging Days
4, 7, 8, 9, 20, 30

Virgo | May

Relaxation and Recreation

The Sun and Mercury will spend time in earthy Taurus and your solar ninth house this month, Virgo, urging you to close the gap between you and someone you adore who's been much too far away for much too long. If you can manage it yourself, a surprise trip may be in order. If not, how about mailing them a ticket to come to you?

Lovers and Friends

If you have family, getting away for a romantic weekend probably isn't always easy to do, Virgo—so take matters into your own hands. You've definitely saved up some sick days or personal days, so why not lure your sweetheart into hiding out with you on May 9 or 31? You might be able to tuck a weekend's worth of affection into one extremely long, luxurious day off.

Money and Success

Dealing with authority figures on your terms isn't something that's often possible, Virgo, but this month, an easy trine between Saturn and Uranus on May 19 will give you several shots at the title. If you're out to make your name and your skills known, look to the New Moon of May 25 to set it up—but don't expect it to happen without a challenge.

Tricky Transits

Fiery Mars in cerebral Gemini will spend the month in your solar tenth house of career matters and dealings with higher-ups and authority figures, Virgo, which is certainly good news if you have a tough project to finish that's critical to your career. Just don't take yourself too seriously, and don't snip at anyone who offers their opinion, because they really want to help.

Rewarding Days

2, 9, 10, 15, 18, 24, 31

Challenging Days

5, 6, 16, 22, 25, 27

Virgo | June

Relaxation and Recreation

Neptune will station to go retrograde on June 16 in Pisces, creating a weekend that was tailor-made for relaxing, Virgo, especially if you can manage to do it by the water. Saturn has kept you tied to duties and responsibilities both on the job and at home—and we all know how you feel about fulfilling your responsibilities. Enough. You're officially off duty. Let the Universe treat you.

Lovers and Friends

Loving Venus will set off for touch-loving Taurus on June 6, an earth sign like your own that's an expert at finding just the right spots for optimum pleasure. If you're at the beginning of something new, you two may not want to interrupt your delightful explorations by leaving the bedroom if it's not absolutely necessary. Do be sure to stock up on candles and snacks before you hang the sign on the doorknob.

Money and Success

Arguments over financial issues are possible on June 2, 15, and 19, Virgo, and you may find yourself in the position of defending decisions you made recently that you're quite sure were the right ones. Don't let anyone shake you. If you've been honest and forthright and you know exactly why you handled things the way you did, that's enough.

Tricky Transits

The Full Moon on June 9 will occur in expansive Sagittarius and your solar fourth house, Virgo, accompanied by a station from excessive Jupiter himself. An expenditure you weren't expecting could be on the agenda, possibly due to a crisis that a child or family member is going through. On the other hand, a new arrival may be en route—in which case, money will be no object.

Rewarding Days
1, 3, 13, 16, 24, 25

Challenging Days
4, 5, 15, 27, 28, 29

Virgo | July

Relaxation and Recreation

The Full Moon on July 9 in dutiful Capricorn will light up your solar fifth house of playmates and lovers, Virgo, and a family gathering that's really mandatory could be on your agenda. The good news is that as per usual, even if you're a bit grumpy about having to attend, once you're there you'll be glad you did.

Lovers and Friends

A relationship that's been strictly platonic up until now may become a whole lot more intimate this month, Virgo, especially around July 1 or 9. You may not be expecting it, but don't immediately reject the idea of taking it to another level without some serious thought. Long-term romantic partners are supposed to double as best friends, aren't they?

Money and Success

If you end up spending more than you'd planned around July 27 or 28, it will probably be due to an urgent situation a family member has been trying unsuccessfully to get through for some time that's finally come to a head. I don't need to tell you to do everything you can, but I'd like to remind you not to hurt yourself in the process.

Tricky Transits

On July 20, red-hot Mars will storm off into theatrical Leo and your solar twelfth house of secrets, Virgo, marking the start of a two-month trek. Over the course of this time, you may see a secret you've been holding on to exposed, and it will be tough to see it coming. Consider this your heads-up. If you're doing something you shouldn't be, back off.

Rewarding Days

1, 7, 14, 18, 19, 23, 25

Challenging Days

4, 5, 9, 16, 17

Virgo | August

Relaxation and Recreation

Your ruling planet, Mercury, will move retrograde through your sign and your solar first house of personality and appearance from August 12 through August 31, Virgo, making it a bit tougher than usual to keep track of details. You're only human, so snafus will happen, but exercising your innate ability to troubleshoot could make all the difference in the world.

Lovers and Friends

Staying in touch with dear ones may not be easy this month, Virgo, so don't take it personally if you can't connect for a day or two at times. With Mercury retrograde, all kinds of misunderstandings and miscommunications are possible. Don't add to them by imagining that a dear one is deliberately avoiding you. Sit tight. You'll hear the story soon.

Money and Success

If you're in a bad spot financially, Virgo, don't be surprised if a family member offers to help before you can muster up the nerve to ask. An easy sextile aspect between Jupiter and Saturn on August 27 will inspire at least one person who knows you well to understand your position and recognize what you need. No fair feeling guilty. Just pay it back promptly.

Tricky Transits

Two eclipses will make this a month to remember, Virgo, especially if you've been thinking about switching jobs. A secret tip that's shared by a fellow employee or higher-up who's fond of you could put you in line for the job you want with the hours you'd love. Just don't leave your present position until you know the new spot is yours.

Rewarding Days

1, 2, 10, 11, 20, 22

Challenging Days

4, 5, 12, 16, 18

Virgo | September

Relaxation and Recreation

If you've been trying to get away and have some fun but haven't found the time yet, Virgo, stop putting it off. Take the weekend of September 15 off and prepare to truly enjoy yourself. Spending time with the one you love is primary, of course, but put some time aside for family and friends who haven't seen you in far too long.

Lovers and Friends

On September 25, an argument between you and a friend you actually consider family could turn things quite cold between you. If it's over a truly petty issue, think before you speak. Is there a hidden or underlying reason they're so upset with you, or you with them? Get to the bottom of it before you say anything you might regret.

Money and Success

Venus rules not just money but also love, Virgo, and she'll be in the mood to do business on September 12 and 15. Get your resumé together and call for an appointment. Better still, polish it up first, so once you have a certain higher-up's attention, you'll be confident that your accomplishments and skills are obvious.

Tricky Transits

The Full Moon of September 6 will occur in your solar seventh house of one-to-one relationships, Virgo, all done up in woozy, sentimental Pisces. This tenderhearted energy could bring along an extremely surprising emotional revelation—about a secret admirer, for example. Just be sure not to let anyone take advantage of your trusting nature. Even Virgos can fall prey to sob stories every now and then.

Rewarding Days

6, 9, 10, 12, 15, 22

Challenging Days

13, 14, 16, 25, 27, 29

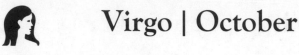 # Virgo | October

Relaxation and Recreation

Easy trine aspects between loving Venus, red-hot Mars, and sexy Pluto on October 1 and 3 will get your month off to the right start, Virgo. In fact, if you haven't yet taken a vacation, this would be the perfect time to go. It's also a terrific time to plan a getaway, make reservations, and put down deposits to hold your spot at conferences or retreats.

Lovers and Friends

Four planets will pass through charming, partner-loving Libra this month, Virgo, all of them intent on fixing you single folks up with someone perfect—possibly around the New Moon of October 19. If you're already spoken for, there'll be a whole lot of flirting going on, but at the very least you'll make the acquaintance of a sociable, funny new friend.

Money and Success

A money matter could turn ugly pretty darn quickly around October 27, Virgo, but if you're honest and open, you might just be able to turn it around before there's no going back. Of course, you're not responsible for what anyone else does, but refusing to add fuel to the fire is always a good idea in these situations.

Tricky Transits

Jupiter will set off for intense, focused Scorpio on October 10, Virgo, which will put him in your solar third house of thoughts and communications for the entire coming year. You're already terrific with details, but this guy is the ultimate detective. Heaven help anyone who's foolish enough to try pulling the wool over your eyes. They'll have their work cut out for them.

Rewarding Days
1, 3, 12, 16

Challenging Days
5, 8, 9, 11, 19, 27

Virgo | November

Relaxation and Recreation

The holiday season is off to a wonderful start, brought to you courtesy of an easy trine aspect on November 11 between Saturn and Uranus, two cosmic heavy hitters who are capable of conjuring up all kinds of magic—like bringing old and young together for warm and wonderful family gatherings. You may not get much rest, but your heart will be full and happy.

Lovers and Friends

An easy trine between loving Venus and dreamy Neptune will put romance in the air on November 16, Virgo. This is the stuff that falling in love all over again is made of—but it's also the magic that attracts you in the first place. Deep spiritual connections of all kinds are possible now. Pay attention to even the briefest encounters. Guardian angels are on patrol.

Money and Success

If you're out and about doing holiday shopping—especially if it's before November 7, Virgo—it's a good bet that you'll wreak some serious havoc on your credit cards or checking account before all is said and done. The good news is that you'll probably find exactly what you're looking for that a dear one will just love. Just don't go too far overboard.

Tricky Transits

Mercury and Saturn will get together in your solar fourth house of home and family matters on November 28, Virgo, a brutally honest and unemotional team that needs to be handled with care. Be sure that your matter-of-fact tone and no-nonsense words don't scare away someone important to you for good. Hold your tongue and count to ten before you utter one single word in anger.

Rewarding Days
3, 4, 9, 11, 12, 16, 21

Challenging Days
7, 8, 13, 19, 27

Virgo | December

Relaxation and Recreation

Just in case you're having trouble slowing down long enough to enjoy the holidays, Virgo, your ruling planet, Mercury, has made an executive decision on your behalf. He'll move retrograde from December 3 through December 22, tossing snags in the direction of all of your carefully laid plans and precise schedules. Don't get frustrated. Enjoy every moment.

Lovers and Friends

With four planets in your solar fourth house of home and family matters, Virgo, you'll probably be in the mood to do some serious entertaining at your place—and as good as you are at creating the right ambience for any gathering, you'll have plenty of visitors. Mercury retrograde may even bring along a few familiar faces you haven't seen in a while.

Money and Success

After inspiring you toward indulging in one last bout of binge-spending, Mars will tiptoe quietly into Scorpio and your solar third house of conversations and communications on December 9, Virgo. Now, this is the stuff that superpowers like x-ray vision are made of, so don't question yourself if you suddenly start to believe you're reading someone's thoughts. You may be right.

Tricky Transits

Saturn will set off for Capricorn on December 19, Virgo, which is home turf for this serious guy. He'll stay put there for the next two and a half years, inspiring you to come up with a five-year career plan you can realistically put into action during 2017. Be on the lookout for elders, higher-ups, and authority figures who can advise and support you along the way.

Rewarding Days

9, 10, 16, 20, 24, 25

Challenging Days

1, 2, 3

Virgo Action Table

These dates reflect the best—but not the only—times for success and ease in these activities, according to your Sun sign.

	JAN	FEB	MAR	APR	MAY	JUN	JUL	AUG	SEP	OCT	NOV	DEC
Move	12, 15, 19	12			20, 25	13, 14		4		10		6, 17
Start a class				24	9, 24			13, 14, 15	14, 15			
Join a club									3, 30			
Ask for a raise	20		12		9, 10			10			22, 23	
Get professional advice	23		27			1, 24		27		12	11, 27	
Get a loan		23		17			24	11		26, 27	11	
New romance	3, 12, 23	3, 4			19		17, 18					24, 25
Vacation				26, 27		25, 26			27, 29			

Libra

The Balance
September 23 to October 22

♎

Element: Air

Quality: Cardinal

Polarity: Yang/masculine

Planetary Ruler: Venus

Meditation: I balance
conflicting desires

Gemstone: Opal

Power Stones: Tourmaline,
kunzite, blue lace agate

Key Phrase: I balance

Glyph: Scales of justice,
setting sun

Anatomy: Kidneys, lower back,
appendix

Colors: Blue, pink

Animals: Brightly plumed birds

Myths/Legends: Venus,
Cinderella, Hera

House: Seventh

Opposite Sign: Aries

Flower: Rose

Keyword: Harmony

The Libra Personality

Your Strengths, Gifts, and Challenges

We're all here to learn our Sun signs, Libra. The one you chose to perfect this time around just so happens to be in the business of keeping things balanced. Basically, your soul signed up to be in and around some pretty unbalanced situations over the course of your lifetime, all in the name of finding that sweet spot that keeps the seesaw in perfect balance. Now, this certainly does explain why you've had what may feel like hundreds of dysfunctional relationships, or why you always feel that you're putting far more into a partnership than The Other, whoever they might be. Unfortunately, much as you love balance, if everyone around you was fair, cooperative, and willing to do whatever it takes to get along perfectly well, how could you ever hone your skills? No, you need to learn negotiation, mediation, and all the other skills that are necessary to effect fair and equitable compromise, so being around disputes and disagreements is part of the deal.

The good news is that while learning to juggle needs, emotions, and attention isn't easy, it's a part of your job description that you probably excelled in just about immediately. In fact, it might actually be that you played the part of mediator/peacemaker within your immediate family when you were just a child or that you watched someone else struggle to keep the peace. At any rate, you're in the process of becoming an expert at making nice. Your mission is to be sure that you don't forget about your own needs while you're playing the part of the eternal cruise director to family, to friends, and, of course, most importantly, to your Other, upon whom the sun rises and sets. Still, if you want to make others happy, make yourself happy first. Put yourself at the top of your priority list. The very top.

Romance, Friendships, and Casual Relationships

First of all, Libra, you're a flirt—a very serious flirt. And you're good at it. Of course, one-to-one relationships are your sign's specialty, but as you no doubt learned quite early on, keeping relationships on an even keel is the toughest thing on the planet—and the more you care about making them work, the tougher the process can be. The thing is, your Sun sign— so aptly represented by that earthy goddess with the blindfold and the scales—is in the business of learning how to instinctively restore balance.

With regard to relationships, that doesn't necessarily mean you'll be good at finding or maintaining the balance between the needs of you versus yours—especially during your younger years—but it won't be for any lack of trying on your part. If your early relationships are far from perfect and possibly even tempestuous and/or amazingly out of whack, don't worry. Just think of each of those experiences as a class you took toward your graduate degree. It might not have been a good time, but if you've learned a lesson from each of them, that time was well spent. Now, however, when you're out looking for a companion you can actually be with peacefully, you're often drawn to the other air signs—chatty Gemini or Aquarius, the genius. Fiery Leos and Sagittarians are fun, though, and while Leo will bring a bit of drama into the mix, they'll spoil you so badly you'll be willing to give them a pass every now and then.

Career and Work

One-to-one relationships are your *raison d'être*, Libra—your reason for living. There's absolutely nothing that fascinates, enthralls, and never ceases to amaze you as much as other human beings, complete with all the faults and foibles that go with each package. That enthusiasm makes you an expert at charming us into revealing ourselves, too, so you probably hear a whole lot of personal things from others that most of us don't. Does this make you an expert in the field of "interviewing"? Sure does, and it only makes sense. There's something about that ultra-personal exchange of intellectual energies that makes you feel alive—so of course you'll know how to do it well. Professions in counseling or mentoring suit you just fine, as do occupations that bring you into the relationships of others—say, professional wedding planning, for example. Regardless of what you choose to do, you'll probably have a partner—because, after all, everything is better when you share it, right?

Money and Possessions

Your ruling planet is Venus, who holds planetary jurisdiction over both love and money, Libra. Now, you folks tend to focus on relationships, but you do still have a very impressive knack for finances, especially when it comes to the management of joint finances. That said, as easy as it is for you to manage the money matters of others, it may not be so easy for you to keep track of your own personal financial matters. Your best bet is to have a financial advisor on retainer who has only your best interests at heart. It might be your best friend who's a whiz at refinancing credit balances so you keep the lowest finance rate possible. Or maybe you stumbled upon an absolute financial genius last time you had your taxes done. Either way, hang on to them—and treat them to lunch quite often.

Your Lighter Side

Anything that involves pleasant sights, sounds, and smells makes your heart happy, Libra, so when it comes to unwinding, start with aesthetically pleasing surroundings. Being out by the water at sunrise or sunset certainly fits the bill. If you've chosen a concert or a visit to an art gallery to occupy your leisure hours, you'll enjoy yourself a hundred times more if you share the experience with a very special someone. And do yourself a favor. When you do manage to take a bit of time off, be sure to spend it in drama-free circumstances with drama-free friends, rather than unofficially mediating a dispute between warring factions. Even Libras need a break every now and then from keeping the peace and making nice.

Libra Celebrities

Barbara Walters, Will Smith, Michael Douglas, and Catherine Zeta-Jones get your list started, Libra—all of whom were born on September 25, by the way. Johnny Carson is also among the famous relationship-oriented folks you keep company with, along with John Lennon, Linda McCartney, and Sharon Osbourne. And take a peek at these other talented folks: Kate Winslet, Sting, Bruno Mars, Viggo Mortensen, Hugh Jackman, and Susan Sarandon.

Words to Live By for 2017
It's time to put my own needs first.

The Year Ahead for Libra

Your ruling planet, the lovely lady Venus herself, has chosen to spend no less than three full months in your solar seventh house of one-to-one relationships, Libra—which is an awful lot of partner-oriented energy to pack into such a partner-oriented place, to put at the disposal of such a partner-oriented sign. Now, she'll be all done up in Aries, however, a sign that does tend to be a whole lot less self-effacing than your own, so chances are good that this may be the year you learn to draw the line between what you're willing to do to please someone and what you need to do to please yourself. The thing is, you're famous—and adored—for giving your all to keep the peace, but every now and then you can go a bit too far with that mission. But as Venus makes her way through Aries—from February 3 through April 2 and again from April 28 through June 6—you'll be a bit more likely to actually utter the word no if you feel you're being asked to do something that's not fair to you. This will probably come as a shock to close friends and relatives who have been trying to tell you for decades to take care of you first, but with startling Uranus also on duty in this sign and house, you'll enjoy raising a few eyebrows every now and then.

Lest you worry that this new me-first attitude might scare off others, however, let's not forget that expansive Jupiter is holding court in your charming sign. He's been there since last fall, so don't worry about being lonely. This generous guy will continue leading an entourage of admirers before your throne for your perusal, and the parade won't be over until October 10, when he'll take off for sexy, intense Scorpio and your solar second house of money matters. From that point on, keeping your finances balanced will be the name of the game—and you can count on it taking up quite a bit of time and some considerable energy, too. Not to worry, though. With generous Jupiter in this house, it will probably be that your income has increased and you suddenly need to find productive ways to invest—which certainly could be a whole lot worse. Just be sure not to go overboard with your spending. Even if you delay payments until the end of the year, at some point that bill will come due. Be as practical as possible and do your best to live within your means.

Jupiter also has jurisdiction over higher education and long-distance travel, by the way, so you may be inclined to take off for a romantic vacation with a new flame—or perhaps you'll finally find time to be alone with your partner in an exotic location. Either way, your mission is to be totally and completely hedonistic and to allow yourself to be very, very spoiled. It's your turn now.

Saturn

Now, with Jupiter in your sign emphasizing relationships so grandly for us all during 2017, in many ways you'll feel as if you're on home turf, Libra—and totally in your element. But there's a second area of life you should probably be paying some attention to before fall arrives. Serious

Saturn has been on duty in your solar third house of thoughts since 2015, but come December, he'll set off for Capricorn and your solar fourth house, where home and family matters are handled. Now, it might seem premature to begin planning for his visit early in the year, but trust me—there's nothing that makes Saturn happier than preparation, and when he makes his way into this private, personal area of your life, you'll want him to be happy. How to do that? Well, take stock of what you need to do to keep your home base safe, secure, and out of financial danger. That might mean installing a security system, but it could also be that a certain someone who's been taking advantage of you needs to be told that it's time to strike out on their own. In the meantime, as Saturn spends his last year in your solar third house of thoughts, don't allow yourself to become too deeply serious or overly concerned with the weight of every syllable you exchange with another. You've probably been a bit cynical about the motives of others for a while, but don't allow yourself to become jaded. Share your hopes, doubts, and fears with a trusted confidant—an elder, a solid authority figure, or a professional who understands your situation.

Uranus

If you were born between October 12 and October 23, Libra, your Sun is currently experiencing the effects of an opposition from startling Uranus, who loves nothing better than initiating complete and total change—in sixty seconds or less. The earlier in your sign your birthdate happens to be, the more familiar you'll be with this situation, but that doesn't mean you won't still be coming to terms with all of the sweeping life changes you've made recently and trying to restore balance to your life. This energy has probably been primarily concentrated on your one-to-one relationships, not just because that's always your primary concern but also because Uranus is making his shocking way through your solar seventh house, where one-to-one connections are dealt with—so, of course, you've been attracting some rather unusual types who most definitely aren't your usual type. The thing is, Uranus's mission is to free us from anything that's holding us back from being true to ourselves, so anyone who's left your life recently—or anyone you can tell isn't fitting into your world any longer—really does have to go. Your mission is to cooperate with this fast-moving energy. As soon as you feel the urge to cut loose, do it. It might seem sudden to others, but it's nothing you haven't been considering for a very long while. The good news is that your horizons will continue to be broadened on a delightfully amazing ongoing basis by a parade of unusual people who'll keep you entertained and endlessly amused.

Neptune

For the past six years, Neptune has been on duty in Pisces, her very own sign—and the one she's most powerful wearing. That puts her right smack dab in your solar sixth house of work, relationships with coworkers, and health habits, Libra. Now this is the house that basically describes the rhythm of your day, and ever since Neptune arrived, her dreamy, woozy energy has probably made it increasingly tough for you to stick to anything even remotely resembling a schedule. Oh, and that goes double for those of you born between October 1 and October 7. In your case, Neptune is also forming an uneasy inconjunct aspect to your Sun, which makes it prime time for confusion with respect to physical routines and the work you do on a daily basis. If you know your health habits aren't positive but you're so deeply entrenched in your everyday rut that you can't see a way to break or alter them, think again. Forget about going by the rules—which includes the schedule you've built your life around. It's time for you to trust your gut. If it's telling you to slowly back away from your current lifestyle and replace your habits entirely—albeit slowly—listen up. Your body is speaking to you. It might not be easy, but you can do this—the thing is, you really have to want things to be different. Envisioning your goals through a daily meditation won't hurt, either, but just listen to your body. That should do the trick.

Pluto

You folks who were born between October 9 and October 15 are in the midst of some pretty serious changes—which, at this point, I know you don't need me to tell you. What I can tell you is that whenever Pluto squares a planet, which is what he's doing to your Sun right now, the point is to make you molt. Yes, I said "molt." It's time to shed your emotional skin and grow a whole new you. This could mean letting go of physical habits, but since Pluto does his best work underground, it's your deepest, most private core self that will undergo the most remarkable changes, some of which won't become apparent to you for at least a year or so. Material things may also have to go—and relationships, too, if they're no longer productive for you. The good news is that the more you let go of now, the more new life you'll experience in the very near future. That goes for all life departments. Pluto's tactics aren't gentle, but the point is to help you reinvent yourself, regenerate and rejuvenate your spirit, and give you a fresh look at who you really are, underneath all those expectations. Be cooperative.

How Will This Year's Eclipses Affect You?

Eclipses are celestial exclamation points. They amp up the volume on ordinary life whenever they occur, but the signs and degrees they activate also bring along events and circumstances that are quite intense. Eclipses occur in pairs, six months apart. Solar Eclipses are supercharged New Moons. They bring the Sun and Moon together, marking peak times for planting spiritual seeds and announcing our intentions to the Universe. Lunar Eclipses are high-energy Full Moons, and just like these monthly oppositions between the Sun and the Moon, they signal times of dramatic culmination and fulfillment.

On February 10, the first Lunar Eclipse of the year will arrive, Libra, in your solar eleventh house of group affiliations and friendships. This fiery lunation will occur in dramatic, theatrical Leo, urging you to end something in grand fashion. It might be that the time has come for you to find a whole new peer group whose beliefs more closely mirror your own. If you don't feel comfortable with a group, it's time for the wrap party. Take a bow and leave your audience and your fellow cast members wanting more.

The first Solar Eclipse of 2017 will occur on February 26, all done up in Pisces and your solar sixth house of work and health matters. If you've been silently making plans to change your habits—even if you've been thinking it might be more of a dream than a plan—well, give it a shot, right now. The Universe is fully prepared to support you, especially if what you're doing ends up making you a clearer channel for spiritual energies. Be wary of taking up new habits that might initially seem to make it easier for you to connect with others. You can manage that all on your own. Stay clear, and stay focused on your goals.

August will play host to the second set of eclipses for the year, Libra. On August 7, a Lunar Eclipse will occur in the sign of Aquarius, which will put this burst of energy in your solar fifth house of lovers, playmates, and leisure-time activities. You could develop a real fondness for computers and other electronic gear right around now—so much so that you decide to begin a class or certificate program. On the other hand, you might decide to meet someone you've known only via online venues. This could work—but be safe. Be sure you're in a public place, let several people know where you are and who you're with, and keep your wits about you.

The last Solar Eclipse of the year will occur on August 21, bringing the Sun and Moon together once again in playful Leo and your solar eleventh house of groups. If you ended your affiliation with a group back in winter, not to worry. Your new kindred spirits, if you haven't already met them, are right around the corner. Accept all invitations that seem amusing.

Libra | January

Relaxation and Recreation

With Jupiter in your sign, life is pretty darn sweet—in most departments, anyway—and adventures haven't been hard to come by. You could be off for yet another this month on a truly delightful trip with your best friend or your sweetheart—or maybe you're traveling solo but are en route to visit at least one someone you haven't seen in far too long. Regardless, enjoy!

Lovers and Friends

Venus and Mars are long-time lovers, set to spend January together—in romantic Pisces, no less. All relationships are important to you, but none so much as the one you share with your primary partner. Well, this team is set and ready to inspire you to fall in love all over again. Oh, and if you're single, someone who might actually be perfect for you could be along shortly.

Money and Success

Negotiating a loan or mortgage or dealing with an inheritance could turn into a confusing power struggle around January 6, Libra—in which case, rescheduling the matter will be your best bet. At the very least, aim for well after Mercury turns direct on January 8, and if you can put it all off until January 20, so much the better.

Tricky Transits

Dreamy Neptune will come together with red-hot, passionate Mars as the year begins, turning up the heat on what might have been a casual thing. If you two continue keeping company all month, you might begin to believe that you're in love—which might well be. Remember, though, that your fondness for being in love can work against you. Reserve judgment until after the pink smoke clears.

Rewarding Days
1, 2, 3, 20, 21, 23

Challenging Days
6, 7, 8, 11, 17, 19, 27

Libra | February

Relaxation and Recreation

If you haven't yet done any long-distance traveling, the Lunar Eclipse on February 10 could push you out the door rather suddenly, Libra. A very long weekend might be in order—say, four or five days, including Valentine's Day? After all the extra work you've done lately and all the added responsibilities you've taken on, you most certainly deserve it. Don't forget the champagne.

Lovers and Friends

Speaking of bubbles, you'll be pleased to know that the emotional Moon will be holding court in your very own romantic sign on February 14, Libra—the perfect time to spend some quality time alone with your favorite hot-tub buddy. A steamy situation would be lovely, but it really doesn't matter where you are. You'll be on the receiving end of some absolutely delightful attention.

Money and Success

Don't allow yourself to be drawn into messy financial situations this month, Libra. With two eclipses set to occur and the fact that Venus, your ruler, is in impulsive Aries, money matters could change quite quickly. That means no offering to negotiate any disputes involving finances, even if a loved one asks for your help. Find someone who's professionally qualified to advise you.

Tricky Transits

February 8 could be a tough day for you, Libra, so listen up. The emotional Moon will activate a battle of sorts that could involve your partner, your family, and perhaps even your professional life as well. If you sense that a situation is turning volatile, back off. Just because you're invited to an argument doesn't mean you have to accept.

Rewarding Days
3, 4, 11, 13, 14, 20, 23

Challenging Days
2, 8, 10, 21, 26, 27

Libra | March

Relaxation and Recreation

Passionate Mars will storm off into sensual Taurus on March 9, Libra—which already sounds pretty nice, right? Well, get this—he'll also be spending the next six weeks in your solar eighth house of intimate encounters. Yes, indeed. If you don't have one of those Privacy, Please signs for your doorknob, this would probably be a good time to invest in one.

Lovers and Friends

Your ruling planet, lovely Venus, will stop in her tracks to turn retrograde on March 4, Libra, possibly bringing an old flame back into your life for a second shot at the title. If you're seeing someone new and you're happy, think twice before you return to what's familiar just because it's familiar. You're a real catch, and you deserve the best. Trust your gut

Money and Success

Excessive Jupiter and Venus—who holds the planetary purse strings—will be moving retrograde this month, Libra, so holding off on any major investments would be best, especially if taking on a partner is part of the deal. No one's saying you can't eventually follow through on your plans—but for now, do some really thorough research before you sign anything.

Tricky Transits

Startling Uranus will oppose Jupiter on March 2, initiating an astrological tug of war that will activate your relationship axis in a very big and possibly very sudden way. If you're single, someone from out of town with a delightful accent could catch your fancy. Just don't get attached until you know for a fact that they'll be around for a while.

Rewarding Days

5, 9, 10, 16, 19, 29

Challenging Days

1, 2, 4, 12, 17, 23, 30

Libra | April

Relaxation and Recreation

Loving Venus will spend most of the month in woozy, dreamy Pisces and your solar sixth house, Libra, where your daily habits and schedules are handled. If you have some time on your hands, you might be tempted to spend it hibernating on the couch with the television on and an adult beverage in hand. Don't do that. It only takes three weeks to create a habit.

Lovers and Friends

You've already had plenty of astrological inspiration to retrace your steps with regard to relationship issues, Libra—but there's more on the way. On April 9, thoughtful Mercury will turn retrograde in sensual Taurus and your solar eighth house of intimate partners—and suddenly, one particular touch is the one you'll be longing for. Okay, so maybe the physical thing was perfect. What about the rest?

Money and Success

Business deals of the joint financial kind and/or negotiations that involve shared possessions or inheritances could be problematic this month, Libra. Don't try to go it alone, especially if you're pretty sure you're in over your head. Find yourself a professional who's familiar with your situation. You need to know exactly where you stand legally before you move an inch.

Tricky Transits

The Full Moon in Libra on April 10 will join forces with outgoing, generous, and oh-so-excessive Jupiter to put you in the mood for romance—which will probably be quite available. The thing is, it may be with someone from the past who's a bit too comfortable and familiar to turn away—even if your relationship wasn't at all positive for either of you. Regardless, think it over before you put your engine in reverse.

Rewarding Days
10, 12, 16, 27, 28

Challenging Days
4, 5, 8, 9, 21, 30

Libra | May

Relaxation and Recreation

If there's something you've always wanted to try, Libra—something that's maybe just a tad risky—you'll be especially drawn to giving it a shot this month. Well, on May 11 and 12, serious Saturn and generous, lucky Jupiter will combine forces to provide you with a safety net that's the best of all astrological worlds. Bungee jumping, though? Really?

Lovers and Friends

Mercury has been retrograding through your solar seventh house of one-to-one relationships since April 20, Libra, bringing you a chance to hear some voices you haven't in a very long time. High school teachers? Maybe. Friends who moved far away? Possible. Old lovers who still aren't over you? Definitely! Don't tease them if you're really not willing to try it again.

Money and Success

The Full Moon on May 10 will occur in privacy-loving and often secretive Scorpio—which just so happens to be your solar second house of finances. This bright light will illuminate this area of life, so there'll be no more hiding. You could hear something now that will convince you that your antennae are as keen as ever.

Tricky Transits

You're usually the very soul of charm and tact, Libra, but right around May 19—well, maybe not so much. Solid, stoic Saturn and rebellious Uranus will form an easy trine aspect, and suddenly, regardless of what the question might be—or the probable reaction of the person who asked it—your bluntness will know no bounds. Prepare to gleefully and deliberately raise some eyebrows.

Rewarding Days

2, 9, 11, 12, 18, 30

Challenging Days

5, 6, 10, 19, 25, 27

Libra | June

Relaxation and Recreation

Good news, Libra. An unexpected chance to hug a dear friend and/or family member you haven't seen in far too long could be along on June 12, when the emotional Moon sets off for Aquarius. If you're only up for a visit or just passing through because you're curious, however, don't pretend otherwise.

Lovers and Friends

On June 6, when loving Venus enters Taurus and chatty Mercury enters equally chatty Gemini, there'll be a whole lot of conversations going on that center around relationships—of all kinds, from intimate to professional. You, of course, are the expert in the field, and you'll be hard-pressed not to offer up your advice, but before you do, be sure you have your facts in order.

Money and Success

If ever there was a time that seemed astrologically tailor-made for financial arguments, the early part of this month might be it, Libra—especially for your sign. This doesn't mean that you're destined to have a fight, but someone who's been trying to draw you out will really amp up the volume on their efforts to irritate you. Stay calm.

Tricky Transits

Between June 4 and June 6, Mercury, Venus, and Mars will all change signs, so "the regulars" in at least three areas of your life will probably also change. Nothing drastic, you understand, and nothing to be nervous about. It's just that you're stretching and growing, so anyone who isn't will cease to amuse you—which will be grounds for at least temporary dismissal.

Rewarding Days

1, 3, 12, 13, 14, 18, 26

Challenging Days

10, 11, 15, 24, 25, 27

Libra | July

Relaxation and Recreation

With Venus, the Queen of Feeling Good, all done up in playful Gemini from July 4 on, we'll all be looking for a bit of intellectual stimulation—which goes double for you, since Venus will be in your solar eleventh house of groups and friendships based on common ideals. If you're feeling even a teeny bit bored, get thee to a class or seek out a gathering of like-minded others.

Lovers and Friends

Venus will spend most of the month in outgoing, thoughtful, and fun-loving Gemini and your solar ninth house, Libra. Now, this is where issues pertaining to the big picture are handled, so you just might find that you're suddenly a lot more willing to listen up and even try to understand the opinions and points of view of others. Stay open. You might learn something. No, wait. Stay open and you will learn something.

Money and Success

You've been juggling a few things to stay afloat financially for a while now, Libra, but there's really no reason for you to worry about it any longer. The Universe has provided two really good days for you to negotiate and make deals this month. Look to July 7 or 18 for the right moment to plan money-oriented meetings.

Tricky Transits

The Full Moon on July 9 will illuminate your solar fourth house of home and family, Libra, and duties and responsibilities you've been putting off discussing won't wait any longer. It might not be fun and it definitely won't be easy, but with intense Pluto on board, this time out, if you have the guts to deal with the actual heart of the matter, you can make some serious headway.

Rewarding Days

1, 6, 7, 18, 19, 25

Challenging Days

2, 3, 4, 16, 23

Libra | August

Relaxation and Recreation

With two eclipses due this month, no one will really be getting a whole lot of rest, Libra—but you, my dear, will at least find a way to juggle a few naps in between dramatic episodes. That said, be careful not to nap too much, especially if you're feeling down. Talk to a professional around August 13 if you've reached a low point.

Lovers and Friends

On August 7, a Lunar Eclipse will activate your solar axis of friends and lovers, Libra, and someone may switch places. That is, someone you think of as a friend may decide it's time to tell you that they're interested in a whole lot more from you. On the other hand, if you've been seeing someone casually and it's become clear that you're not meant for each other, it might be time to restore that friendship.

Money and Success

Jupiter is on duty in your sign, Libra, a generous and often excessive energy that never fails to make mountains out of molehills—for better or worse. On August 27, however, he'll meet up with Saturn, a cautious kind of guy—and between the two, you'll be able to talk just about anyone into just about anything. Ready or not, it's time to make your case.

Tricky Transits

On August 4, mighty Jupiter will get into an energetic square with intense Pluto—and this, friends, is the stuff that power struggles can be made of. In your case, it might be that higher-ups are pressing you to do more than you were hired to do. In this case, you'll need to decide just how willing you are to go above and beyond to make a name for yourself.

Rewarding Days
1, 2, 10, 11, 20, 22

Challenging Days
3, 4, 5, 7, 12, 21, 24

Libra | September

Relaxation and Recreation

The Full Moon on September 6 will join forces with red-hot Mars in precise Virgo and Mercury in Leo—who'll be stationing, by the way—to call your attention to something that needs to be fixed. Now, most likely, it's going to be a relationship that's in need of repair, and only you can get the show on the road. Just try not to become too absorbed in the project.

Lovers and Friends

You'll probably be far too busy with group responsibilities and commitments to tend to what's nearest and dearest to your heart for a week or two, Libra, but once Venus and Jupiter get into an energetic, friendly sextile aspect on September 15, all that will change. The best part is that your sweetheart will be understanding and supportive until your time is once again your own.

Money and Success

You'll probably be a bit more prone to spending your hard-earned cash around the weekend of September 22, Libra and an urgent or pressing situation brought to you by a loved one could be the reason. Woozy Neptune will be quite powerful toward the end of the month, however, so be sure you're getting all the facts before you start digging through your rainy day fund.

Tricky Transits

On September 28, an opposition will form between Jupiter (the Great Exaggerator) and Uranus (the Great Rebel). These two will activate your solar relationship axis in a very big, very sudden way, so you should probably buckle up and be prepared for a bit of a bumpy ride over the coming weekend. Not to worry, though. All should be well within a week.

Rewarding Days

9, 10, 12, 15, 17, 22

Challenging Days

3, 4, 5, 13, 14, 16, 25

Libra | October

Relaxation and Recreation

Five planets will make their way through your charming sign and your solar first house of personality, Libra—and this is quite the magnetic crew. Needless to say, if you're single and you don't want to be, it's prime time to get out there and mingle. By the New Moon of October 19, things could be very, very different.

Lovers and Friends

Venus—your ruling planet and the Goddess of Love—will set off for your sign on October 14, Libra, ushering in a month's worth of pleasant encounters with both interesting new friends and long-term dear ones who've been tried and true to you for as far back as you can remember. Your mission is not to hold on too tightly to new acquaintances who obviously love their personal freedom.

Money and Success

The Sun in your sign will get into an energetic, supportive sextile with serious Saturn on October 16, Libra—which is really good news for those of you who are in the process of making a financial deal with a higher-up or authority figure. What a terrific time to present your resumé, whether it's for an entirely new position or for a raise or promotion within your current work situation.

Tricky Transits

Jupiter has been on duty in your sign for the past year, Libra, bringing you love, luck, and lollipops every time you've turned around. Well, he'll be moving into Scorpio on October 10, but lest you think that romantic roll you're on is about to come to an end, consider this: Scorpio is a very sexy sign that just adores intimacy. Doesn't sound too bad, does it?

Rewarding Days

1, 2, 3, 12, 13, 16, 28, 29

Challenging Days

6, 8, 9, 10, 11, 15, 19

♎ Libra | November ♎

Relaxation and Recreation

With red-hot, passionate Mars charging through your sign and your solar first house of personality and appearance, Libra, it's not hard to imagine you raising a few eyebrows this month. Mars doesn't have time to be discreet, so even though tact is one of your most famous skills, you'll probably have a bit more trouble trying to conjure it up.

Lovers and Friends

Honesty is refreshing, Libra—even if it's not always conducive to immediate agreements. That said, it's now officially time for you to be blunt and perhaps even painfully truthful in your dealings with others. That goes double if you've been angry for quite some time for a very good reason. Clear your throat and let it out, in no uncertain terms.

Money and Success

The Sun, Mercury, Jupiter, and Venus (your patron planet) will pass through your solar second house of personal finances this month, Libra, all of them wearing intense Scorpio. Now, this certainly could mean you're in for some money-oriented arguments or disputes over possessions, but if you're not willing to play dirty, you might just have to opt to not play at all.

Tricky Transits

The Full Moon of November 4 will set up shop in your solar eighth house of shared resources and jointly held possessions, Libra, so rest and relaxation may be tough to come by—at least until the weekend is over. Carry out any negotiations you're feeling comfortable with on November 9, 11, or 21, when chances are best that all parties concerned will at least try to be fair.

Rewarding Days
9, 11, 17, 21, 27

Challenging Days
2, 3, 8, 18, 19

Libra | December

Relaxation and Recreation

Four planets, including impulsive Mars, are set to dash merrily through Sagittarius this month, Libra, which will put this crew in your solar third house of conversations. Now, Sagittarius is notoriously blunt, so if you have something to say, resistance will be futile—but I'm betting no one will mind. Sagittarius planets are pretty darn entertaining, especially when they're completely unleashed—and Mars doesn't do leashes.

Lovers and Friends

On New Year's Eve, the emotional Moon will make her way through witty, intelligent Gemini and your solar ninth house of long-distance relationships and far-off loved ones—and she's set to meet up with startling Uranus, who just loves to bring along the last thing anyone would ever expect. In your case, you should probably expect at least one voice from the past—even if it's only via a call at midnight.

Money and Success

You will probably have happy professional news to share with your loved ones on December 25, Libra, thanks to a conjunction of Venus (your patron planet) and Saturn (the planet of career matters). Now, Saturn can be quite the wet blanket at times, but with charming Venus on board, the news can't help but be good. In any case, enjoy the holiday!

Tricky Transits

Mercury will station to turn retrograde on December 3, about halfway through a two-month trek through fiery, funny Sagittarius and your solar third house. Now, this is a very long visit, and Sagittarius planets are experts at inspiring candor, so unvarnished, no-nonsense straight talk will be the order of the day—or the month, actually. Being nice is one thing, but being honest is always a good thing.

Rewarding Days

6, 7, 8, 15, 17, 20, 25, 31

Challenging Days

2, 3, 12, 13, 21, 22

Libra Action Table

These dates reflect the best—but not the only—times for success and ease in these activities, according to your Sun sign.

	JAN	FEB	MAR	APR	MAY	JUN	JUL	AUG	SEP	OCT	NOV	DEC
Move	6, 10, 11				8, 9, 31			4, 5	3, 4	10, 17, 22		
Start a class		13		2, 3	25		26, 27	13, 14			6, 7	3, 30
Join a club		23, 26					28		3, 15, 17		10, 11	
Ask for a raise	6		9			9						
Get professional advice	15		12, 23, 29			24, 26, 27				27, 28, 29	10, 20	
Get a loan	20			26	15, 24, 31		19		10, 11			
New romance	19, 27	14		10, 11		15, 16, 18	10, 11			22, 23		3, 30, 31
Vacation		5, 6	11, 18, 19		25, 26			27, 28, 29				

Scorpio

The Scorpion
October 23 to November 21

♏

Element: Water

Quality: Fixed

Polarity: Yin/feminine

Planetary Ruler: Pluto (Mars)

Meditation: I let go of the need to control

Gemstone: Topaz

Power Stones: Obsidian, garnet

Key Phrase: I create

Glyph: Scorpion's tail

Anatomy: Reproductive system

Colors: Burgundy, black

Animals: Reptiles, scorpions, birds of prey

Myths/Legends: The Phoenix, Hades and Persephone, Shiva

House: Eighth

Opposite Sign: Taurus

Flower: Chrysanthemum

Keyword: Intensity

The Scorpio Personality

Your Strengths, Gifts, and Challenges

Your ruling planet is intense, mysterious Pluto—which certainly explains a lot. You never do anything "just a little." You're either in, which means you're totally rapt, or out, which means you really don't care either way. You're magnetic, determined, and impossible to ignore, and when you enter a room, everyone knows you're there before you've so much as uttered a single word. Your perceptive abilities are second to none, which means you're also a detective, and heaven help anyone who thinks they can outsmart you—because that, my darlings, just doesn't happen. Body language and vocal inflections tell you everything you need to know, and you're not afraid to stare. That stare, of course—even if it's just because you're interested and not because you're planning someone's untimely demise—is what makes you a tad intimidating to the average bear. Ah, well. Anyone who isn't up for a challenge won't hold your interest for long, anyway, so go ahead and stare and let the Universe weed out the lesser souls.

Of course, focus often turns to obsession, and you can most definitely become obsessed, not just with individuals but also with activities—and not just with sexual activities, either. The thing is, once you're interested, you want to know absolutely everything there is to know about your subject. Just do yourself a favor every now and then. Distract yourself long enough from your current passion to nap, or better still, to sleep through the night.

Romance, Friendships, and Casual Relationships

Intense? Who, you? Oh, maybe just a little, Scorpio—but honestly, if a deep, honest, emotional give-and-take is all you're after in a relationship, what's the problem? Shouldn't we all be willing to share our heart, soul, and deepest secrets with our partner? Well, yes, and in a perfect world, that's how it would be. In the world as we know it, however, coming by the type of trust that entails isn't easy, especially for those of us who weren't born with your perceptive talents and don't have the innate ability to sniff out someone's true motives in a matter of seconds. That's not to say that you trust easily, but only that when you've decided to let down your guard, you let it all the way down. That said, when you're in the market for a true, trustworthy, long-term soulmate—not just some delightful but temporary company, that is—your "interview" methods can be a bit intimidating. Maybe it's that way you have of locking eyes with someone that lets them know you're rummaging around in their soul—but it might also be the fact that when you're interested, you're really, really interested, and quite attentive. Sometimes even to a fault.

Yes, once you become involved with someone, they become your main focus, emotionally and physically. And speaking of physical things, let's chat for a moment about sex, one of your favorite topics. Anyone who hopes to keep your intense little self interested on a long-term basis had best be quite the powerhouse in the boudoir, because sexuality falls under your sign's jurisdiction, and you don't often deny yourself. For all these reasons, Taurus is often your first choice in a mate—which only makes sense. You guys are the astrological owners of sexuality, and they're the astrological owners of sensuality. Talk about a match made in heaven! You might also find a nice fit with the other water signs, Cancer and Pisces. They'll understand and appreciate your moods—which honestly is no easy task at times but is always well worth the effort.

Career and Work

Whatever you do for work, Scorpio, it's pretty much a given that you're either really, really good at it and aiming to get better every day or just going through the motions to earn your daily bread. In your book, there's just no room for in-betweens, and that most certainly does apply to career and professional matters. In fact, regardless of where you work or what you do, if you're not already at the very tip-top of the food chain, you're probably setting plans in motion to get there. You have the patience for endless research and the stomach for dealing with careers that most of us shy away from, including businesses that deal with sexuality and even death. If there's a component of secrecy involved, your work might also become your hobby. Try not to let that happen, though. There's a lot more to life than digging around in the dark for answers. Take sex, for example...

Money and Possessions

When it comes to financial matters, Scorpio, you can go one of two ways. Your naturally obsessive nature might inspire you to hoard the money you have and refuse to let go of it, even if you really need something. Don't do that. Yes, it's good to have a financial safety net, but being afraid to use it when necessary is akin to having nothing at all, which most definitely defeats the purpose. On the other hand, since your solar chart hosts excessive Sagittarius on your second house cusp, you might overspend on a regular basis, sure that one way or the other, the Universe will provide. Well, the Universe does provide, but giving it a hand doesn't hurt, so if you're not an expert at finances—well, at yours, anyway—find someone you trust who can advise you or, better still, handle all your money matters.

Your Lighter Side

What's fun for someone as intense and private as you? Well, other than the obvious behind-the-scenes activities, your fascination for mysteries and secrets might make you a crime-story aficionado—in which case, you're probably quite familiar with the ID Channel. Unraveling puzzles, solving problems, and finding answers to your questions online may also keep you busy—that is, if you're ever alone long enough to indulge in anything that doesn't involve a delicious partner.

Scorpio Celebrities

Sexy? Oh, maybe just a touch—and sexual, for certain. Take Julia Roberts, Ethan Hawke, former Playboy model Jenny McCarthy, Leonardo DiCaprio, and Matthew McConaughey, for starters—not to mention Bo Derek, who starred in the movie 10, for obvious reasons. And speaking of sexuality in general, how about Caitlyn Jenner and RuPaul. Activists like Whoopi Goldberg, Mark Ruffalo, and Neil Young are also fellow Scorpios.

Words to Live By for 2017
Take what you need and leave the rest.

The Year Ahead for Scorpio

Excessive, extravagant Jupiter has been on duty in partner-oriented Libra and your solar twelfth house of Privacy, Please since last September, Scorpio—and honestly, as much as you enjoy quality time alone with a delicious partner, you've probably had to invest in several of those signs to hang on the doorknob. Yes, if you're attached, your sweetheart probably hasn't arrived at work in the morning without an ear-to-ear grin in...well, probably never, actually, but even more so lately.

And since Jupiter will stay snuggled up in this secretive, sexy place until October of this year, you two might want to at least set up a regular schedule for contacting friends who may not see you very often—just so they don't worry.

If you're not attached but you've been happily "dating," the smorgasbord of lovers the Universe has been sending along will continue—but be careful. One of them might catch your fancy. In fact, keep your eyes open for a fiery new coworker or business associate, especially if you cross paths with them from February 3 through April 2 or April 28 through June 6. Why then? Well, it seems that the lovely lady Venus will be storming through impulsive Aries during those astrological windows—and when Venus is in this fast-moving, impatient sign, it doesn't take long to fall in love. Whether or not you'll stay in love is another story, of course—but what fun it will be to fully investigate the possibility with an exciting new lover! Lest we forget, however, Venus also holds the planetary purse strings, so keep an eye on your spending while she's in the mood to impulse-shop. The really big news of 2017—for you in particular—is the fact that Jupiter will set off for your sign on October 10. A year full of love, luck, and lollipops? Yep. Hopefully you'll have enough energy left over to enjoy it.

Saturn

Well, Scorpio, Saturn will spend one final year in Sagittarius, busily putting the finishing touches on his current project: your solar second house of possessions and personal money matters. He set up an office in that house back in 2015, intent on inspiring you to cut back, get organized, and rid yourself of anything you really don't need. Obviously, if you haven't already gotten yourself on a budget, you should get to work on that right away—before he does it for you. Saturn's mission here is to trim back what's unnecessary to help you remain financially solvent—but honestly, he's been known to do his job a bit too well at times. The good news is that even if circumstances have forced you to live on a shoestring for the past year and a half, you've probably come to realize just how little you really need to get by. At this point, you may even have learned to appreciate how much freer you've become without so many financial responsibilities. If you need to do any major spending this year, opt for quality over quantity, invest in warranties, and pass on frivolous extras. Now, Saturn also rules career matters and dealings with higher-ups, so if you've been working diligently and waiting patiently for a raise, bonus, or promotion, your efforts could pay off before the end of the year—but don't be shy. If the authority figures you need to impress don't come to you, take the bull by the horns. Make an appointment, polish up your resumé, and present your case. Oh, and remember—the better prepared you are, the better off you'll be. Saturn just adores preparation.

Uranus

Startling, unpredictable Uranus will continue on his trek through your solar sixth house this year, Scorpio, where issues of health and work are handled. Now, this is the start of his seventh year in this house, so at this point, you've probably come to expect the possibility that all your best-laid plans could come undone at a moment's notice—which means you've probably also learned a very valuable skill: troubleshooting. Then again, this freedom-loving guy may have already convinced you to ditch anything even remotely resembling a schedule and take your show on the road by becoming self-employed. If you've had the urge to get out from under the thumb of authority figures, superiors, and higher-ups and you haven't yet acted on it, this may well be the year you do. Of course, if you're going to break the rules, you've got to learn them first, so before you literally quit your day job, be sure you know exactly what it will take for you to successfully strike out on your own. Just don't wait too long to investigate your options. When Uranus is on duty in this house, it's easy to become a bit of a rebel, which your boss may not appreciate—which could end up getting you relieved of your duties. Yes, I mean fired. Sure, that may be what you were after all along, but again, be prepared. All this goes double for those of you born between November 11 and November 23. This year, you'll also be dealing with a tricky inconjunct aspect from Uranus to your Sun. This is the stuff that uncomfortable or confusing dealings with coworkers are made of—which might be the final straw that pushes you out the door.

Neptune

Well, Scorpio, you're set to enjoy yet another year of the lovely lady Neptune's company in your solar fifth house of lovers and playmates—and when it comes to Neptune transits, the news could most definitely be worse. This romantic, dreamy energy is famous for dissolving boundaries, making intimacy easier to come by—and not just the sexual kind, either. As you well know, there are many types of intimacy, from intense conversations at the kitchen table in the wee hours of the night to physical encounters that touch you on a deeply spiritual level—and you'll have plenty of chances to continue experiencing them all. Yep. Like I said, it could be worse. The thing is, Neptune also carries rose-colored glasses wherever she goes, so you'll need to be sure that you're not taken in by someone who wants to take advantage of your kind heart and generosity. Fortunately, your antennae are nothing if not super-sensitive, so sniffing out someone's true motives is usually a piece of cake. If you're doubtful, though, consult an earthy friend who loves you enough to tell you the unvarnished truth. If you were born between November 1 and November 7, your Sun is currently receiving a trine aspect from Neptune, so your personal magnetism—not to mention your natural sexiness—will be tough to rein in and impossible to resist. Just be sure to aim this stuff in the right direction. Magnets attract all kinds of things.

Pluto

Intense, sexy Pluto himself—who just so happens to be your ruling planet—is currently on duty in your solar third house of conversations and communications, Scorpio. So needless to say, while finding equally intense, sexy playmates has never, ever been a problem for intense, sexy little you, Pluto's energy in this house will make it even easier—say, tenfold or so—because every word you utter will emerge sounding like an irresistible invitation to get to know you better. Okay, a more irresistible invitation. The thing is, Pluto isn't in any hurry to leave this house. I mean, you're looking at another eight years or so. Obviously, if you haven't already, you'll need to learn how to control your words—not to mention the tone of your voice. At times, that might mean not speaking much at all, especially if you're getting "I'm interested" vibes from someone and the feelings aren't mutual. If you were born between November 8 and November 14, all that goes double for you, since your Sun is also currently enjoying a stimulating, energetic sextile from Pluto. Now, when the average bear—not a Scorpio, that is—receives this transit, it feels like being temporarily gifted with a superpower—the power to seduce just about anyone into doing just about anything. As we've already discussed, however, you already own this gift. Talk about irresistible! Your mission is to be fair and honorable when you're using it. Don't focus this energy on easy targets, and don't play games with anyone's heart just because you can.

How Will This Year's Eclipses Affect You?

Eclipses are celestial exclamation points. They amp up the volume on ordinary life whenever they occur, but the signs and degrees they acti-vate also bring along events and circumstances that are quite intense. Eclipses occur in pairs, six months apart, over a two-week period. Solar Eclipses are supercharged New Moons. They bring the Sun and Moon together, marking peak times for planting spiritual seeds and announcing intentions of all kinds to the Universe. Lunar Eclipses are high-energy Full Moons, and like these monthly oppositions between the Sun and the Moon, Lunar Eclipses signal times of dramatic culmi-nation and fulfillment.

The first Lunar Eclipse of 2017 will occur on February 10 in fiery, dramatic Leo and your solar tenth house of career matters, marking a perfect time to wrap things up with regard to a professional project you've been working on quite diligently for some time now. It's no secret that you do tend to be a tad obsessive every now and then, and when you're set on doing a task perfectly, it's often tough for you to let go and allow your efforts to stand on their own. This time around, however, you can rest assured that if you feel confident, your labors will be well received by higher-ups and authority figures. Do yourself a favor. Turn in your work, clock out, and invite some friends to join you in a toast to a job well done.

On February 26, the first Solar Eclipse of the year will arrive, bring-ing the Sun and Moon together in woozy, romantic Pisces and your solar fifth house of lovers. Yes, this could mark a drastic change in your relationship status, and yes, it could mean that you're just now getting started on a new one—but you may also decide not to move forward with your current flame. Together with the fact that intuitive Neptune is also on duty in this house—and since, FYI, she's the astrological owner of Pisces—well, if your antennae tell you that even though this feels nice now, it isn't the right long-term fit, listen up. If memory serves, the only time your intuition ever got you in trouble was when you didn't pay attention to it.

The second Lunar Eclipse of the year will arrive on August 7 in your solar fourth house of home, family matters, and domestic situations, illuminating rebellious Aquarius and urging you to break free of restric-tions. Now, depending on your current circumstances, this could mean that you're ready to move out and make it on your own—or that you're ready to cohabitate. Regardless of what you choose, as long as you're honest with yourself, this will be an exhilarating, exciting time, during which you'll get to know yourself all over again. The happier your living arrangement ends up being, the more productive and positive your life will be. Get busy making that happen—even if you have to break a few rules along the way.

The last eclipse of the year will be a Solar Eclipse on August 21, bringing the Sun and Moon together once again in fiery Leo and your solar tenth house of professional matters. If you left a less-than-satisfying work position behind back in February with hopes of eventually starting up your own business or at least moving on to a better position, this could well be the time your efforts begin to bear fruit. It's time for a new beginning, at any rate, and with creative, outgoing Leo on board, you can't help but be noticed by the powers that be. Don't be shy. Step out into the spotlight and take a bow.

Scorpio | January

Relaxation and Recreation

With loving Venus set to make her way through woozy, dreamy Pisces this month, Scorpio, I might ordinarily say you'd have tons of time to kick back and relax—but given the fact that she and her passionate partner, Mars, will be making their way through your solar fifth house of lovers—well, not so much. Doesn't sound too painful, though. Try to nap occasionally.

Lovers and Friends

One of the people you've been seeing lately may become a tad needy this month, Scorpio. If you're not really interested in the long haul, you may need to take a step back—before they begin getting too attached. That urge to free yourself will be especially strong around the New Moon of January 27, all done up in independent Aquarius and arriving in the company of a no-nonsense Venus-Saturn square.

Money and Success

Be careful not to lose money this month, Scorpio—not just figuratively but literally. Keep an especially careful eye on your purse or wallet around January 12, 15, and 16. At the same time, be sure not to allow anyone to take advantage of you. Your perceptive abilities are astounding, to say the least, but even a Scorpio can fall prey to a convincing sob story every now and then.

Tricky Transits

Venus will get together with Jupiter on January 26, Scorpio—which always means that excess is in the air. The thing is, the aspect between them is an uncomfortable inconjunct, so while you may be able to have everything you want, you could also end up with more than what you bargained for. Be careful what you wish for.

Rewarding Days

2, 3, 20, 21, 23, 29

Challenging Days

12, 15, 16, 26, 27

Scorpio | February

Relaxation and Recreation
Here comes Venus in Aries, a fiery, energetic energy that lives for adrenaline rushes—accompanied by her partner, Mars, who wrote the book on the subject. No, there won't be much downtime during February, but you'll have some exciting experiences with this passionate pair on duty. Passion can go either way, though. Check your temper, especially around February 8.

Lovers and Friends
If you're not already spoken for, you might be happily surprised to meet a new coworker or business associate who's anything but shy about their feelings—including the ones they're having regarding you. The heavens will be full of impulse in the department of love, but whether or not it lasts is another story. Ah, well. Enjoy the investigation!

Money and Success
If you're in the mood to do some serious impulse-shopping around February 8, think twice before you hop in the car with a pocket full of plastic. Be sure you're not just trying to distract yourself to avoid thinking about a nagging problem or to sidestep a much-needed meeting with someone you're thinking of phasing out of your life. Talk to them. Then shop.

Tricky Transits
A partner-oriented, romantic Libra Moon will be on duty on Valentine's Day, Scorpio, putting everyone in the mood to partner up and share something sweet—and I'm not talking only about chocolates. The thing is, if Jupiter has kept you as busy as I think he has, then whittling down your guest list to just one might be a challenge. Try not to hurt anyone's feelings.

Rewarding Days
4, 5, 6, 11, 12, 13

Challenging Days
7, 8, 10, 21, 26

Scorpio | March

Relaxation and Recreation

If you're up for a spontaneous weekend away this month, Scorpio, the weekend of March 24 looks just dandy. Five planets will conspire to provide you with the energy, curiosity, and boldness to visit a new place or try something new and interesting. Of course, since startling Uranus is on board, one never knows where or what that might be—but who cares? Go for it!

Lovers and Friends

The lady Venus, Goddess of Love, will turn retrograde on March 4, Scorpio, and, together with a sentimental meeting of Mercury and Neptune, might just inspire you to pick up the phone or dash off an email to someone you haven't seen in a very long time. Before you do, however, be sure you're not thinking fondly of the good times and conveniently forgetting the bad.

Money and Success

If you have the feeling that a certain career-oriented situation is temporarily out of your control around March 30, don't question your own judgment. You're probably right. Now, you really don't care for the concept of not being in control, but before you fly off the handle or say something you'll regret, wait. Just a bit. This, too, shall pass.

Tricky Transits

Extravagant Jupiter and Uranus—Mr. Unpredictable himself—will join forces this month to put surprises and last-minute U-turns on the agenda for us all—but in your case, Scorpio, most especially in the department of secrets. Now, this can be terrific—if, say, someone plans a surprise party for you—or not so terrific, if you get caught doing something you shouldn't be doing. Careful!

Rewarding Days

1, 5, 6, 7, 9, 29

Challenging Days

2, 4, 12, 17, 21, 23

Scorpio | April

Relaxation and Recreation
The Full Moon on April 11 will team up with expansive Jupiter to activate your solar twelfth house in a really lovely way, Scorpio. In fact, if you've been trying to figure out the right time to lure your sweetheart away from the madding crowds for a very serious conversation about the future, wonder no longer. This is the stuff that memories are made of.

Lovers and Friends
The Sun, Mercury, and Mars will take turns passing through sensual Taurus and your solar seventh house of one-to-one relationships this month, Scorpio. Needless to say, if you're attached, you and your sweetheart probably shouldn't overbook your social schedule. Why put yourself in the position of having to tell stories to friends who won't believe a word of it anyway?

Money and Success
Yes, April 15 is Tax Day, and yes, you're often one of the last to make it to the mailbox, but you really shouldn't push your luck this year, Scorpio. Venus, the ruler of not just love but also money, will station that day—and when planets station, they're insisting on attention. Why set yourself up for an audit or examination? Get it taken care of early.

Tricky Transits
Mercury will stop in his tracks to turn retrograde on April 9, Scorpio, and from his spot in Taurus and your solar seventh house of relationships, he'll inspire you to contact someone you've been thinking of quite a lot lately but haven't seen in a very long time. That said, since Venus will also be retrograde until April 15, give yourself time to think over whether or not you want them back in your life.

Rewarding Days
2, 10, 11, 12, 16, 27

Challenging Days
4, 7, 8, 9, 20, 21

Scorpio | May

Relaxation and Recreation

The Full Moon on May 10 will illuminate your sign and your solar first house of personality, Scorpio, turning up the volume on all those qualities we so love about you. Your unbridled, unabashed sexuality, for example, but also your perceptivity, which makes you a natural-born detective. If you're introduced to someone by a dear friend and your antennae twitch, even once, don't worry about offending anyone. Start digging.

Lovers and Friends

With Mercury and Venus moving direct in fiery, impulsive Aries—after both spent time retrograde, an extremely frustrating thing for Aries planets, by the way—well, you'll be ready to give something a second shot, Scorpio. What kind of something? Well, Aries is quite impatient. The two planets will be in your solar sixth house of work situations, which includes relationships with coworkers. Nuff said?

Money and Success

The urge to either change fields entirely or at least switch positions within your current company hasn't gone away, has it? Well, if you've stayed put, waiting for a better offer, an easy trine aspect between Saturn and Uranus on May 19 could bring you the situation you've been dreaming of. No more waiting or dreaming, though. Get your resumé together and make an appointment.

Tricky Transits

Assertive Mars is currently storming through talkative Gemini and your solar eighth house of shared resources, Scorpio, so you may need to have at least one sit-down with dear ones to discuss either joining your assets together or splitting them up. Either way, the deals will be fiery and feisty and possibly also quite full of confrontations. Buckle up.

Rewarding Days
2, 7, 11, 23, 24, 31

Challenging Days
3, 5, 9, 10, 16, 27

Scorpio | June

Relaxation and Recreation
Your solar fifth house describes what's fun for you, Scorpio—and right about now, the star of that show is the lovely lady Neptune, purveyor of escape hatches and dissolver of reality. You've been intently focused on practicality and following the rules for quite a while now. It's time to kick back and chill out. Just don't get too comfy. There's still work to be done.

Lovers and Friends
You'll have two chances this month to make friends with a certain some-one you've been admiring from afar, Scorpio—at the very beginning and at the tail end of June. That doesn't mean you can't continue to grab their attention whenever the opportunity arises—only that if you really want to make an impression, June 1, 3, and 30 aren't bad times to make your intentions known.

Money and Success
The Full Moon on June 9 will bring a very bright astrological spotlight into your solar second house of personal resources and possessions, Scorpio, asking that you take steps to cut back on your expenses in a very big way. Now, this may mean doing without some things you were sure you couldn't, but if you want to make serious Saturn happy—and trust me, you do—you'll at least give it a shot.

Tricky Transits
On June 23, the New Moon in home and family-loving Cancer will arrive in your solar ninth house of long-distance relationships and far-off places, Scorpio, probably bringing along news of a new arrival or happy event. If you can't make it there, don't be sad. Send along your good wishes—and, if you can, a ticket to bring your loved ones home to visit.

Rewarding Days
6, 20, 21, 23, 24, 25

Challenging Days
3, 4, 15, 19, 28, 29

Scorpio | July

Relaxation and Recreation

The weekend of July 7 was tailor-made for recreation, Scorpio—the kind you're especially fond of. A romantic sextile between Mercury in passionate Leo and loving Venus will start you off, but with the Full Moon due to arrive the next day, it's not hard to imagine you in the arms of your special sweetheart. Just be sure your work is done before you leave.

Lovers and Friends

With Venus in lighthearted, playful Gemini and your solar eighth house of intimate encounters as of July 4, Scorpio, this month may be just as hot indoors as it is outside. If you're not seeing anyone at the moment, the Universe will be happy to send along some new playmates—the kind who probably won't mind having some casual fun without any strings attached.

Money and Success

On July 18, Venus will get together with generous Jupiter—and this pair, Scorpio, is the astrological stuff that wealth is made of. That goes double since Venus is on duty in your solar eighth house of joint finances. If you've been thinking of investing, this is the time for it. A solid, grounded trine aspect between thoughtful Mercury and practical Saturn on July 19 will inspire you to make wise choices.

Tricky Transits

The Sun and Mars will storm off into fiery, dramatic Leo and your solar tenth house of career matters late this month, Scorpio, so if you've been trying to gain the attention of a higher-up or authority figure, you'll most certainly have it then. The thing is, the spotlight will illuminate everything you've done, for better or worse. If you're hiding something, it might not stay hidden for long.

Rewarding Days

6, 7, 8, 14, 18, 19

Challenging Days

2, 5, 9, 16, 20

Scorpio | August

Relaxation and Recreation

A pair of eclipses will activate your solar axis of home and family versus career matters this month, Scorpio. These lunations don't mess around, so don't be surprised if urgent circumstances force you to juggle your time and energy at a moment's notice. Do your best, and don't let anyone make you feel guilty about what you're just not capable of handling.

Lovers and Friends

Mercury will stop in his tracks on August 12 to begin a three-week retrograde period, Scorpio, and since he'll be in your solar eleventh house of friendships and group affiliations, you should probably expect to hear at least one dearly-missed voice from the past. Of course, there's really no better time for an all-out reunion. See if you can't manage to get the whole gang back together.

Money and Success

The first three weeks of August will probably be quite unpredictable when it comes to money matters, Scorpio, but not to worry. Sit tight and let the storm pass. On August 27, an evenhanded sextile between generous Jupiter and practical Saturn will bring along the information you need to make sound decisions for all parties concerned.

Tricky Transits

On August 4, a rather testy square will occur between your ruling planet, Pluto himself, and Jupiter, who never fails to expand the energy of any planet he touches. Now, Pluto tends to be a tad controlling at times, and while you're used to dealing with his energy, this time around what seemed like a minor situation could turn into a major power struggle. Buckle up.

Rewarding Days

10, 11, 13, 20, 22

Challenging Days

7, 9, 12, 15, 18, 21, 24

Scorpio | September

Relaxation and Recreation

If you've ever thought about performing, Scorpio, three planets in fiery, dramatic Leo might just convince you to give it a shot this month. Of course, you tend to prefer behind-the-scenes positions in general, but every now and then, even your secretive sign has the urge to show off. If it hits you now, why not give in and have some fun?

Lovers and Friends

The Full Moon on September 6 will illuminate your solar fifth house, Scorpio, where love affairs are handled. It will occur in romantic Pisces a day after Mercury turns direct, so if you've been trying to get back together with someone but not having much luck, listen to your intuition. Are you really meant to be together? No one can decide that but you.

Money and Success

With charming Venus in impossible-to-ignore Leo and your solar tenth house of career matters until September 19, you're all set to make some wonderful first impressions on higher-ups and authority figures—and the news just gets better. On September 15, generous Jupiter will get in touch with Venus to give you a lucky break. Pay attention. Timing really is everything.

Tricky Transits

An elder may ask more from you than you can reasonably give on September 13, Scorpio—and you'll just have to let them know that you're only human and can only do so much. It looks like there'll be a fair amount of guilt tossed your way, but it will only get to you if you let it. Don't obsess over anything they say. If you know you've done all you can, let it go.

Rewarding Days

2, 6, 8, 9, 12, 15, 22

Challenging Days

4, 5, 13, 20, 25

Scorpio | October

Relaxation and Recreation

Five planets will take turns hiding out in your solar twelfth house this month, Scorpio, so going out to party might not be your top priority. If you've recently been run through the mill, don't feel bad about taking some time to regroup, regenerate, and revitalize. If anyone needs time alone every now and then, it's you. And FYI—keeping company privately with someone you trust will work just as well.

Lovers and Friends

Venus will square off with no-nonsense Saturn on October 8, Scorpio, so if you've reached the breaking point with a friend who's turned out not to be much of a friend at all, you'll be ready to cut all ties with them and move on. If you're convinced they haven't done anything to hurt you deliberately, go easy on them when you make your exit.

Money and Success

Jupiter will head off into your sign on October 10, Scorpio, bringing you good luck, good timing, and the ability to make contact with successful others who'll be happy to provide you with the benefit of their experience to help you along your professional path. The break you've been waiting for is right around the corner. The best part is that you'll enjoy this energy for an entire year. Congrats!

Tricky Transits

The Full Moon on October 5 will arrive in the company of a Venus-Mars conjunction, Scorpio—a rather tricky combination of astrological energies. On the one hand, if you're infatuated, your passions will be running on high—in a most delightful way. If the bloom is off the rose, however, an argument may provide you with the last straw you've been looking for to end it.

Rewarding Days
1, 3, 10, 12, 16, 21

Challenging Days
5, 8, 9, 11, 15, 19

Scorpio | November

Relaxation and Recreation

An easy trine between career-minded Saturn and independent Uranus will arrive on November 11, giving you the opportunity to happily mix work with play and achieve some pretty amazing results in the process. Your creativity will be running on high, so if you haven't already figured out how to turn your hobby into a tidy part-time income—at the very least—you'll be able to make it happen now.

Lovers and Friends

Better take your vitamins regularly, Scorpio. On November 13, loving Venus will get together with expansive, excessive Jupiter, both of them in your very own sexy little sign and your solar first house of appearance and personality. Magnetic? Oh, yeah. Even more than usual—way more than usual, in fact. If you're not happily attached, you can expect a veritable parade of delicious new companions to choose from.

Money and Success

The Sun and Mercury will spend time in your solar second house this month, Scorpio, all done up in lucky Sagittarius. Together with the fact that Jupiter is on duty in your sign, this wouldn't be a bad time to pick up a lottery ticket. Aim for November 11, 17, or 25 to make your purchases—but don't get crazy. Remember, it only takes one to win.

Tricky Transits

The Full Moon on November 4 will set up shop in your solar seventh house of one-to-one relationships, Scorpio, accompanied by three planets with rather diverse ideas on the subject. Your mission is to think outside the box, with regard to all your relationships. Just because everyone else handles a situation a certain way doesn't mean it's the right way.

Rewarding Days
11, 16, 17, 25, 27, 29

Challenging Days
3, 4, 14, 19, 30

Scorpio | December

Relaxation and Recreation

Talk about merry! With charming, sociable Venus in league with Jupiter—the heavens' answer to Santa Claus—in the oh-so-upbeat sign of Sagittarius, this December just has to turn out to be a month to remember. The icing on the cake, in your case, might just be a reunion of sorts. Who is it you haven't heard from in far too long? Reach out. It's time to catch up.

Lovers and Friends

All the merrymaking you'll enjoy early this month will keep your heart warm and a smile on your face. And the news only gets better after December 25 arrives. Venus will step into solid, practical Capricorn—a sign that just loves enduring relationships—and then meet up with Saturn. Treat yourself to the reassuring warmth of familiar loved ones.

Money and Success

From December 3 through December 22, Mercury will be moving retrograde in your solar second house of personal finances and money matters, Scorpio, so if you're out and about doing your last-minute holiday shopping, do yourself a favor and save every single receipt. Chances are good it won't fit, the color will be wrong, or they'll already have one. Trust me on this.

Tricky Transits

Mercury will turn direct on December 22—which really should clear up the whole delays/roadblocks/stalls situation you've been dealing with recently, Scorpio. The thing is, it might take a few days to kick in. Your patience is legendary, so even if it's been tried to the limit, conjure up a bit more to get through the holidays. Ah, well. 'Tis the season. Relax and go with the flow.

Rewarding Days

1, 5, 14, 21, 24, 25

Challenging Days

10, 13

Scorpio Action Table

These dates reflect the best—but not the only—times for success and ease in these activities, according to your Sun sign.

	JAN	FEB	MAR	APR	MAY	JUN	JUL	AUG	SEP	OCT	NOV	DEC
Move	27, 28		22, 23			23, 24		6, 7				
Start a class					12, 13, 17	23	4, 5, 9	10, 11		12	3, 5, 13	
Join a club					23, 24			24				9, 10
Ask for a raise	23, 29			16, 17					15, 17	10	17	
Get professional advice	15, 16, 20	3, 8	12, 17, 23	8				13	12, 13		20	19, 21
Get a loan		10			9, 24, 31	18	24, 25	27		10	20, 21	
New romance		12		25, 26	9, 10, 11		13, 14	22		10	16, 17	
Vacation	12		1, 4, 6			24, 25, 26			26, 27			22, 24, 25

Sagittarius

The Archer
November 22 to December 21

↗

Element: Fire	Glyph: Archer's arrow
Quality: Mutable	Anatomy: Hips, thighs, sciatic nerve
Polarity: Yang/masculine	Colors: Royal blue, purple
Planetary Ruler: Jupiter	Animals: Fleet-footed animals
Meditation: I can take time to explore my soul	Myths/Legends: Athena, Chiron
Gemstone: Turquoise	House: Ninth
Power Stones: Lapis lazuli, azurite, sodalite	Opposite Sign: Gemini
	Flower: Narcissus
Key Phrase: I understand	Keyword: Optimism

The Sagittarius Personality

Your Strengths, Gifts, and Challenges

"Nothing exceeds like excess." Arguably, it's the second-best-remembered line of dialogue from the movie *Scarface*, but it also doubles beautifully as a motto for your sign, Sagittarius. Your ruling planet is Jupiter, the ancient Roman King of the Gods who's currently famous for being the largest planet in our solar system. In the astrological world, as the heavens' main purveyor of expansion, generosity, and exaggeration, he's equally hard to miss. Obviously, anything even remotely resembling moderation isn't his strong suit, and as his personal astrological property, it stands to reason that having just a small slice of anything isn't your specialty, either.

Truth is, you're quite fond of the concept of growth and expansion. In your Jupiterian mind, if one is good, two must surely be better—and following that logic, ten should be just fabulous. Yes? Well, yes—but if only one of what you're after is available, then that particular one had better be the biggest and most elaborate one of all. Fortunately, this celestial affinity with the concepts of "much," "more," and "many" applies most of all to your higher mind's quest for knowledge. Your curiosity is every bit as insatiable and relentless as Gemini's, and once you've learned something—again, just like Gemini—there's just no better high for you than sharing it. So in addition to being a perpetual student, you're also a born teacher. Of course, you might tend to expound on subjects you're not quite as well versed in as you think you are every now and then—but hey, delivered up via that wonderful sense of humor? Who'll complain? Certainly not the smiling, much-amused entourage of friends, followers, and fans that Jupiter surrounds you with on a regular basis.

Romance, Friendships, and Casual Relationships

Whether you're ready to kick back and relax or paint the town red, the playmates you summon absolutely must be playful, Sagittarius, in the truest sense of the word. That means they must be big fans of laughter, but more importantly, they need to be sharp enough to feed your brain. You absolutely can't stand being bored, and when you are, it's not all that hard to spot. The tapping, fidgeting, and endless eye rolls give you away. But it's only natural. In your mind, regardless of the day or the moment, there's no time to waste. You are on a ravenous, lifelong quest for knowledge and are perpetually on the prowl for new information—preferably delivered up via interesting others with odd, thought-provoking stories to tell and unusual experiences to share.

That's what you're looking for in relationships—all of them. With what you're willing to offer in return, it's not too much to ask—right? Well, on a temporary basis, sure. Anyone who answers to the previous description will be properly doted on, but let's face it—that will only last as long as you're amused, and you're oh-so-easily bored. This doesn't mean you can't commit at all, but with regard to lasting relationships of any variety, you're not just after an intellectual distraction. You want the real deal—basically, someone who might just be your mental and/or spiritual match.

This year, you'll probably be especially focused on finding a true partner, and since you're already so fond of Librans, you could end up with one of those charming Venus-ruled envoys as a BFF, at the very least. Your rebellious side, however, has always been fond of impulsive, impetuous Aries, and the fire in you loves dramatic, theatrical Leo too—just as long as they're not too high-maintenance. Oddly enough, your best match could be airy Aquarius, whose righteous, rebellious streak will always keep you on your toes.

Career and Work

Okay, let's be clear: the whole concept of "work" leaves you cold, Sagittarius. As far as spending a third of your day to earn your daily bread goes—well, if it's absolutely necessary, you'll get through it, but if it feels like hard labor, you're outta there. You're nothing if not flexible, so changing job duties or even professional fields suits you just fine—until you discover a daily activity that's not just tolerable but actually enjoyable as well. Anything that involves learning more about a skill you already have or teaching what you already know is terrific, but regardless of what you do, doing it without anyone looking over your shoulder is an absolute must. Rules are one thing, but freedom is your number-one priority. Oh, and since you've always been fond of animals, working in the veterinary field is a nice fit, and your fondness for exotic accents and foreign languages makes you an excellent candidate for work as an ESL instructor.

Money and Possessions

You're the child of excessive, impulsive Jupiter, so you probably weren't born with a gift for managing your resources moderately, Sagittarius. In fact, you're probably far more familiar with feast-or-famine syndrome. This year, however, you stand a very good chance of discovering the magic behind keeping a leash on both your habits and your spending. This might mean that very soon, you'll actually have money to manage— in which case, a trusted advisor is an absolute necessity. In fact, depending on just how much you've accumulated and/or just how extravagant you've been lately, you might even need two—one to advise you emotionally and the other to point out the facts. The thing is, you've never been famous for self-restraint, and that won't be changing any time soon. Find someone with impeccable credentials, sign them up, and hand over the keys to the kingdom.

Your Lighter Side

Anyone or anything that expands your horizons is always welcome in your world, Sagittarius. That includes attending classes taught by entertaining teachers you'll soon be sharing a dinner with, as well as mingling with interesting new people over coffee or wine. Long-distance globe-trotting is the best, especially if you have time to explore. Being bored is the only thing your restless little heart just can't tolerate.

Sagittarius Celebrities

You're always ready to have some fun, Sagittarius, and if one of you fiery, funny, bigger-than-life folks is in the vicinity, that's a guarantee. Yes, Sagittarius, you keep company with the likes of Jon Stewart, Bette Midler, Frank Sinatra, Sarah Silverman, and Richard Pryor. Other playful Sagittarian spirits include Walt Disney, Criss Angel, and Steven Spielberg. And then there's Tina Turner, Taylor Swift, Scarlett Johansson, Britney Spears, Christina Aguilera, Miley Cyrus, and Nicki Minaj.

Words to Live By for 2017
Moderation. Moderation. Moderation.

The Year Ahead for Sagittarius

You probably didn't have much time for fun during 2016, Sagittarius— but I'll bet you got a whole lot done. Your ruling planet is expansive, outgoing, and oh-so-generous Jupiter, and he spent most of the year in hardworking Virgo and your solar tenth house of authority figures, career, and professional matters. He kept your attention focused primarily on work matters for the duration, but last fall, this outgoing, affable fellow set off for charming Libra and your solar eleventh house of group affiliations and friendships—quite a different energy with quite different ideas on how you should be spending your time. Yes, even if you still have to devote much of your energy to keeping your career on a steady path, Jupiter will be happy to continue providing you with all kinds of opportunities to have some fun, just the way you like it—with quite the varied cast of characters.

Of course, with Saturn set to spend yet another year in your sign and your solar first house of personality and appearance, you'll be a bit more serious than usual at times—but definitely not all the time! Then, too, loving Venus will take her time moving through Aries this year, spending a total of three months in this fiery, impulsive sign—which will put her in your solar fifth house of recreation, playmates, and lovers, by the way. If you're attached, it's a good bet you two will be pursuing some extremely unusual, high-energy activities together, all of them designed to amp up your adrenaline and let you know you're alive. Sounds exciting, but be sure that any risks you take during 2017 are well calculated.

You single folks are in for a real treat, by the way, thanks to Venus. For starters, you will enjoy a parade of high-energy admirers who'll actually hold your interest for more than just one date. But you may also cross paths with someone who possesses an array of distinctly Aries-like qualities—or, basically, a bold, fiery soul who stands their ground and doesn't back away from confrontation. The thing is, folks like this are usually looking for a lover who's also a worthy opponent, so if you're not a fan of confrontation, keep your eyes open for signs that the new warrior in your life may be a bit too fond of fighting to keep around long term. That doesn't mean you can't enjoy their company every now and then, of course. Just keep the relationship in perspective.

Saturn

Well, Sagittarius, if you haven't already gotten yourself organized, you'll have one more year to work it out. Saturn will stay on duty in your sign and your solar first house of personality and appearance until December 19, giving you plenty of time to put some serious structure in your life—or to restructure it, as the case may be. Remember, Saturn is the purveyor of self-discipline, patience, and endurance, and quite a career-oriented fellow as well. Three of this year's eclipses will set to work reshaping your beliefs and changing your mind on all kinds of things—which can be extremely unsettling. But with Saturn in attendance, you'll be able to make changes sensibly and cautiously with an eye toward rebuilding yourself from the ground up.

Of course, if you're perfectly happy with your current position in life and confident that you're right where you should be, so much the better. In that case, Saturn will be happy to provide you with rewards for the time you've invested in living your life in a reasonable and productive way. That goes double for career and professional matters, where you're due to receive the recognition and respect you've earned—even if it's because you've chosen to pursue an entirely new path. Saturn also has a lot to do with our dealings with elders and authority figures, so at this point, if you've taken the time to develop and tend carefully to relationships of this kind, you may actually be invited into a respected circle.

Uranus

Saturn will continue doing his best to keep you on a practical, organized, and steady path this year, Sagittarius—but he'll have his work cut out for him. It seems that startling Uranus will continue storming through fiery Aries and your solar fifth house of creative endeavors and recreational pursuits, determined to convince you that change is a positive, necessary, and exhilarating process. Now, if any planet can affect your intellectual attitude, it's this cerebral fellow, so buckle up and expect the unexpected, possibly delivered up via sudden or drastic circumstances. It's more likely, however, that the parade of interesting, unusual, and oh-so-inspirational people you've been enjoying for years now will keep on making their way into your life. No, that doesn't sound bad at all, and you most certainly won't be bored.

You may continue to raise some eyebrows with what spills from between your lips, however, or even with the way you've chosen to express the brand-new you. If you were born between December 10 and December 22, your Sun is also receiving Uranus's energy via an easy trine aspect—which might actually mean that you'll suddenly decide to demonstrate those inner changes through some rather radical adjustments to your physical appearance. Ah, well. Dye washes out, hair grows back, and wardrobes are replaceable. Go for it. Let the world see the new you—but do try to go easy on the piercings and tattoos. Remember, this too shall pass. If you want physical proof of it, take some pictures.

Neptune

You're currently enjoying the presence of the lovely lady Neptune in your solar fourth house of home, family, and domestic matters, Sagittarius, and this is a planet who turns us all into emotional sponges whenever she visits. As such, it's a given that a family member or child will manage to tug mightily on your heart strings at least once this year. The good news is that it may be for entirely delightful reasons, such as the birth of a child or a happy event—a wedding, maybe? Regardless of the circumstances, you might expect that your earliest emotional memories will be triggered, so a bout or two with nostalgia and sentimentality may be on your agenda as well.

If you were born between December 1 and December 7, your Sun is also receiving a rather testy, insistent square from Neptune, and since she's the Queen of Spirituality, what she really wants is for you to surround yourself with kindred spirits who'll be supportive and helpful in your quest to find your own personal spiritual truth. What motivates you most on an internal level? What causes inspire you? Find like-minded others and keep company with them. Getting back to the fact that you're also quite the psychic sponge right about now, it's even more important to pay attention to what not to surround yourself with—which basically amounts to negativity on any level. Avoid loud music, harsh light, and volatile people, and try not to indulge in escapist behaviors that will harm you in the long run.

Pluto

You've been dealing with intense, powerful Pluto in your solar second house of money matters and personal finances for years now, Sagittarius—since 2008, in fact. Now, Pluto's job is to eliminate what's not necessary, so you've probably had to give up a thing or two over the years—and since Pluto is in practical, rational, and oh-so-frugal Capricorn, living on a shoestring has become second nature—yes, even for a sign that's famous for being a tad on the excessive, extravagant side. The good news is that you've probably also come to realize what's truly important to your happiness—and what's really not. That goes double for those of you born before December 7, who've also experienced the effects of a semisextile aspect between Pluto and your Sun. If you were born between December 7 and December 12, you're going through that transit right now, so do yourself a huge favor and be cooperative. Whittle down your expenses as much as possible, put yourself on a budget, and get rid of what's not necessary or productive. You need to let go, but that doesn't mean you're losing anything. Think of this as a time to shed the past, and look forward to the new growth that will come along down the road.

How Will This Year's Eclipses Affect You?

Eclipses are celestial exclamation points. They amp up the volume on ordinary life whenever they occur, but the signs and degrees they activate also bring along events and circumstances that are quite intense. Eclipses occur in pairs, six months apart, over a two-week period. Solar Eclipses are supercharged New Moons. They bring the Sun and Moon together, marking peak times for planting spiritual seeds and announcing intentions of all kinds to the Universe. Lunar Eclipses are high-energy Full Moons, and like these monthly oppositions between the Sun and the Moon, Lunar Eclipses signal times of dramatic culmination and fulfillment.

The first Lunar Eclipse of the year will arrive on February 10, illuminating the sign of Leo and your solar ninth house of long-distance travel, education, and opinions on the big picture. An event could occur around that time that's powerful enough to force you to reexamine your deepest belief systems—but not to worry. If anyone is open to change—even sweeping change—it's the mutable signs, a group of which you're a card-carrying member. Of course, it may be that a trip you take opens your eyes to a new way of life or an opportunity to start over, or you may choose to widen your horizons through classes or certificate programs.

The first Solar Eclipse of 2017 will occur two weeks later, on February 26, activating your solar fourth house with a strong dose of sentimental, compassionate Piscean energy. Since this house pertains to home and family matters, you may be moved to help a family member or child solve a problem, possibly related to an addiction or a negative behavior they seem to be legitimately interested in changing. Do what you can to help, but keep in mind that Pisces energy often makes it difficult to separate fact from fiction. If you're not convinced that this person is being completely honest, ask an impartial third party for their thoughts on the matter.

On August 7, the second Lunar Eclipse will occur, this time in your solar third house of thoughts, communications, and siblings. This lunation will take place in startling Aquarius, a sign that just loves to rebel. It may be that the new opinions you formed back in February are now challenged, and you may even need to defend yourself—but not to worry. If anyone is up for it, you will be, especially since Saturn will still be on duty in your sign, ready to help ground you and give you confidence. If a dear one seems to be refusing to conform to anything even remotely resembling the status quo, whether they're just going through a stage or this new attitude is permanent, do your best to support them.

Finally, on August 21, the second Solar Eclipse will arrive, once again activating Leo and your solar ninth house. Solar Eclipses are all about high-energy beginnings, you'll remember, so at this point, you'll be ready to take what you learned back in February and make a major life change. You may decide to move long-distance, or someone from a distant shore may take a primary, permanent position in your life. Regardless of how it happens, this lunation can absolutely make you feel born again. Your mission is to use it to recreate yourself in positive, productive ways.

⚹ Sagittarius | January ⚹

Relaxation and Recreation

Loving Venus and red-hot Mars are all done up in romantic, sentimental Pisces and planning to spend the month in your solar fourth house of emotions and domestic matters. This team's mission is to convince you to stop doing whatever you're doing long enough to take a look around and realize exactly how good you have it.

Lovers and Friends

Your ruling planet, expansive Jupiter, is currently on duty in sociable, friendly Libra and your solar eleventh house of groups—which certainly does explain why you've been burning the candle at both ends so enthusiastically of late. Don't be surprised if you're asked to take the reins and lead your tribe on a very important quest.

Money and Success

With the Sun in authoritative Capricorn and your solar second house of money matters, you should be feeling very much in control of your finances at the moment. If you're not, stop what you're doing, think about where you want to be a year from now, and put a plan in motion. In this case, there really is no time like the present.

Tricky Transits

Mercury will finally turn direct on January 8, Sagittarius, marking the beginning of the end of a long wait to get the information you need to make a sound, rational decision on a personal issue that's been problematic for at least the past three weeks. Excellent news—except for the fact that you might not be delighted with what you learn. Ah, well. Knowing the truth is always best.

Rewarding Days

3, 4, 8, 20, 22, 23

Challenging Days

6, 7, 11, 15, 19, 27, 31

↗ Sagittarius | February ↗

Relaxation and Recreation

Loving Venus will take off for fiery, impulsive Aries and your solar fifth house of recreational pursuits on February 3, Sagittarius, so yes, finally, after all that overtime you've been putting in, it's actually time to play. You, of course, know exactly who to call to maximize your recreational time. Better keep them on speed dial this month—or better still, keep them close!

Lovers and Friends

A partner-loving Libra Moon will be on duty in the heavens above you this Valentine's Day, Sagittarius, urging you to pull out all the stops and see to it that your sweetheart never forgets this special day. Of course, you've had a plan up your sleeve for some time now. Just be sure to put it in motion on time!

Money and Success

Your ruling planet, expansive Jupiter, will stop in his tracks on February 6, right smack dab in a lovely, cooperative, and extremely stimulating sextile aspect with cautious, practical Saturn. You know how they say that timing is everything? Well, it is, and this month you'll have a knack for sensing the right moment for just about everything—most especially money matters and career decisions.

Tricky Transits

The Solar Eclipse on February 26 will occur in woozy Pisces and your solar fourth house of emotions from the past, Sagittarius—so what you remember best about a certain relationship might not be an entirely accurate account. If a decision needs to be made and you think you might be suffering from selective memory syndrome, ask a practical friend for their honest opinion.

Rewarding Days
3, 6, 9, 11, 13, 14, 22, 23

Challenging Days
1, 2, 7, 8, 21, 26, 27

♐ Sagittarius | March ♐

Relaxation and Recreation

Talk about a good time! The lovely lady Venus will spend the entire month in fiery Aries, which puts her charming, assertive energy in your solar fifth house of recreation. Yes, indeed. There will be no holding you back from trying anything new during March—the more exciting, the better. Bring on the adrenaline!

Lovers and Friends

That certain someone you were pretty sure had gotten away? Maybe not. Venus will turn retrograde on March 4, giving you the chance to find out. Of course, it may be you who is pursued for a second or even third time. Before you decide to try to revive the past, however, be sure you're not just seeking out what's familiar.

Money and Success

Once Venus turns retrograde in impulsive Aries on March 4, you'll need to keep an especially cautious eye on your money, Sagittarius. You may be in so much of a hurry to buy something that you don't realize you're not getting your money's worth—and yes, you could even misplace your wallet. Invest in warranties and save your receipts.

Tricky Transits

Taking a chance on something new can be scary—but talk about exhilarating! Keep that in mind around March 2, when Jupiter and Uranus will combine energies to push you out of the nest—ready or not. Examine the true motives of anyone who tries to discourage you from experiencing a new side of life or a new type of relationship.

Rewarding Days

5, 7, 9, 18, 19, 25, 26

Challenging Days

2, 3, 4, 11, 12, 17, 23

⚹ Sagittarius | April ⚹

Relaxation and Recreation

A playful Gemini Moon will be holding court in the heavens on April 1, so if you're in the mood to play a prank on someone, she'll be happy to help. Just be sure that nothing you do can be interpreted as mean-spirited. A joke is a joke, but making someone feel foolish isn't funny.

Lovers and Friends

Your ruling planet, Jupiter, will spend yet another month in partner-oriented Libra—and on April 10, a Full Moon in that same sign will join forces with this expansive fellow. Obviously, this lineup could put you in the mood to sign up for a long-term commitment. Wait, though, just a bit—just until after Venus turns direct on April 15.

Money and Success

Mercury and Venus will both be retrograde from April 9 through April 15. If there's any way you can avoid making a major purchase during that time, put it off. If you can wait until next month, so much the better. You may not be getting your money's worth, and it will be all too easy to fall prey to a smooth-talking salesperson.

Tricky Transits

Venus will back up into sentimental, nostalgic Pisces on April 2, aiming to spend the last leg of her retrograde trek in your solar fourth house of home and family matters. You may be about to hear a voice you've been missing for a very long time. If they don't beat you to it, why not reach out and restore a precious connection?

Rewarding Days

16, 17, 23, 24, 27

Challenging Days

7, 8, 9, 20, 21, 30

Sagittarius | May

Relaxation and Recreation

The lovely lady Venus is moving forward again and is set to spend the month in impulsive Aries and your solar fifth house of playmates, lovers, and recreation. This fiery energy will undoubtedly inspire you to push some envelopes, just as she did back in February and March. This time around, though, be sure any risks you take are well calculated—and have fun!

Lovers and Friends

The New Moon on May 25 will occur in your solar seventh house of one-to-one relationships, Sagittarius, all done up in fun-loving Gemini. If you're not seeing anyone, it's time to get out there and mingle—big time. If you're happily attached, an entertaining new friend you'll both enjoy could be along shortly. Either way, it's time to play

Money and Success

On May 9 and May 31, the Sun and Mercury will take turns meeting up with intense, powerful Pluto, activating your solar house of money matters and your solar house of work. Yes, that raise, bonus, or promotion you've been waiting for could be right around the corner. If you haven't yet made it clear that you're ready for more responsibility, there's no time like the present.

Tricky Transits

The Full Moon on May 10 will occur in secretive Scorpio and your solar twelfth house—which is a pretty darn secretive place itself. That said, since Full Moons illuminate, you should probably expect a secret to literally come to light. If you're involved in something that's not quite ready for public consumption, better slow it down. In fact, applying the brakes would be best.

Rewarding Days

7, 9, 12, 13, 18, 30, 31

Challenging Days

5, 10, 11, 26

Sagittarius | June

Relaxation and Recreation

The Sun, Mercury, and Mars will skip this month through lighthearted Gemini, a fun-loving sign you've always been quite fond of. This chatty, energetic trio will pique your curiosity in at least one department, so much so that a return to school or a bit of travel could be on your agenda. It's time to broaden your horizons—which happens to be your specialty.

Lovers and Friends

The Full Moon on June 9 will activate your relationship axis, Sagittarius. Together with a lovely, energizing sextile aspect between Venus and Mars—well, let's just say that if you've been thinking about taking a casual relationship to the next level, this combination will be all the inspiration you'll need to make the leap. Don't be scared. Full-time playmates are wonderful to have around, yes?

Money and Success

The New Moon on June 23 will bring the Sun and Moon together in your solar eighth house, Sagittarius, where issues of joint finances and shared resources are handled. Prepare for a family member—possibly a child—to come along with a financial request. You'll want to help, and if you decide their needs are genuine, you'll pull out all the stops to help them get back on their feet.

Tricky Transits

Serious Saturn will spend the month retrograding through your sign, Sagittarius, urging you to take charge of work-oriented projects. This is your chance to finish up anything you've left undone before an authority figure you're trying to impress comes along, notices, and asks you some tough questions. Don't blow the meeting before it happens with a bad first impression. Get busy.

Rewarding Days

1, 3, 8, 9, 10, 11, 12

Challenging Days

2, 15, 16, 18, 28, 29

Sagittarius | July

Relaxation and Recreation

If you haven't yet set the dates of your vacation, Sagittarius, the weekend of July 7 would be a terrific time to get the show on the road. If work responsibilities are preventing you from traveling, that doesn't mean you can't still have fun. A sky full of home-loving Cancer energies will provide the perfect astrological ambience for entertaining at your place.

Lovers and Friends

Jupiter—your patron planet—has been on duty in your solar eleventh house of friendships and group affiliations since last fall—and you've enjoyed every single moment in true Sagittarian style. Parties and spontaneous gatherings at your place—it's been fabulous, and it's not going to end just yet. Look to July 7, 14, or 18 for a wonderful, delightfully unplanned evening.

Money and Success

The Sun in Cancer may have you thinking about remodeling, adding on a room, or moving to another home entirely, Sagittarius. The thing is, you may not be able to manage it financially until next month—and if that's the case, you may actually have to practice the ancient art of patience. If you're adding another pet or person to your family, however, making room for them will be a pleasure.

Tricky Transits

The Sun, Mercury, and Mars will take turns this month passing through Leo—your playful, extremely dramatic fire-sign cousin who's impossible to ignore. You'll have endless energy when it comes to socializing, but do remember that sleep is a necessary component of playing well with others. Treat yourself to at least six hours a night—not counting naps.

Rewarding Days

6, 7, 10, 11, 18, 19, 24

Challenging Days

2, 4, 8, 9, 17

Sagittarius | August

Relaxation and Recreation

The Sun and Mars are astrological fireballs. They're the prime purveyors of oomph and enthusiasm, Sagittarius, and they're set to spend a whole lot of time in dramatic, theatrical Leo this month. Now, Leo is your fire-sign cousin, and like you, Leo never knows when to quit. Obviously, you may not get much rest, but you can count on being just fine with that.

Lovers and Friends

Venus in home and family-loving Cancer is currently on duty in your solar eighth house of intimate relationships and joint finances, Sagittarius, urging you to stay close to home as much as possible this month—but that doesn't mean you'll be bored, much less lonely. You may, however, have to gently suggest to someone especially needy that it's time to go home.

Money and Success

You may be tempted to act impulsively with regard to a financial matter around August 17, Sagittarius—but please don't. In addition to Mercury being retrograde, there's an extravagant and not all that realistic Venus-Jupiter square forming up, and moderation was never this team's strong suit. Take some time to go over your numbers—say, three weeks?

Tricky Transits

Mercury will slow down to turn retrograde on August 12, all done up in precise, meticulous Virgo—and passing through your solar tenth house of career matters. Don't be scared. If you have professional meetings on the agenda, chances are good you'll have to reschedule—okay, at least once, which can be irritating—but if you're smart, you'll use this extra time to make sure you have your ducks in a row.

Rewarding Days

1, 2, 10, 13, 20, 22, 27

Challenging Days

3, 4, 5, 7, 12, 16, 18, 21

✠ Sagittarius | September ✠

Relaxation and Recreation

Work, work, work, and work. All those diligent Virgo planets will insist that you see to your duties and get your chores done before you even think about going out to play. Just between us, though, if you can manage it, the weekend of September 15 is the perfect astrological time to escape and actually have some fun.

Lovers and Friends

It's been close to a year since your ruling planet, Jupiter, set off for ultra-social Libra and your solar eleventh house of groups and friendships, Sagittarius—and it's probably been a very warm and lively year. You've only got a few more weeks of this energy to enjoy, however, so if there's someone you really want to get to know, set up a lunch date soon.

Money and Success

Four planets passing through Virgo and your solar tenth house will make this an important month for you career-wise. Until a few days after Mercury turns direct on September 5, however, taking time to go over your resumé to make sure all your accomplishments are duly noted is really your best bet. The New Moon on September 20 is a terrific time to make your case to higher-ups.

Tricky Transits

On September 5, Mercury will turn direct—which certainly sounds like the right time to move forward, right? Well, not so fast. Whatever snafus you've been dealing with will definitely begin to unravel that day, but it may not be until September 12 that the light at the end of the tunnel is apparent—and even then, an authority figure may hold your feet over the fire.

Rewarding Days

9, 10, 12, 15, 16, 17, 22

Challenging Days

5, 6, 8, 13, 24, 25

↗ Sagittarius | October ↗

Relaxation and Recreation

Duets are the name of the game now, Sagittarius, so no matter how you spend your leisure time this month, you'll enjoy it a whole lot more if you share your experiences with one particular person. If you're not attached and you want to be, get out with a trusted wing-person and mingle. The New Moon on October 19 is prime time for finding a soulmate.

Lovers and Friends

Five planets will make their way through charming Libra this month, making your solar eleventh house of groups and friendships a very busy place (busier than usual, even, which is really saying something). If you find that you're spending an awful lot of time with someone you think of only as a friend, don't be surprised when they announce that they're really interested in more than just friendship.

Money and Success

Negotiations over career matters will go best if you aim to schedule them around October 12, 16, or 29, Sagittarius, when authoritative Saturn will be in a far more supportive and far less judgmental frame of mind. At the very least, you'll make a positive first impression, and at best, you might just land yourself a nice fat raise, bonus, or promotion.

Tricky Transits

Buckle up, Sagittarius. On October 10, after a year in charming, chatty Libra, your ruling planet, Jupiter, will tiptoe quietly into secretive Scorpio. Will this put a dent in your social schedule? Maybe—but if you're attached, keep in mind that Scorpio is a very sexual sign, so if you two are missing in action from a few gatherings every now and then...well, who could blame you?

Rewarding Days

1, 3, 12, 16, 29

Challenging Days

5, 6, 8, 11, 23, 26

♐ Sagittarius | November ♐

Relaxation and Recreation

Conservative Saturn will get into an easy trine with rebellious Uranus on November 11, making it possible for you to blend the experiences from your past with your hopes for the future. To activate this lovely combination, decide where to aim your energies, then talk to an elder or professional higher-up who knows how to think outside the box.

Lovers and Friends

If you're involved with someone delicious, Sagittarius, you two may not see much of the outside world this month—deliberately, of course. The lovely lady Venus is in sexy Scorpio, as is your ruler, expansive Jupiter—and there's nothing about these two that even remotely smacks of moderation in the department of pillow talk. Be sure to check in with the outside world every now and then.

Money and Success

A pack of intense Scorpio planets—your own Uncle Jupiter included, by the way—will turn your attention toward shared resources this month, Sagittarius. In fact, as early as the Full Moon on November 4, you may need to make a major decision about a joint financial matter. When in doubt, invest in the advice of a trusted professional.

Tricky Transits

Mercury and Saturn will come together on November 28 in your sign, a pair that was tailor-made for making tough choices with an eye toward permanence and announcing your decisions with confidence. If you've been mulling over a career change, you'll know exactly what to do in short order. Be fair. Be sure to give the proper amount of notice.

Rewarding Days

9, 10, 11, 16, 17, 25

Challenging Days

7, 8, 13, 19, 27

♐ Sagittarius | December ♐

Relaxation and Recreation

It's a good time to be you, Sagittarius. The Sun, Mercury, and Venus are dashing merrily through your sign and your solar first house of personality and appearance, and even though Mercury will spend much of December moving retrograde, the worst you can possibly expect might be a traffic jam or flat tire—but the best will be hearing from at least one someone you've been sorely missing.

Lovers and Friends

If you're not attached, Sagittarius, someone delightfully interesting who's most definitely not from your neck of the woods could be along shortly to change all that. Keep an ear out for a wonderful storyteller with a fascinating accent. Oh, and don't fret about the success rate of long-distance relationships. People move cross-country and even overseas every day. Relax and see what happens.

Money and Success

Serious Saturn will return to his home turf for the first time in almost thirty years on December 19, Sagittarius—which will put him in your solar second house of personal finances for the next two and a half years. If you haven't already, put financial planning right up there at the very top of your list of New Year's resolutions. Trust me on this.

Tricky Transits

Loving Venus will get together with Saturn on December 25, putting tradition, manners, and respect for your elders on everyone's list. In your case, don't be surprised if a wave of appreciation washes over you while you're spending time with family or dear friends this holiday season—and by all means, don't be shy about expressing it.

Rewarding Days

3, 6, 7, 8, 16, 17, 20, 24, 25

Challenging Days

1, 2, 11, 12, 22

Sagittarius Action Table

These dates reflect the best—but not the only—times for success and ease in these activities, according to your Sun sign.

	JAN	FEB	MAR	APR	MAY	JUN	JUL	AUG	SEP	OCT	NOV	DEC
Move	1, 3			2, 5				12, 13			3, 4	
Start a class		10, 11		6, 7	1, 2		14, 15		12, 14		14	
Join a club		11, 22		10, 11		3, 8, 22		26				
Ask for a raise	12	23	29		15		7, 8		9, 12		13	
Get professional advice	6, 10, 12		12, 17, 29	24		8	24	27	17	12, 16		17, 22
Get a loan		8, 9	30		10, 11			4	22	17, 18		
New romance		5, 6			19, 26		4			5		
Vacation			7, 8, 9			13, 14, 16		22	29		25, 26	24, 25

Capricorn

The Goat
December 22 to January 19

♑

Element: Earth	Glyph: Head of goat
Quality: Cardinal	Anatomy: Skeleton, knees, skin
Polarity: Yin/feminine	Colors: Black, forest green
Planetary Ruler: Saturn	Animals: Goats, thick-shelled animals
Meditation: I know the strength of my soul	Myths/Legends: Chronos, Vesta, Pan
Gemstone: Garnet	House: Tenth
Power Stones: Peridot, onyx diamond, quartz,black obsidian	Opposite Sign: Cancer
	Flower: Carnation
Key Phrase: I use	Keyword: Ambitious

The Capricorn Personality

Your Strengths, Gifts, and Challenges

You're always prepared, Capricorn. Does this make you a lifelong honorary Girl Scout or Boy Scout? It certainly does—and as anyone who knows you will be happy to swear, the similarities don't end there. You work hard to be honest, trustworthy, and thrifty, and even harder to keep earning symbolic merit badges. Awards. Diplomas. Certificates. A picture on the mantle in a very nice frame showing you and the mayor shaking hands. Whether it's conscious or not, gaining recognition from authority figures—and maybe even earning rewards, every now and then, for performing especially well—well, it's second nature to you. This concept was probably drummed into your head during childhood by a parent who made it their business to be sure you developed a strong work ethic, with a special emphasis on the results—the sweet, satisfying feeling of an official and/or public pat on the back for a job well done. That said, you can be a bit too "motivated" to gain that approval at times—or, in a word, a bit too ambitious. You'll know this is the case if your sweetheart, friends, and family all keep begging you to chill out. If that's the case, please do chill out. You have a wonderfully dry sense of humor, and when you let go and let your hair down, unbeknown to most, you're most definitely the life of the party. Oh, and once you do allow yourself to get out there and have some fun, don't you dare let anyone talk you into taking charge of the game or organizing the players.

Romance, Friendships, and Casual Relationships

Dependable. Reliable. Responsible. Hardworking. You're the real deal, Capricorn, the partner absolutely everyone is looking for—especially since all those wonderfully earthy qualities come wrapped up in a delightfully wry, witty, and personable package. You have a reputation for being a tad on the cool and calculating side, but that description tends to be shared only by those who don't know you well. The lucky ones in your inner circle tell an entirely different story. You're warm, loving, and oh-so loyal to family and friends you consider family—to a fault, actually. You sometimes blame yourself for their shortcomings and wonder what you could have done to have stopped them from going astray. Stop that. Seriously. You're responsible for you. Period. It's lovely that you care about your dear ones, but please do learn to care about yourself—enough to take some time for recreation. There's fun to be had out there and playmates to have fun with. Taurus and Virgo are terrific pals, earth-sign cousins who also often make solid, easygoing long-term partners. If you're looking for someone to settle down and have a family with, home-loving Cancer might be your best bet—happy to tend the home fires while you're out conquering the world. When it comes to entertaining friends who'll inspire you to relax and kick back, look to fiery, funny, and always philosophical Sagittarius.

Career and Work

What do you want to be when you grow up? You folks tend to know the answer to that question quite early on—and whatever that answer is, it tends to stick. That said, with authoritative Saturn as your ruler, no matter what path you've chosen, you'll be doling out orders from your executive office upstairs in no time flat. Matter of fact, even before you've made it up there, even if you're just sixteen and treading water for a paycheck at a pizza parlor, your managerial potential will still shine through—and inevitably, someone will ask if you'd like to train for management. You were born to lead. Just remember the climb when you get to the top.

Money and Possessions

As per the influence of your frugal ruling planet, Saturn, you don't often indulge in excess, Capricorn, and you have no problem whatsoever living on a budget. That doesn't mean you enjoy cutting back to the bare bones, however—only that when it has to happen, you can most definitely handle it. Fortunately, you're pretty darn good with money—for the most part, anyway—so once you have a decent position, you won't lack for much. You're also a wise shopper and quite respectful of those carefully chosen possessions you're moved to purchase. The thing is, you have unpredictable, impetuous Aquarius on your solar second house, so every now and then, a good binge-spend just has to happen. If it happens this spring, fine. Just hang on to every single receipt.

Your Lighter Side

You work hard and most certainly deserve time off, but you probably feel guilty when you're not on the job—even if it's just for a few hours, much less for a week or more. Obviously, you're not exactly a natural when it comes to relaxing, Capricorn, but if anyone desperately needs to unwind, it's you. A weekend might be a nice compromise, once you've been convinced to delegate duties and you're sure you can cover all your bases. The funny thing is, much as it's not easy to talk you into it, once you've shut off your phone—well, stand back, because the party is on! It's all about laughter, late nights, and good old-fashioned hedonistic fun. If you have your way, it will start with a good soak and a good meal. That's just before you set out to wreak havoc on an unsuspecting city with intelligent friends who know how you get when you're actually off duty. No matter how you unwind, don't let anyone talk you into running the show. Mention that you're officially off duty, smile pretty, and walk away.

Capricorn Celebrities

Take a look at this impressive lineup of your compatriots, Capricorn. Let's start with those who are ageless and timeless, who've made such an amazing impression on the world that they'll never be forgotten—like Janis Joplin, David Bowie, Betty White, Elvis Presley, and Stephen Hawking, for example. You folks just adore the idea of mastery, so much so that you strive for it in all you do—so pat yourself on the back for being forged from the same celestial stuff as celebrities like Diane Keaton, Annie Lennox, Mel Gibson, and Jim Carrey, all renowned experts in their fields.

Words to Live By for 2017
It's time to take control of my relationships.

The Year Ahead for Capricorn

Last September, Jupiter in partner-loving Libra made his way into your solar tenth house of career matters, authority figures, and dealings with higher-ups on the job—where he'll remain until October 10 of this year. When Jupiter visits, it's kind of like having Santa Claus on duty, and while you may or may not actually receive presents from your superiors, you can rest assured that if you need someone of authority to have your back, they'll be right there. In fact, someone has probably already performed that task, most likely from behind the scenes. Now, as I already mentioned, Libra is an extremely partner-oriented sign, so if you've been thinking of starting a business, a partnership might be the way to go. Just be sure they're as committed to success as you are—and if they happen to be your romantic partner...well, sit down and have a long, serious chat about whether or not your relationship will benefit from spending so much time together. Again, the secret is being sure you're equally committed to the project.

Of course, you may be starting that business in a very different location, thanks to Venus, who'll spend three months in your solar fourth house of home and family matters, all done up in fiery, impulsive Aries. This fast-moving, independent energy might just prompt you to move—and if so, since she'll be working in cahoots with shocking Uranus, chances are good it won't be just across town. If you manage to stay put, you can count on this fiery lady to keep your domestic life "interesting" from February 3 to April 2 and again from April 28 through June 6. If you're single and a family member insists on introducing you to someone they're sure is just perfect for you, don't you dare refuse—no matter what happened last time. Agree to meet, even if it's only for lunch—or maybe even just a quick coffee.

Saturn

Saturn is your ruling planet, Capricorn, a rather stern fellow who's in charge of our dealings with authority figures—not to mention all matters pertaining to social status, career, and profession. It's a natural fit—after all, you've always been driven to achieve and excel, and you're nothing if not respectful of authority figures and elders. So this year, as Saturn finishes up his trek through Sagittarius and your solar twelfth house of secrets and Privacy, Please, you may feel a bit conflicted. On the one hand, you'll want to get up, get going, and work steadily to accomplish your goals, ignoring all obstacles and moving forward, as per usual. You may even be working at home, intent on finishing a project that's kept you busy for the better part of two years. On the other hand, you'll be drawn inward at times, possibly because you're a bit depressed. Now, everyone needs time alone every now and then to recharge the old batteries, but if you're spending more time at home alone in the dark—well, it's time to take care of that situation. Depression can become quite serious quite quickly. Fortunately, there are medical solutions to be had, so all you really have to do is get yourself to a trusted professional—the thing is, you'll need to do it early on in the process. Don't hesitate to call on a friend or family member to help you figure out what type of help you need, and drag them along to ask the questions you might not be thinking of at the moment. There's nothing to be ashamed of, and you have no reason to feel guilty. Let those feelings go and get yourself back on the path toward enjoying life again.

Uranus

Back in 2010, this startling planet set off for impulsive, fiery Aries and your solar fourth house, Capricorn, where home, family, and domestic issues are handled—and ever since, keeping you and yours on any type of regular schedule has become a bit of a battle. In fact, at times, it's been quite the battle indeed. You may have been dealing with shaky or uncertain living situations, or with family members or roommates who are erratic or unstable. The thing is, the fourth house is our emotional foundation, and when Uranus is here, that foundation often feels as if it's undergoing earthquakes. Now, you're a veritable rock, so you've no doubt handled all this well, but that doesn't mean you need to do it alone. Contrary to popular opinion, you aren't responsible for what others do—even if they live with you or they're related to you. Besides, if you allow yourself to become too encumbered by others' burdens…well, with this impulsive, radical energy here, you just might throw a few things in a suitcase one fine day and head on down the road for parts unknown. Yes, permanently. Of course, that might not be the worst thing in the world. Long-distance moves are exhilarating—which could be exactly what you need right now. If you were born between January 9 and January 19, your Sun will be receiving an action-oriented square from Uranus this year, so all of the above goes double for you. Fasten your seatbelt and prepare for a wild, exciting ride.

Neptune

Your solar third house is currently being inhabited by the lovely lady Neptune, who's been on duty here since 2011. Now, her specialty is dissolving boundaries, and this house deals with communication via the senses—all six of them—as well as navigating through your immediate environment. That said, it's easy to understand how even a solid, grounded creature like yourself might have become a bit more sensitized to negative energies in your neighborhood, and to bright lights and loud sounds in general. The thing is, you're learning to open up and connect with your environment. You've become a psychic sponge, so harsh sensory experiences might actually hurt—yes, even physically. If you were born between January 6 and January 11, your Sun will be further influenced by Neptune via an easy, stimulating sextile—and this is the stuff that psychic abilities are made of. So if you suddenly discover that you're able to predict what others will say about 90 percent of the time, don't question your sanity—but don't necessarily share the news with anyone you don't trust implicitly. It will be especially easy to make contact with the muse of your choice now, so if you're feeling creatively blocked, sit still for just a few moments and pay attention to your breathing. Okay, yes, that's meditating, but I didn't want to scare you off by using the word. Now that it's out on the table, though, this is a terrific time to take up the metaphysical activity that's most to your liking.

Pluto

Your solar first house has been entertaining intense, penetrating Pluto in your very own sign since 2008, Capricorn—which certainly does explain a lot. I mean, you've always been a bit on the intense side, but at this point, I'll bet when you walk into a room, even if it's on tiptoe, everyone notices immediately. If you were born between January 6 and January 12, Pluto will form a conjunction with your Sun this year—and this is where it gets really intense. The thing is, you're currently exuding sexuality, passion, and power without saying a word or moving a muscle, and that kind of stuff is hard to miss, so whether you're single or quite happily attached, fascinated admirers will be along on a regular basis. Now, some may be a bit more determined than others, and deciding how to deal with each of them will, of course, be your decision. Remember, though, that all transits work both ways, so if you have the feeling that someone is trying to control or "handle" you, remind yourself that you're in charge now. Period. Don't let anyone prey on you by taking advantage of your good nature and innate sense of decency. You can invite others in or dismiss them without any explanation—it's all up to you. Oh, and if anyone foolishly pushes you too far to see what you're made of? Don't hesitate. Release the Kraken. Hey, they asked for it.

How Will This Year's Eclipses Affect You?

Eclipses are celestial exclamation points. They amp up the volume on ordinary life whenever they occur, but the signs and degrees they activate also bring along events and circumstances that are quite intense. Eclipses occur in pairs, six months apart, over a two-week period. Solar Eclipses are supercharged New Moons. They bring the Sun and Moon together, marking peak times for planting spiritual seeds and announcing intentions of all kinds known to the Universe. Lunar Eclipses are high-energy Full Moons, and like these monthly oppositions between the Sun and the Moon, they signal times of dramatic culmination and fulfillment.

The first Lunar Eclipse of 2017 will occur on February 10 in fiery, dramatic Leo and your solar eighth house of joint finances, Capricorn, possibly bringing a money-related issue to a head in an equally fiery and dramatic way. If you've been trying to keep the peace and hoping this whole situation would blow over, you probably won't be able to do that much longer—and to be honest, putting this off any longer really isn't in your best interest, anyway. It's time to sit down with a certain person and let them know exactly what you expect from them, most especially with regard to sharing responsibilities of the financial kind. Put your foot down and refuse to be taken advantage of.

On February 26, the first Solar Eclipse of the year will arrive, all done up in woozy Pisces. This lunation will occur in your solar third house of conversations and communications, Capricorn. Now, you're usually pretty much on your game when it comes to keeping track of who said what to whom, but Pisces energy has been known to space out on a detail or two every now and then. A miscommunication or misunderstanding that happens around this time may seem harmless enough at first, but don't let it slide. Tiny mix-ups could turn into major issues in very short order. Fortunately, you have the ability to nip this thing in the bud. Be very clear in all your conversations and be sure your intentions are understood.

On August 7, the second Lunar Eclipse of the year—in startling Aquarius, no less—will activate your solar second house of personal finances and possessions, Capricorn. Now, this could bring along a major change in your financial situation, but don't fret too much just yet. If you're prepared and you have a safety net in place—and honestly, when don't you?—it might just turn out to be a minor bump in the road due to an unexpected expense. On the other hand, sudden financial change can go either way. A windfall? Sure, maybe. That raise, bonus, or promotion you've been waiting for? Yep. One never knows.

The last Solar Eclipse of 2017 will arrive on August 21, once again in Leo and your solar eighth house. This time around, however, unlike last February, rather than bringing closure to a financial issue, you may have the chance to start all over again—pretty much from scratch, in fact. Now, don't panic. That doesn't mean you'll be financially devastated, but it does mean you'll need to rethink just about everything concerning your budget, spending habits, and long-term obligations. Refinancing loans, consolidating credit card balances, and trimming the fat from wherever you can is a good idea. Matter of fact, don't wait for this eclipse to occur—be proactive. Get your financial paperwork done well ahead of time.

Capricorn | January

Relaxation and Recreation

Getting a plan to come together could be tough up until January 8, since Mercury will be moving retrograde. If you have to move your plans around, don't get frustrated. You might quite happily find that the rain date ends up being the best date you could possibly have chosen. Yes, every now and then it's good to let go and let the Universe drive.

Lovers and Friends

The Full Moon on January 12 will occur in your solar seventh house of one-to-one relationships, Capricorn, all done up in home-loving Cancer. If you're not already living with someone, this lunation could inspire one of you to bring up the idea of cohabitation. Think carefully before you sign up. Are you really ready for this?

Money and Success

With generous Jupiter in your solar tenth house of career matters since last September, Capricorn, there's been very little you've been able to do that's wrong—in the eyes of your superiors, that is. The extra effort you've invested has definitely paid off career-wise. This month, though, your family and friends just might raise a bit of a ruckus about not seeing you nearly enough.

Tricky Transits

Fiery Mars and dreamy Neptune will come together on January 1 in your solar third house of conversations and communications, Capricorn, urging you to put every bit of that passion you're feeling into every syllable you utter. You may make someone mad, but you'll most certainly feel good about yourself afterward. Go ahead. Raise some eyebrows.

Rewarding Days
2, 3, 10, 12, 20, 23

Challenging Days
6, 7, 11, 15, 27, 31

Capricorn | February

Relaxation and Recreation

Valentine's Day will arrive with a loving, romantic Libra Moon in tow, so even though you're not usually much for sentimentality, you just might be moved to do something quite special for someone quite special. The good news is that this one particular gesture will probably make the rest of the month just wonderful.

Lovers and Friends

Venus and Mars will storm through Aries this month, and since Venus is in charge of attracting what we love and Mars is in charge of pursuing what we want—well, this is an unstoppable duo. Oh, and they're making their way through your solar fourth house of emotions from the past. Time to give someone a second chance? Maybe. You decide.

Money and Success

Anyone who challenges your authority around February 22 has issues of their own you'll never truly understand, Capricorn. Still, backing away won't be an option—and you're quite a competitive soul, anyway, and not a stranger to conflict. Your mission is to resist the urge to completely destroy them after you've proved your worth once again to the powers that be.

Tricky Transits

On February 8, the heavens will host a war of sorts, involving four extremely assertive and determined planets. We'll all feel the tension. In your case, however, it just may turn out that a sudden set of circumstances sets you free from responsibilities you weren't sure you could handle for much longer. It may be unsettling, but wait for the end result.

Rewarding Days

5, 6, 7, 9, 13, 16, 23

Challenging Days

2, 3, 8, 21, 26, 27

Capricorn | March

Relaxation and Recreation

A pack of active cardinal energies will keep you moving this month, Capricorn—so much so that by the New Moon on March 27, you may actually be willing to slow down just a bit and delegate some duties. You don't do this often, so don't feel guilty. Everyone gets overwhelmed every now and then. You're a force to be reckoned with, but do allow yourself a break.

Lovers and Friends

The Sun, Mercury, and Neptune will take turns passing through Pisces and your solar third house of conversations and communications this month, Capricorn, turning all your encounters into emotional exchanges that come straight from the heart. If a certain someone apologizes—or tries to, no matter how awkwardly—do both of you a favor and accept. There's nothing to be gained from holding on to a grudge.

Money and Success

Venus is the Goddess of Love and Money, Capricorn, and she'll turn retrograde on March 4, urging you to review your finances and figure out whether or not your current career is supporting you in the style you want to become accustomed to. If you're happy, wonderful. If you're not, get out there and shake some hands.

Tricky Transits

Jupiter will square off with intense Pluto on March 30, Capricorn, activating a bit of tension between you and a higher-up, elder, or authority figure. If you know you're wrong, the best way to handle this will be to admit it, apologize, and move on. If you know you're right, though— well, heaven help anyone who tries to dismiss you without hearing your side of the story.

Rewarding Days
5, 7, 9, 16, 18, 19

Challenging Days
1, 2, 11, 12, 17, 23, 30

Capricorn | April

Relaxation and Recreation

Dividing your time equally between work-oriented situations and domestic matters may not be easy this month, Capricorn, but you really will have to find a way to work it out. Fortunately, the Full Moon in Libra—the sign that's best at juggling—will come along on April 11, temporarily endowing you with the superpowers necessary to keep both departments running smoothly.

Lovers and Friends

Venus will back up into woozy Pisces and your solar third house on April 2, Capricorn, urging you to restore a connection with someone you've been missing for way too long. No matter why you've been estranged from each other or whether it's been two months or two years—well, buck up, swallow your pride, and get this done. Life's too short for this nonsense.

Money and Success

If you've been trying to find the right day to sit down with an elder, higher-up, or authority figure you need to ask a favor of, Capricorn, April 5 is the perfect time to make that happen. Assertive Mars will team up with intense, unrelenting Pluto to give you the strength and determination you need to further your cause.

Tricky Transits

On April 8, several planetary culprits will join forces to create the potential for misunderstandings that won't be easily untangled, Capricorn. If you're already feeling confused about the state of a certain relationship, one miscommunication could bring it to an end. If that's what you're after, fine. If not, be warned: it's time to be very, very clear about what you want.

Rewarding Days

5, 6, 16, 17, 18, 27

Challenging Days

7, 8, 9, 13, 21

Capricorn | May

Relaxation and Recreation

The Sun and Mars will take turns passing through fast-moving, impatient Gemini and your solar sixth house of work and relationships with coworkers, Capricorn. If you're partnered up with someone and it's not a good fit, don't pretend everything is just groovy. Mention it to your coworker. You two may be able to work something out. If not, approach the higher-ups together.

Lovers and Friends

Great big changes are en route for you in the relationship department, Capricorn, and I'll bet you can feel them coming. Sit tight until May 9, when a lovely trine between the Sun and Pluto could bring along the news you've been waiting for from a lover, playmate, or child. Don't make any decisions until you have all the right information.

Money and Success

The emotional Moon in quirky Aquarius will connect with Jupiter on May 17, Capricorn, creating the perfect astrological storm for the formation of luck—lots of it, arriving in sudden fashion. So now that you know the Universe will have your back if you take a well-calculated risk on that day, hopefully you'll use this energy wisely—for something more ambitious than just buying a scratch-off.

Tricky Transits

An easy, prosperous trine will occur on May 19, Capricorn, bringing together old-fashioned Saturn and rebellious, futuristic Uranus. Now, Saturn is your ruling planet, so you know how to cooperate and negotiate. Any attempts to communicate those skills to the rest of us now would be much appreciated.

Rewarding Days
2, 9, 12, 17, 18, 31

Challenging Days
5, 10, 11, 25, 27

Capricorn | June

Relaxation and Recreation

The heavens are still fairly bursting with action-oriented cardinal energies, Capricorn, so getting any type of meaningful rest will probably have to wait until next month. The thing is, you'll be having so much fun that chugging down a cup of coffee to give you a second wind won't seem like much of a hardship. Do take naps, though—often, please.

Lovers and Friends

The Sun, Mercury, and Mars will spend time in Cancer and your solar seventh house of one-to-one relationships this month, Capricorn, all done up in family-oriented, warm, and snuggly Cancer. If you're not already attached, you'll be thinking seriously about signing up for that happy condition now—especially around June 1 and again from June 24 on. Think about it carefully. If you're ready, congrats!

Money and Success

Your earth-sign cousins—Taurus, I mean—have a well-deserved reputation for being money magnets. And since you guys are tight, when Taurus planets show up, things start to happen for you too. You've officially been put on alert, then: on or around June 24, Venus in Taurus will send some serious luck your way. Take advantage of this gift.

Tricky Transits

Neptune will stop in her tracks on June 16, insisting that we all stop paying so much attention to facts, figures, and rules—just long enough to appreciate the things in our lives that bring us joy. Make some popcorn, pull on some snuggly socks, and revel in the endearing, familiar comfort of your home and loved ones.

Rewarding Days
1, 3, 13, 24, 25

Challenging Days
4, 11, 14, 15, 19, 28

Capricorn | July

Relaxation and Recreation

The Sun, Mercury, and Mars will all spend time in fiery, playful Leo this month, Capricorn, urging you to chill out, relax, and have some fun. Of course, in order for that to happen, every single one of your responsibilities will need to be properly taken care of. Fine. Once that's done, however, turn off all electronic devices and enjoy the company of those amusing three-dimensional creatures right in front of you.

Lovers and Friends

The Full Moon on July 9 will illuminate your sign, Capricorn, and your solar first house of personality and appearance. If you've been thinking of making changes—perhaps to attract someone new—well, don't only make changes to the outer you. Adjust your attitude so that you'll be drawing successful, grounded types. You know, the kind of person who actually deserves you.

Money and Success

That same Full Moon on July 9 will draw the attention of important higher-ups your way, Capricorn—for only the best of reasons. If you've been trying to make an impression on someone, this is most definitely the time to set up an appointment. Be sure your resume is updated, at the very least. If you're feeling like a whole new person, though—well, why not put together a whole new you on paper?

Tricky Transits

On July 20, fiery Mars will set off for equally fiery and extremely dramatic Leo. This will occur just as the Sun in your solar seventh house of relationships gets into a bit of an argument with startling Uranus—which can end up exactly as it sounds. If you don't feel like a fight, ditch anyone volatile as soon as possible and table the issue.

Rewarding Days

7, 8, 11, 18, 19

Challenging Days

4, 5, 9, 16, 17, 23

Capricorn | August

Relaxation and Recreation

Balancing time spent at work and time spent on familial and domestic responsibilities has never been easy for you, Capricorn, so when that issue raises its nasty little head once again this month, you'll need to figure out a solution—for the short term, at the very least. If you can work it out, though, a more permanent fix is most definitely in order.

Lovers and Friends

If you're trying to get in touch with a long-distance loved one, better make a special effort to find them and reestablish contact before Mercury turns retrograde on August 12. You may need to jump through some hoops to make it happen, and it may not be easy. If time is of the essence, don't waste a single moment more.

Money and Success

Generous Jupiter will get together with Saturn on August 27, who just so happens to be your ruling planet. This is a combination that's all about fortunate timing—or basically, being in the right place at the exact moment the Universe is about to pass out a treat. You can be there to collect. Your mission is to pay attention to the details you so love.

Tricky Transits

On August 4, excessive Jupiter will square off with intense, sexy Pluto—and since squares push us into action, it's easy to see how you might be tempted to take a whole weekend off to spend in a most intimate fashion with your sweetheart, with very little regard for your work-oriented duties. Well, good for you. It's certainly about time.

Rewarding Days
10, 11, 13, 19, 20, 22

Challenging Days
3, 4, 5, 7, 12, 21, 24

Capricorn | September

Relaxation and Recreation

Four planets will make their way through Virgo and your solar ninth house this month, Capricorn, a lovely indication that you may be on your way to finding an entirely different path in life. Might be that you'll move and become a whole new person in the process. Might simply be that your views will change on an issue that's near and dear to your heart, making you feel like a whole new you.

Lovers and Friends

If you're thinking of taking off for a weekend to finally spend some quality time with your sweetheart, the weekend of September 15 is perfect for your needs. The emotional Moon and Venus—the Goddess of Love, thank you very much—will be on duty in your solar eighth house of intimate encounters, all done up in passionate, romantic Leo. Any questions?

Money and Success

Your solar eighth house will be a very busy place this month, Capricorn. Remember, this is also where matters of joint finances and shared resources are handled, and with Leo energies involved, it's challenging but important that you don't allow your pride to interfere with your business sense—much less your common sense. Sit tight. You'll have the applause and acclaim you're after quite shortly.

Tricky Transits

Expansive Jupiter will face off with impulsive Uranus on September 28, urging you to make some drastic changes with regard to your career life and your home life. Yes, at the same time. Don't hesitate to ask a benevolent higher-up or elder for help. They'll be happy to support you. You may even end up with a benefactor.

Rewarding Days

2, 9, 10, 12, 15, 17, 22

Challenging Days

3, 4, 5, 13, 16, 25

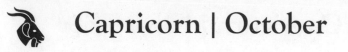

Capricorn | October

Relaxation and Recreation

You'll have plenty of chances this Halloween month to get your adrenaline pumping, Capricorn. You're not usually much for getting into disguise, but right about now, wouldn't it be excellent to be a kid again, even if it's only for a night? Sure it would. Make that magic happen for you and yours on October 31.

Lovers and Friends

If someone you've only thought of as a friend suddenly begins to invade your thoughts on a regular basis—well, I think you should just give in and admit that there's something more there than friendship. Not to me, though—it's time to admit it to them. Don't worry. At the very least, they'll be flattered. At best, you may have found your next partner.

Money and Success

Venus will square off with Saturn on October 8 and fiery Mars will follow suit on October 11, activating what could turn out to be a very nasty fight over money. You've probably seen this coming, but still, even if you're eminently prepared for battle, if it's really below you to keep this going, don't. Walk away with your pride intact.

Tricky Transits

On October 10, after a full year in sociable, chatty Libra, Jupiter will set off for intense, investigative Scorpio and your solar eleventh house of groups and peer circles. If you've been feeling unwelcome, overworked, or unappreciated, you won't hesitate to find yourself a whole new tribe now. As well you should, by the way. They're out there. Keep looking.

Rewarding Days

1, 2, 3, 12, 16, 28, 29

Challenging Days

4, 6, 11, 23, 26

Capricorn | November 🐐

Relaxation and Recreation

You can probably expect a motley crew to show up for this year's holidays, especially if you have an extra seat or two available at the table on November 23. The emotional Moon will be all done up in startling Aquarius, set and ready to bring along some extremely "interesting" folks for your perusal. Bet you'll enjoy every moment.

Lovers and Friends

The New Moon on November 18 will occur in intense, determined Scorpio, urging you to accept yourself as you truly are—even if you have to change peer groups or group affiliations to make it happen. If you've been thinking about meeting some new people for some time now, stop playing around. Investigate—and when you discover where your kindred spirits mingle, get thee there.

Money and Success

On November 13, Venus and Jupiter will get together, creating the possibility of creating wealth—and we're talking great wealth here. Now, not all of us have the capacity to understand the messages these two financial geniuses are whispering—but you? Well, you understand their language. If your gut tells you to invest—on any level—go for it.

Tricky Transits

After what will probably turn out to be a lovely weekend for you and yours, fiery Mars and determined Pluto will square off on November 19, Capricorn, marking the start of a rather testy workweek. Your mission is to stay put and not stalk off into the sunset unless and until plan B is ready to be employed.

Rewarding Days

3, 4, 9, 11, 21, 25

Challenging Days

7, 8, 13, 19, 26, 27

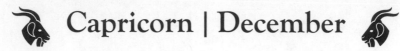

Capricorn | December

Relaxation and Recreation

A pack of planets in outgoing, personable Sagittarius will gang up on you in a most delightful fashion from their spot in your solar twelfth house of secrets this month, Capricorn, determined to entice you out of the dark, no matter how tough it might be for you. The holidays are tough for us all at one time or another. You know who to call. Don't let your pride stop you.

Lovers and Friends

December 25 will be just delightful for you, Capricorn. For starters, loving Venus will be on duty in your sign, bringing elegance, respect, and an appreciation for loyalty into all your encounters. And your ruling planet, Saturn, will be keeping quite close company with her over the holiday. There's something just lovely about being surrounded by tried-and-true loved ones. Make sure that happens.

Money and Success

Venus will hold court in outgoing, excessive Sagittarius until December 25, and since she's in charge of money matters and Sagittarius has never been famous for being especially moderate—well, you should probably plan on spending a whole lot more than you'd planned this holiday season. Keep the receipts, though. They may already have one.

Tricky Transits

Mercury will spend from December 3 through December 22 moving retrograde through Sagittarius and your secretive solar twelfth house, Capricorn—so yes, if you're doing something surreptitious, you should expect to be exposed late this month. If you're planning something sweet and secretive for someone you love, keeping it under wraps will take some effort!

Rewarding Days

6, 7, 10, 16, 20, 24, 25

Challenging Days

1, 2, 5, 11, 22

Capricorn Action Table

These dates reflect the best—but not the only—times for success and ease in these activities, according to your Sun sign.

	JAN	FEB	MAR	APR	MAY	JUN	JUL	AUG	SEP	OCT	NOV	DEC
Move	5, 6, 7		26, 27, 28			1, 3	2, 3		27, 29	5	3, 4, 5	
Start a class		12, 13, 16	15, 16		10, 11		7			1, 3		25, 26
Join a club	20, 21			11, 12	11	6, 7	7, 24	10				
Ask for a raise		13, 22			17		10, 11		3, 30	8, 9		22, 24
Get professional advice		23, 24		7, 8, 9			24			21		
Get a loan	12, 13	11	21, 29			15, 24		18	6			
New romance	20		18, 19		25, 26	24, 27, 28		10, 11				27
Vacation		12		17, 18, 19			25	22		10, 11		

Aquarius

The Water Bearer
January 20 to February 19

≋

Element: Air	Glyph: Currents of energy
Quality: Fixed	Anatomy: Ankles, circulatory system
Polarity: Yang/masculine	Colors: Iridescent blues, violet
Planetary Ruler: Uranus	Animals: Exotic birds
Meditation: I am a wellspring of creativity	Myths/Legends: Ninhursag, John the Baptist, Deucalion
Gemstone: Amethyst	House: Eleventh
Power Stones: Aquamarine, black pearl, chrysocolla	Opposite Sign: Leo
	Flower: Orchid
Key Phrase: I know	Keyword: Unconventional

The Aquarius Personality

Your Strengths, Gifts, and Challenges

You're the fixed air sign of the zodiac, Aquarius, an intensely intellectual creature with no shortage of opinions and absolutely no fear of
expressing them. Of course, radical, rebellious, and oh-so-unpredictable
Uranus is your ruling planet, so it only stands to reason that you'd raise
a few eyebrows every now and then—and that you'd secretly enjoy every
single disruptive minute. Not to worry, though. As Uranus's child, it's
your job to challenge the status quo, point out what's wrong with the
system, and open up as many of our eyes as possible to what's really happening in the world. So if, in your often not-so-subtle way, that means
directly contradicting a belief or tradition long held by others and
maybe even by you—well, that's what it takes to make progress, right?
Right. Matter of fact, take a look at the list of celebrities at the end of
this section, many of whom are members of your tribe who quietly and
rationally nudged us out of collective ruts. Will you be next? You most
certainly can be. All you have to do is fix your mind on a positive goal—
with the emphasis on *positive*—and put one foot in front of the other.
Your sign understands the point A to point B plan, and you're plenty
determined and objective enough to make it happen.

Romance, Friendships, and Casual Relationships

Obviously, once you decide to sign up long-term, Aquarius—which is
often a rare thing for you—it absolutely must be with someone who
shares your opinions on the big picture. That includes but is not limited
to politics, religion, social justice, and the law. You may decide to let
someone slide if they don't share your views on say, the Beatles—but
when it comes to an issue you feel is truly important, if you're not on
the same page intellectually, you won't be thinking about anything even
remotely resembling permanence. The truth is, you may even begin
plotting your escape as soon as you hear the news. When it comes to
choosing a partner, freedom-loving, socially conscious Sagittarius is
often a good match, and your fellow air sign, Gemini, is curious and
witty enough to hold your interest for a good long while. Libras may
appeal to you, too, especially because they're ready and willing to try
to be everything to their partners—which, of course, would include the
position of best friend, an absolute deal breaker for you.

Career and Work

You're a cerebral being, Aquarius, an unparalleled expert at thinking outside the box. In fact, I'm convinced that phrase was invented by someone who was watching a member of your astrological tribe tackling a supposedly insurmountable problem. You firmly believe that no matter what the intellectual challenge, there are always options—and when they're not immediately apparent, it's only because we're not asking the right questions. That, of course, is the stuff that genius is made of (another word that seems to be among your personal properties), so no matter what field you choose to pursue, if you find it interesting, you'll excel at it. If not—well, you'll go through the motions until something better comes along, but when it does, you'll be outta there, computer under your arm, in a matter of moments. The thing is, being bored for eight hours a day—multiplied by five—is intolerable for you. It's just not an option. Odd or unusual occupations are extra fun. What's better than the surprised look on someone's face when you tell them you're an astrologer, astronaut, robotics technician, or storm chaser? Not much!

Money and Possessions

Before we get into money matters, Aquarius, let's talk about your favorite things—which, as anyone who knows you will attest, are almost always and almost entirely electronic gadgets. Computers, smartphones, tablets, smartwatches, virtual reality devices—you name it. It doesn't matter what they do or if their uses overlap. If you don't already have the cutting-edge version of the ones you love, you're coming up with a plan to own them soon—and man, once they're in your hot little hands, are you good at using them! Of course, you're the first to admit that you're roughly half computer anyway, so "bonding" with them easily only makes sense. Be kind—and patient, please—with those of us who aren't as tech-savvy. Heaven knows we're trying!

Now, on to money matters. First off, your toys aren't cheap, and they're upgraded all the time, so to support your e-habit, you'll need to earn a tidy sum. Fortunately, you can put your natural affinity for the tech fields to work for you. If you don't write the manuals for a living, you most certainly could. Careful, though. You do have unassuming Pisces on your solar second house, so don't settle for less than you know your skills are worth when you're negotiating salary. You're a valuable commodity. Price yourself accordingly.

Your Lighter Side

What makes you really, really happy, Aquarius? Well, aha moments are right at the top of the list. In your book, there's nothing more thrilling than when a flash of insight zips through your brain—and suddenly, you get it. Yep. That's the best. Doing battle with authority is great fun, too, especially if it's on behalf of a group whose members are odd or eccentric. Computers, phones, and other electric contraptions are fabulous toys that you think of as extensions of your brain, and since you're also the most group-oriented sign in the heavens, social-networking sites can keep you amused for hours. Just don't forget to turn off your gadgets every now and then to enjoy the experience of a live conversation with another person—the kind that doesn't involve typing.

Aquarius Celebrities

You're in terrific company, Aquarius. Take a look at the rule breakers, rebels, geniuses, and social activists born under your sign: Rosa Parks, Oprah Winfrey, Charles Darwin, Ellen DeGeneres, Alice Cooper, Wolfgang Amadeus Mozart, Ayn Rand, Joe Pesci, John Belushi, John McEnroe, Yoko Ono, and Kerry Washington. Currently, however, there's just no better living example of how amazingly, radically nonconformist you can be than the politically incorrect atheist/libertarian Bill Maher—who, by the way, doesn't believe in astrology.

Words to Live By for 2017

Setting up rules I can live with is my first priority.

The Year Ahead for Aquarius

You'll be doing a whole lot of communicating this year, Aquarius, thanks to the joint efforts of startling Uranus, no-holds-barred Jupiter, and Venus, the Goddess of Love and Money. If you're thinking this sounds like it might be the perfect astrological recipe for winning the lottery and/or love at first sight, you're right. Both of those lovely things are entirely possible with this crew on board. After six years, you've pretty much gotten used to having Uranus on duty in your solar third house of communications and conversations, so at this point, sudden and unexpected news has to be absolutely stunning to get a rise out of you. But during 2017, Venus will spend three full months with Uranus—and when these two conspire, relationships become a bit trickier than usual to navigate. Add in a heaping dollop of expansive, excessive Jupiter in partner-oriented Libra and it's clear that any relationship changes will be great, big relationship changes. Ordinarily, this could be a rather unsettling time, but with Uranus as your ruling planet, you're naturally prepared for anything—which means you'll sail through this, enjoying exciting adventures with interesting new friends and seasoned loved ones who share your love of the unexplored.

Now, back to the love-at-first-sight thing. Venus in Aries will have you on high alert for the presence of your next meaningful relationship from February 3 through April 2 and again from April 28 through June 6, so if you cross paths with someone delicious and/or fascinating, don't hold back. Smile and say hi—and don't let them escape without exchanging numbers. And speaking of numbers, if you're feeling lucky, grab a lottery ticket. One. It only takes one ticket to win.

Saturn

Serious Saturn has been making his way through your solar eleventh house of friendships and group affiliations since early 2015, Aquarius, and he won't be done with this trek until December 20 of this year. Over the course of this time, you've no doubt been handed all kinds of duties and responsibilities you weren't counting on—but then, the spontaneous side of life is what gets your adrenaline going, so being tapped to take charge probably didn't bother you one little bit. Fact is, you may actually be enjoying it, at this point. If this promotion to honorary principal or denmother/denfather hasn't happened so far, sit tight. The year isn't over yet. Now, all this pertains to the groups you're willingly and happily a part of, but you may also be hit with added responsibilities you're not quite so happy about, possibly due to family members who aren't doing such a terrific job on their own. No, you don't tend to have much patience with anyone who hasn't mastered the concepts of independence and self-sufficiency, but if this is the first time you've needed to step in for a loved one, do try to be understanding. Learning how to take care of ourselves doesn't happen overnight. Now, when it comes to the groups you associate with in general, if you no longer feel that you're spending your time with kindred spirits, it might be time to look around. You're an extremely social creature, so it takes you next to no time to make friends. Get out there and find your tribe.

Uranus

This unpredictable, rebellious fellow is your ruling planet, Aquarius—which isn't all that surprising. Uranus just loves inspiring last-minute U-turns, breaking the rules, and challenging authority—all of which I'm sure sounds quite familiar. The thing is, ever since Uranus took over the helm in your solar third house of thoughts—and it's been six years now, by the way—sudden change and rebellion have probably become the norm in your life. On an interpersonal level, these changes may have occurred within your relationships with neighbors or siblings—or your neighborhood in general may have gone through some rather drastic physical changes. Internally, however, it's really you who'll change, and the process isn't nearly over, so don't get comfy just yet.

You're experimenting with opinions, mindsets, and belief systems, and until you find the one or ones that fit just right, nothing about your world will be set in stone. That goes double for those of you born between February 7 and February 18, since your Sun will be enjoying an energetic, enthusiastic sextile from Uranus in impulsive Aries this year. Stay open to new people and new experiences. You may flit from peer group to peer group and circle to circle, but think of the medley of encounters you'll have with interesting, unusual individuals—and every single thing that happens will help you form long-term opinions on the big picture—politics, religion, education, and so forth. Just be sure not to push your changing views on others. Allow them the freedom to explore new viewpoints—or to hold on to the ones they hold dear.

Neptune

If you were born between January 27 and February 5, your Sun is currently being influenced by a semisextile aspect from dreamy, woozy Neptune in Pisces. Now, this isn't ordinarily an especially strong influence, and given that it's Neptune who's involved, it would be easy to miss. The thing is, Neptune has been on duty in your solar second house for years now, where issues of finances, possessions, and money matters are handled—and she's the Queen of Illusions. This could mean that you're not spending your money wisely, or you're spending more than you should because you haven't looked around for a better deal. It might even mean that you've actually lost or misplaced money or had it stolen, or that someone has taken advantage of you. When Neptune contacts the Sun directly, all this goes double, so now more than ever, it's time to trust your cerebral little antennae. If a deal sounds too good to be true, it probably is. If someone comes to you for financial help with a story that sounds too melodramatic to be true, that, too, might just be the case. The best way to use this transit constructively is to see to it that the work you do reflects your personal beliefs. If you're not happy with how you spend your days, a paycheck won't make it any better. Just don't quit your day job until you have plan B in motion.

Pluto

Pluto is a secretive, powerful kind of guy who's never cared much for bright lights, much less the spotlight. He's been holding court in your solar twelfth house since 2008, a highly secretive place where Privacy, Please is primary. Ever since then, you may have been put in the position of holding on to a secret—at times, maybe even without your knowledge. Well, that's not going to change any time soon—at least, not until 2024, anyway. If you haven't already learned how to make the distinction between what truly isn't fit just yet for public consumption and what really needs to be unceremoniously announced, prepare yourself, because the Universe is probably going to toss you some brand-new opportunities to figure it out during 2017. If you were born between February 6 and February 11, that goes double for you. Your Sun will be contacted by Pluto via a semisextile aspect, urging you to keep quiet about just about everything. As vocal as you are about your causes and the organizations you wholeheartedly support, however, that's virtually impossible—but every now and then, if you have the feeling that blunt honestly might not be the best policy, don't say a word. Take your time and decide when the time is right to mention what you know. Oh, and that urge you have to join a secret society of some kind? Sure, it might be fun, but before you get yourself too deeply involved, be sure there's nothing dangerous or even slightly illegal in their rulebook. Apply that to sexy, fascinating individuals with shady pasts who unexpectedly tickle your fancy as well.

How Will This Year's Eclipses Affect You?

Eclipses are celestial exclamation points. They amp up the volume on ordinary life whenever they occur, but the signs and degrees they activate also bring along events and circumstances that are quite intense. Eclipses occur in pairs, six months apart, over a two-week period. Solar

Eclipses are supercharged New Moons. They bring the Sun and Moon together, marking peak times for planting spiritual seeds and announcing intentions of all kinds known to the Universe. Lunar Eclipses are high-energy Full Moons, and like these monthly oppositions between the Sun and the Moon, they signal times of dramatic culmination and fulfillment.

The first Lunar Eclipse of the year will occur on February 10, Aquarius, illuminating dramatic Leo and your solar seventh house of one-to-one relationships. Now, you're not usually much into huge displays of emotion—you tend to make faces when they happen, actually—but this time around, you may not have a choice in the matter. A certain someone who's always been a tad on the theatrical side may suddenly decide to let their feelings known in a very big, very embarrassing way—so big, in fact, that if you've been on the fence about whether or not to continue seeing them, there'll no longer be any doubt in your mind that the time has come. The same ending may come about in other relationships in less vivid fashion, too. The point is to toss aside anyone or anything that's not helping you lead a productive and happy life. Oh, and FYI—the closer to February 11 you were born, the more suddenly you'll take action.

The first Solar Eclipse of 2017 will arrive on February 26, all done up in woozy Pisces and your solar second house of possessions and money matters—which could make it a bit harder than usual to keep track of your finances, Aquarius. No fair panicking, though. Eclipses bring startling changes but not necessarily losses. Remember that lottery ticket you bought last week? Hey, it has to happen to someone, right? Why not you? On the other hand, if, before the eclipse arrives, you have the feeling that someone is playing you or taking advantage of you—well, don't just sit there. You know exactly which sites to explore for clues. Fire up your computer and do some investigating.

The Lunar Eclipse on August 7 will land right smack dab in your sign and your solar first house of personality and appearance, Aquarius, urging you to do something drastic to your physical body—something that will affect the first impression you make on others. Might be you're in the mood for a whole new wardrobe that better reflects who you are right now. Might be that you're thinking about piercing something or getting a tattoo. Fine. Just don't go nuts. What you're feeling right now will pass, but ink lasts forever. At the very least, choose something you're sure you'll always be proud to sport, even in mixed company. The closer you were born to February 4, the more you'll experience the effects of this lunation, but regardless of when you arrived, prepare yourself for startling change.

The last Solar Eclipse of the year will occur in Leo and your solar seventh house of one-to-one relationships. Yes, once again, your closest relationships stand to undergo major change—this time around, however, it will be because you're starting over, not clearing the decks as you were last February. In fact, the sudden events that occur now will make it quite clear to you that the choices you made back then were the right ones. Even if the process is uncomfortable or unsettling then, rest assured that you're on the right track. Look to the future. It's time for a five-year plan, isn't it?

Aquarius | January

Relaxation and Recreation

The year will start with a bang for you, Aquarius—with the emotional Moon on duty in your sign and your solar first house of personality and appearance. The thing is, your emotions will be running on high for another reason: a meeting of passionate Mars and dreamy Neptune. Sounds like you'll be positively feverish—for all the right reasons.

Lovers and Friends

The New Moon on January 27 will set up shop in your sign and your solar first house of personality and appearance, Aquarius, urging you to go even farther out of your way than usual to be sure that the world knows just how unique a snowflake you really are. Fine. Just don't scare away a new admirer in the process. Keep a lid on it.

Money and Success

You'll be chatting up a storm on January 3, Aquarius, and money will likely be the topic. That deal you've been trying to negotiate for what seems like forever? It's all going to come together. You'll have to sit tight until after Mercury turns direct on January 8, but hey- at least you know the deal is in the works.

Tricky Transits

The Full Moon on January 12 will occur in emotional Cancer, so all your feelings will be running very close to the surface, especially with regard to a certain coworker. The thing is, communicative Mercury will set off for Capricorn that day, a practical, no-nonsense sign that doesn't approve of gushing. Not to worry. If anyone can express feelings without going overboard, it's you—but please do express them.

Rewarding Days
1, 3, 11, 20, 23

Challenging Days
10, 12, 17, 19, 27, 31

Aquarius | February

Relaxation and Recreation
With the Sun and chatty Mercury making their way through your sign and your solar first house this month, Aquarius, it's not hard to see you being a bit too busy with social engagements to get much rest. That, of course, won't be a problem. You're of the opinion that sleep is highly overrated—especially if it gets in the way of interesting conversations.

Lovers and Friends
Venus—the Great Attractor—and Mars—her partner, known as the Great Pursuer—will pass through red-hot, impulsive Aries this month, Aquarius, putting them right smack dab in your solar third house of conversations and communications. If you're interested in someone—well, with these two on duty, it won't be a secret for long.

Money and Success
Be very careful with your wallet or purse around February 26, Aquarius. A Solar Eclipse will occur in your solar second house of personal finances and money matters, all done up in woozy Pisces, and you might just misplace your plastic or your cash. Be on guard, too, however, against anyone who comes to you with a sob story you've heard before.

Tricky Transits
A Grand Cross will occur on February 8, Aquarius, involving startling Uranus, expansive Jupiter, and intense Pluto. The emotional Moon will trigger it, and from her spot in Cancer, she won't be in the mood to hold anything back—for better or worse. In your case, that could mean that you'll be a lot more emotional than usual. Prepare to raise some eyebrows.

Rewarding Days
9, 11, 13, 16, 20, 22, 23

Challenging Days
2, 3, 8, 21, 26, 27

Aquarius | March

Relaxation and Recreation

It's almost playtime, Aquarius—but not just yet. You'll have to put off any major plans to be completely hedonistic until your homework is done—which, astrologically speaking, probably won't be until after fiery Mars leaves dutiful, hardworking Taurus next month. That doesn't mean you won't have any fun at all—only that it will take some careful planning to find the time for anything more than lunch.

Lovers and Friends

Your solar ninth house is currently hosting Jupiter in partner-loving Libra, and since this house often brings us encounters with others from far-off places, if you're not attached, someone with a charming accent could be along shortly to change that. Now, you're not one to partner up quickly, but in this case—well, you may just know right away that it's the right thing to do.

Money and Success

The Full Moon on March 12 will work together with a testy square between Mercury and Saturn to help you make a tough decision, probably involving joint finances or shared resources. If you've been taken advantage of and you're all done allowing that to happen, you'll be more than happy to mention it now—probably just before you say goodbye.

Tricky Transits

Expansive and quite often excessive Jupiter will get into it on March 2 with startling Uranus, who just so happens to be your rebellious ruling planet. Yes, if you've been feeling repressed or controlled in any way, you'll act quickly to put an end to it in rapid-fire fashion. Clear the area of innocent bystanders if you feel yourself getting warm.

Rewarding Days

5, 6, 7, 9, 25, 26, 29

Challenging Days

2, 3, 11, 12, 17, 23, 30

Aquarius | April

Relaxation and Recreation

As promised, Aquarius, energetic Mars will set off for your solar fifth house of recreation, playmates, and leisure-time activities on April 21, all done up in ultra-playful Gemini. It's time to push responsibilities aside whenever possible and have some serious fun—and it's certainly not like you haven't earned it. Kick back and enjoy the company of lighthearted friends.

Lovers and Friends

With sturdy Saturn on duty in your solar eleventh house, Aquarius, you've probably developed some really good friendships over the past couple of years—and one of those friends is about to let you know just how loyal they really are. Look to April 4 for a tough situation to be resolved far more easily because a certain someone will have your back—big time.

Money and Success

Venus's retrograde trip through Pisces and your solar second house of money matters will go on until April 28, Aquarius, which could be a tad problematic at times. The thing is, Venus won't turn direct until April 15, so if someone is taking advantage of you, you may not become aware of it until then. Now that you know it's possible, though, it's time to establish some boundaries with anyone you're not quite sure of.

Tricky Transits

Saturn will station on April 6 to turn retrograde, Aquarius, just a few days before Mercury does the same. This is pretty much a guarantee that roadblocks, delays, and unforeseen complications will come along when you least expect them, but rather than getting frustrated, take a look around. Whom have you met and/or what have you seen and enjoyed that wasn't on your schedule?

Rewarding Days

5, 6, 10, 24

Challenging Days

7, 8, 9, 21, 22, 30

Aquarius | May

Relaxation and Recreation

Bet you spent a good amount of time last month with old friends and relatives you hadn't seen much of lately. This month, you'll do just as much socializing, but chances are good you'll be out and about with some pretty darn fascinating new acquaintances. Have fun, but don't forget your tried-and-true loved ones who'll still want a nice chunk of your free time—now that you have some!

Lovers and Friends

The New Moon on May 25 will activate your solar fifth house, urging you to become romantically involved with someone quite independent whom you've only just met. Well, why not? If they're just as freedom-loving as you are, they won't want to exchange any premature promises about the future. Doesn't that sound fabulous? Careful, though. This is the kind of free spirit you might actually want to keep around.

Money and Success

Venus rules money and possessions, Aquarius, not just love. She's on the last leg of her extra-long trek through impulsive Aries, so even if you resisted the urge to binge-spend last month, continuing along that self-disciplined path might not be so easy to do now. That goes double if you happen to spot something a loved one would just adore. Ah, well.

Tricky Transits

The Full Moon will arrive on May 10, Aquarius, all done up in intense, sexy, highly emotional Scorpio. Now, if there's anything you're not, it's highly emotional, so this might be an uncomfortable day or two for you—especially if others create dramatic or even melodramatic circumstances to get a bit of attention. Don't buy into the game. Walk away.

Rewarding Days
2, 9, 11, 12, 18, 30, 31

Challenging Days
10, 15, 19, 27

Aquarius | June

Relaxation and Recreation

The Sun, Mercury, and Mars will dash merrily through your solar fifth house of playtime and playmates this month, Aquarius, all of them wearing lighthearted, fun-loving, and oh-so-curious Gemini. You'll have plenty of opportunities to go out and mingle with new people, and with Jupiter still on duty in ultra-sociable Libra, you won't want to stay home anyway. Go ahead. Boldly go where you've not gone before.

Lovers and Friends

Don't let a misunderstanding that arises around June 26 cause you to questions a dear one's loyalty, Aquarius—at least, not until you have solid proof that you should. Thoughtful Mercury will be in the mood to take things personally and maybe even jump to conclusions. Your mission is to give the benefit of the doubt to anyone who has truly earned it.

Money and Success

The New Moon in Cancer on June 23 will set up shop in your solar sixth house of work situations, Aquarius. If you've ever thought seriously about working out of your home, now may be the time you're actually able to put that plan into motion. If you need advice about how to keep the ball rolling, call on that elder who's been encouraging you all along.

Tricky Transits

Neptune will stop in her tracks on June 16, preparing to turn retrograde in woozy Pisces, her very own sign. Now, this is a potent but invisible energy that can cause a whole lot of misunderstandings in little or no time if you're not paying attention. In your case, it's money issues that could be confusing. Don't go it alone. Get yourself some solid advice.

Rewarding Days
1, 3, 6, 17, 18, 24, 25

Challenging Days
2, 4, 13, 15, 19

Aquarius | July

Relaxation and Recreation

The Sun, Mercury, and feisty Mars will storm through fiery Leo this month, Aquarius, which just so happens to be your solar seventh house of one-to-one relationships. If you're single, someone with a serious flair for the dramatic will likely cross your path. If you're attached, take care not to make your sweetheart too jealous—at least not deliberately.

Lovers and Friends

With Venus in lighthearted, playful Gemini on duty in your solar fifth house of fun and recreation, Aquarius, there's really no way you won't have quite the booked social calendar. Your attitude, however? Bring it! You may even be high-energy enough to squeeze in a long-distance trip to visit a long-lost loved one around July 17, 18, or 19.

Money and Success

Negotiating the right price for a trip will go quite easily this month, so if you and a loved one have a dream vacation in mind, there's no time like the present to put those plans in motion. No one's saying you have to leave right away, or even soon, but once you make a deposit and have an itinerary, the dream will begin to come true. Enjoy the entire process.

Tricky Transits

On July 20, a testy square between the Sun and startling Uranus will stir up some tension in the heavens above, Aquarius. Might be that someone you care for is involved in an unexpected dilemma or that urgent circumstances force you to cancel plans and make yourself available. Either way, you'll rise to the occasion—and they'll be relieved and grateful.

Rewarding Days

6, 7, 14, 18, 19, 24, 26

Challenging Days

4, 5, 9, 13, 16, 17

Aquarius | August

Relaxation and Recreation

With the Sun and Mars on duty in fun-loving Leo, we'll all want to play this month, Aquarius—but you stand an excellent chance of finding the time, resources, and perfect companion(s) to turn a spontaneous day trip into a wonderful memory. If you can sneak away for a bit longer, try to aim for the weekend of August 25, when lovely Venus will add a touch of romance to your agenda.

Lovers and Friends

A sky full of fire and air will make it next to impossible for you to find any time to yourself, Aquarius—but then, you won't want to be alone. This sociable tribe will put you in touch with a new group of friends who totally and completely share your ideals and aspirations for the future—and, after all, other than keeping your independence intact, isn't that what it's all about?

Money and Success

Mercury will stop in his tracks to turn retrograde on August 12, Aquarius, all done up in Virgo and your solar eighth house of joint resources and shared assets. Now, if you've been doing battle over an inheritance or having a tough time getting a loan or mortgage—well, those delays won't end for at least three weeks. The thing is, you may not have all the info you need just yet. Use this time to do your homework.

Tricky Transits

There are two eclipses scheduled for the month, Aquarius, and they're both due to activate your solar relationship axis. Expect sudden impulses and events in this department around August 7 and 21, but remember, the effects of eclipses may take time to unfold. Trust your antennae to inform you when it's time to say goodbye.

Rewarding Days

10, 11, 13, 20, 22, 27

Challenging Days

3, 4, 5, 7, 21, 24

Aquarius | September

Relaxation and Recreation

If you're off around September 12 or 13 and looking to let your hair down and have some guilt-free, non-responsible fun, Aquarius—well, you may have to wait a bit longer for that to happen. The thing is, serious Saturn will be on duty, encouraging others to put you in charge of the day's entertainment or activities. Don't agree if you're really not up for the task.

Lovers and Friends

On September 5, Mercury will turn direct in your solar seventh house of one-to-one relationships, Aquarius, urging you to make up your mind with regard to a certain person who's brought a whole lot of unwelcome drama into your life lately. Don't feel guilty about telling them off—and don't be afraid to be a bit dramatic yourself, if that's what it takes to drive the point home.

Money and Success

Four planets will make their way through hardworking, meticulous Virgo this month, Aquarius—which will put this pack in your solar eighth house of shared resources and joint finances. Now, you're an independent soul, but before you make any money-oriented decisions, you might at least try to pay attention to someone whose wisdom in financial areas is a bit more extensive than your own.

Tricky Transits

When excessive, expansive Jupiter gets together on September 28 with Uranus—your unpredictable, spontaneous ruling planet—well, anything is possible, Aquarius. Chances are good now, however, that sudden events will come about through a sibling or neighbor who might be just a tad too concerned with your affairs. No, you don't care for this, and yes, you should mention that immediately.

Rewarding Days
2, 9, 11, 12, 15, 17, 22

Challenging Days
1, 8, 13, 25, 26, 29

Aquarius | October

Relaxation and Recreation

No less than five planets will make their way through your solar ninth house this month, Aquarius, all of them wearing partner-oriented Libra, a sign that doesn't care much for going solo. They'll activate your urge to expand your horizons in some way, whether by traveling, going back to school, or investigating a different belief system. Keep your mind open to new ventures—and adventures, too!

Lovers and Friends

Passion and intensity will join hands on October 1, Aquarius, thanks to an easy trine between Mars and Pluto—a very, very sexy team. If you're not involved, someone you spot may play a major part in the rest of your October. Your antennae will tell you if and when to begin clearing your schedule to investigate this fascinating new carbon-based unit.

Money and Success

On October 10, Jupiter—who prides himself on being responsible for success, by the way—will move into intense Scorpio and your solar tenth house of higher-ups, authority figures, and career matters. Well! That certainly does bode well for your professional aspirations over the coming year. Get busy using this energy right away. Update your resumé and make some appointments to show it off.

Tricky Transits

The Full Moon in Aries on October 5 will illuminate your solar third house, Aquarius, where conversations and communications take shape. Now, Aries planets aren't shy, you've never been shy, and Full Moons don't allow us to hide anything. Obviously, if you have something to say, it's going to emerge—big time. You may surprise even yourself at how quickly your verbal filter shuts off.

Rewarding Days

12, 13, 16, 27, 28, 29

Challenging Days

4, 5, 6, 9, 10, 11, 23

Aquarius | November

Relaxation and Recreation

A sky full of playful, curious air and fire planets will see to it that you're anything but bored this month, Aquarius—which, as we all know, is the only condition you absolutely cannot and will not tolerate. If you're delayed en route to a party or gathering around November 27, consider the fact that the Universe might just be keeping you from being somewhere you shouldn't be—for your own good, that is.

Lovers and Friends

On November 11, you'll notice that just about everyone seems to be in the mind and mood to cooperate, Aquarius—and, even more importantly, to consider new solutions to old problems that don't necessarily involve anything in the rule book. Excellent. Now, set up an appointment to chat with a certain someone you've been dying to convert to your way of thinking.

Money and Success

The lovely lady Venus—who holds the planetary purse strings, by the way—will come together with excessive Jupiter on November 13, Aquarius. Oh, and this famously lucky duo will be on duty in your solar tenth house of career matters. Obviously, if you're in the market for a raise, bonus, or promotion, this is the time to make your intentions known to the higher-ups in charge.

Tricky Transits

The Full Moon on November 4 will stir things up in your solar fourth house of home and family matters, Aquarius—which could mean you're due for a disruption of sorts in your domestic routine. Fortunately, you've seen this coming—that's if you aren't initiating the process yourself from behind closed doors. Either way, you'll be prepared, if not eager, for sudden change.

Rewarding Days
9, 11, 16, 17, 25

Challenging Days
2, 3, 13, 19, 20, 27

Aquarius | December

Relaxation and Recreation

December's traditional festivities don't make it easy for any of us to get much shut-eye, Aquarius—but there's a whole lot of excessive, fun-loving Sagittarian energy passing through your solar eleventh house right about now, so you'll be lucky to get four or five hours on most nights. Ah, well. 'Tis the season. Enjoy. Participate fully. Collect laughs, love, and hugs.

Lovers and Friends

A certain someone you've been friends with for a very long time may suddenly catch your fancy this month, which is just fine, provided that neither of you has other obligations—a partner or spouse, in other words. If not, think of this as a gift from the Universe during the ultimate gift-giving time of the year.

Money and Success

On December 19 and 21, the Sun and Saturn will cross over the Capricorn county line, putting them both in the mood to set some ground rules on your behalf. If you feel that your privacy has been invaded of late, you'll be able to straighten that out right quick. Careful, though. 'Tis the season to be tactful.

Tricky Transits

Mercury will turn retrograde on December 22, Aquarius, set to stir up some memories in your solar eleventh house of peer groups and friendships. 'Tis the season for bringing loved ones close—especially if you haven't seen them recently and your heart needs a fix. Forget a gift. How about investing in a plane, train, or bus ticket instead?

Rewarding Days

6, 7, 8, 16, 20, 24, 25

Challenging Days

11, 12, 13, 22

Aquarius Action Table

These dates reflect the best—but not the only—times for success and ease in these activities, according to your Sun sign.

	JAN	FEB	MAR	APR	MAY	JUN	JUL	AUG	SEP	OCT	NOV	DEC
Move	6, 7, 8		9, 10, 11	5, 6, 7	3	1, 3		26, 27				
Start a class		9, 10				24, 25, 26		2, 3			3	
Join a club	4, 5			23, 24				2, 3		12	25, 26, 27	
Ask for a raise	20	26	4, 16		18, 19		5, 6		2, 3			
Get professional advice	20, 29		12, 23		18, 19	11		20, 27			13, 14	
Get a loan		12, 13		6, 7			25		15, 17, 22	1, 2, 3		
New romance	3, 24, 25	14, 24		28			28		27			24, 25
Vacation			24, 25, 26		16, 17	13, 14, 18		10, 11		14, 22	21, 22, 23	11, 12, 25

Pisces

The Fish
February 20 to March 20

♓

Element: Water

Quality: Mutable

Polarity: Yin/feminine

Planetary Ruler: Neptune

Meditation: I successfully
navigate my emotions

Gemstone: Aquamarine

Power Stones: Amethyst,
bloodstone, tourmaline

Key Phrase: I believe

Glyph: Two fish swimming in
opposite directions

Anatomy: Feet, lymphatic system

Colors: Sea green, violet

Animals: Fish, sea mammals

Myths/Legends: Aphrodite,
Buddha, Jesus of Nazareth

House: Twelfth

Opposite Sign: Virgo

Flower: Water lily

Keyword: Transcendence

The Pisces Personality

Your Strengths, Gifts, and Challenges

Your ruling planet is Neptune, the Queen of Intuition and Disguises, Pisces—which certainly does explain why your antennae are so amazingly keen and so well hidden. They never fail to alert you well in advance of the arrival of a fraud, cheater, or swindler—an absolutely invaluable trait. At the same time, however, you have a knack for seeing the best in others, regardless of what others tell you or what their current behavior may suggest—another fabulous trait. Obviously, this adds up to an astrological conflict of interests, which tends to come to a head when your tender heart is involved and you go with what you'd like to believe rather than what your alarm system is warning you against. That might mean that in your early years, you might not make the best choices—which is perfectly understandable. You were born with the innate gift for understanding that oftentimes, for better or worse, there are some dances in life that simply must be done. So if you ignore all the bells and whistles and at least try to enter into a relationship you simply can't resist with a positive frame of mind and heart—well, at the very least, maybe you'll both walk away with a life lesson under your belt. That's lovely and heartfelt, and you should be commended for your unending faith in others, but if the dance you're accepting is harmful in any way, don't hesitate to dash off into the sunset. Your first obligation is to you—which is something you really do need to have reinforced on a regular basis. Too many of you can end up as emotional punching bags because you think that's just how the dance is done. It's not. Stand up and say no.

Romance, Friendships, and Casual Relationships

With Neptune on duty as your astrological ruler, Pisces, it's easy to understand why you're so amazingly compassionate, empathetic, and self-sacrificing. This is the planet that breaks down barriers and allows us to realize just how intricately we're connected to everyone and everything else on our lovely planet. That said, if you haven't already learned that due to all those lovely Neptunian gifts, you're an extremely vulnerable soul—well, it's most definitely high time that you did and that you take steps to start protecting yourself. The thing is, since Neptune is in your sign at the moment—for the first time in 164 years, by the way—she's especially powerful and intoxicating. Basically, you're in the mood to fall in love—lovely, yes, but do be sure you're taking that step with someone who's not just charming but also in this thing for the long haul. As per usual, the other water signs, home-loving Cancer and perceptive Scorpio, are your most natural choices and the signs you get along with most easily. But if you're looking for an emotional connection that gives you a bit of fun, don't rule out your next-door neighbors, the Aquarius folks on the block. They may not be as warm and fuzzy as you folks are, but they share a whole lot of your values and beliefs—which, after all, is what counts, right?

Career and Work

Water, water, and water. What could possibly be better than getting paid to spend your time in it, on it, or around it? Nirvana. There's an extremely spiritual side to your nature, however, so you may also make your daily bread doing readings or counseling others. No matter what you do, you'll be much happier—and far more productive, by the way—if it's an occupation that makes you feel like you're making a valuable, positive contribution to the world. It might be working with local merchants in metaphysical or spiritual centers, or maybe striking out on your own to serve as a guru of sorts. That fondness for taking care of those who are wounded, broken, or helpless may also lead you into one-on-one counseling. It might be that you become part of a networking organization that's out to improve the plight of an underdog. It doesn't matter. If you believe in what you're doing, the day will fly by and you'll be happy to have spent every moment just exactly as you did.

Money and Possessions

When it comes to objects, Pisces, your favorites are usually your favorites for wonderfully sentimental reasons. Photos, for example, are especially tough for you to part with. Anything that's attached to an extremely pleasant memory will also need to be pried from your hands. In the department of finances you can also be a tad on the impractical side, but not because you're not good with numbers. No, if you have money issues, it's because you give so much of it away. Your mission from this day forward, then, is to hang on to what you have that you need for yourself—which includes your paycheck. Take care of you, and teach others how to take care of themselves by your example. Keep a careful eye on your wallet, purse, and checkbook, and try not to go nuts with the plastic.

Your Lighter Side

What's fun for you? Well, anything that allows you to escape from the harshness of reality for a while, for starters. Television, music, yoga, art, movies, spiritual groups—oh, and séances. How deliciously terrifying! Being by, in, or around water is also wonderfully relaxing for you—and by the way, if you don't live near a body of water, you should. Always follow your gut when it comes to choosing your companions and surroundings. If you're not comfortable, don't stay where you are just to be polite. You're a sensitive soul who enjoys the softer, more aesthetic side of life, which is exactly what you deserve.

Pisces Celebrities

Spiritualist Edgar Cayce was born under your spiritual sign, Pisces, along with the classical composer Frédéric Chopin, and Michelangelo, who painted the Sistine Chapel. As for actors and actresses, there's Drew Barrymore, Olivia Wilde, Bruce Willis, and Elizabeth Taylor—the classic example of elegance and glamour for decades. Kurt Cobain, Queen Latifah, and Adam Levine are also water-sign cousins.

Words to Live By for 2017
Establishing appropriate boundaries is my mission.

The Year Ahead for Pisces

Back in September of 2016, Jupiter set off for partner-loving Libra and your solar eighth house, Pisces. Ever since then, this excessive, expansive guy—who never did know when to quit—has been doing his best to call your attention to the issues covered by that house, including your most intimate relationships and your most intricate financial partnerships. That said, if, you've begun to feel that a certain someone has been taking advantage of your love, your good nature, and your generosity—well, it's time to put your foot down. No, confrontation isn't your usual m.o., but with the King of the Gods on duty, you most definitely won't be at a loss for words, and your authority will likely go unquestioned as well. If you're living with anyone who isn't carrying their share of the load, your first task for this year will be to put an end to that nonsense. You're dutiful and giving—to a fault, usually. But that doesn't mean that you should allow yourself to be an emotional punching bag—especially not when there are so many wonderful new soulmates you've yet to meet. Toss the trash and look to the future.

And speaking of soulmates, let's chat for a bit about loving Venus, who'll spend three full months in impulsive Aries and your solar second house of values this year—yep, right along with startling Uranus. Obviously, your choice of companions, be they intimate, romantic, or platonic, will very closely reflect the person you're in the process of becoming. So think about this: when you look back in three years, who are the folks you'll think of fondly and be able to reminisce about with a smile on your face? That's your mission for 2017, Pisces—to choose the faces that will appear repeatedly in your emotional scrapbook.

Saturn

If you haven't yet received that raise, bonus, or promotion you know you deserve, Pisces, don't get frustrated. The astrological culprit behind the delay is Saturn, who never fails to make us pay our dues before the goodies are passed out. That's most especially the case now, since he's on duty in Sagittarius and your solar tenth house—aka the department of career, profession, and public reputation—and he's quite at home here. Again, don't get frustrated. Just keep working. Once you've convinced Saturn there's really nothing more you can do to earn kudos, he'll file the appropriate paperwork, make the necessary calls, and let you know how it goes. Be patient, though. Saturn's fondness for paperwork and bureaucracy is legendary. Besides, getting what you deserve from higher-ups isn't a process that can be rushed. On the other hand, if you haven't yet done all you know you can to further yourself in your chosen field, not to worry. There's still time. Saturn won't set off for Capricorn until December 20. In the meantime, your mission is to come up with a plan. Maybe you need a tad more experience, another certificate, or a refresher course. Figure it out and get it done. If you've earned Saturn's approval, you'll have your rewards, probably by the end of the year. Oh, and when Saturn enters Capricorn in December, he'll be in your solar eleventh house of peer circles and friendships, by the way, so prepare yourself to be handed the reins and asked to take charge of a group.

Uranus

That fondness you've developed for electronic gadgets isn't going any-where just yet, Pisces. Uranus—Mr. Wizard himself—just loves electronics, and currently he's set up shop in Aries and your solar second house of possessions, inspiring your current curiosity about the latest techno-logical toys. The thing is, toys like this aren't cheap—and this house also refers to the condition of your financial picture. Uranus is an all-or-nothing kind of guy, so impulsively spending much more than you can reasonably afford is a danger. It doesn't have to only be electronics you're stretching your budget to accommodate, either. Ask a friend or loved one if they think you're overdoing it, and don't get mad if they nod. Sit down and take a look at your financial picture—a practical, realistic look. If you're not sure you're up for doing it alone, a friend who's a whiz with numbers can help.

Wherever Uranus is, drastic change is always just around the corner, so yes, windfalls are most certainly one of the possible outcomes of his visits to the second house—but it's just as possible to lose a lot. All this applies most especially to those of you who were born between March 10 and March 22. Your Sun will also receive a semisextile from this rebellious, unpredictable fellow at some point during the year—and this kind of transit provides plenty of reason to break some rules and challenge some authorities. Choose your battles wisely, though. No fair rebelling just for the sake of rebelling.

Neptune

Neptune dissolves boundaries when she's in the neighborhood, Pisces, and she's been on duty in your sign and your solar first house of per-sonality since 2011. What does this tell us? Well, you're already a tender, vulnerable soul, so this type of visit from Neptune has turned you into what can best be described as a psychic sponge. Your antennae have probably been spot-on accurate for the duration—almost scarily accurate at times. Hopefully, you paid attention to them when they twitched. In that case, you've learned a lot about yourself and even more about why others do what they do—and there's much more to come. On the other hand, if you're having trouble getting in touch with your intuition, take a look at your lifestyle. If you're overindulging in alcohol, drugs, or any other addiction, from television to shopping—well, that might be it.

You're dulling your sixth sense. Stop that. No one's saying you can't use one of Neptune's escape hatches every now and then when reality becomes a tad too harsh, but only that if you aren't aware of what's going on around you for extended periods of time, you'll miss the point of this transit—to learn how to be vulnerable and safe at the same time. This is no easy feat in our world, but you've got those amazing antennae to guide you. Your mission is to listen to the voice of your subconscious. Those of you who were born between February 25 and March 4 are currently enjoying the effects of a head-on visit from the lovely lady Neptune. Multiply all of the previous advice by ten and don't question your sanity when you realize you just actually read someone's mind. It's part of the package.

Pluto

Pluto will spend yet another year in Capricorn and your solar eleventh house of group affiliations and peer circles, Pisces—and let's keep in mind that he's the King of Intensity, and often in the neighborhood when power struggles and major upheavals occur. Needless to say, if you've been going through a bit of turmoil with regard to your group associations, it's perfectly understandable—especially if the whole "who's in charge here?" issue is really at the heart of it. The thing is, while you're not usually a contentious soul, Pluto can turn anyone into a force to be reckoned with, perfectly capable of playing politics with the best of them. If you've tried your best to stay out of the group drama but found that to be impossible, stop dragging your heels. Apparently, the Universe has decided that you're the perfect person to take over the wheel—so grab it and do what has to be done. If you were born between March 6 and March 12, over the course of the coming year, your Sun will also receive an active, energetic sextile from Pluto—the perfect astrological recipe for the creation of benevolent dictators. Now, with all Pluto transits to the Sun, losses are possible. The good news is that in the case of the sextile aspect, chances are really, really good that it's you who'll be doing the letting go, throwing away, and weeding out. Rather than feeling that something has been taken from you, you'll understand the need to clear the decks for new growth and be more than happy to assist the process. It's time to rejuvenate and regenerate, Pisces. Don't be afraid to molt a little to make it happen.

How Will This Year's Eclipses Affect You?

Eclipses are celestial exclamation points. They amp up the volume on ordinary life whenever they occur, but the signs and degrees they activate also bring along events and circumstances that are quite intense. Eclipses occur in pairs, six months apart, over a two-week period. Solar Eclipses are supercharged New Moons. They bring the Sun and Moon together, marking peak times for planting spiritual seeds and announcing intentions of all kinds known to the Universe. Lunar Eclipses are high-energy Full Moons, and like these monthly oppositions between the Sun and the Moon, they signal times of dramatic culmination and fulfillment.

The first Lunar Eclipse of the year will occur in showy, dramatic Leo on February 10, landing squarely in your solar sixth house of health habits, work situations, and work-oriented relationships. Now, this certainly could mean that something will trigger your vanity and set you off on a mission to perfect your physical appearance. Leo does adore the applause and appreciation of a crowd. Plus, Neptune is your ruler and also rules the concept of glamour—and FYI, casting a glamour in the old days was the most popular way of making someone's appearance change. If you've been thinking of changing your habits, dieting, or altering your appearance, this lunation will be happy to make it happen. At the very least, find yourself a comfortable exercise regimen. It will change everything.

The first Solar Eclipse of 2017 will arrive on February 26, all done up in your very own sign and subtly making its presence known in your solar first house of personality and appearance. The closer you were born to this date, the more you'll feel this one, Pisces—but there's really no way any of you can avoid noticing its effects. It seems that a certain illusion you've been perpetuating about yourself is about to be poked at, prodded, and possibly even exposed to the light of day. The good news is that this revelation may just free you up—after all, keeping a secret takes a whole lot of effort. Congratulations! You're about to take one giant step forward toward becoming authentic.

The second set of eclipses will occur during August, with a Lunar Eclipse in Aquarius starting the show on August 7. This supercharged Full Moon will shine her light into your solar twelfth house of secrets, making it entirely possible for a secret part of your life to become public knowledge quite quickly, quite unceremoniously, and without much, if any, warning. If you're indulging in anything that's not quite fit for public consumption and you'd like to keep it a secret, better think more than twice about continuing this behavior over the latter half of the year. Of course, if you want to get caught—which may be exactly what's happening, on some level—don't do a thing. Just carry on. The Universe will arrange a fair, righteous ending.

On August 21, a Solar Eclipse will come along, Pisces, once again activating Leo and your solar sixth house. If you put an end to a bad habit back in February, you'll receive positive celestial reinforcement from the Universe that you were on the right path and that your efforts have been duly noted. It might be that you show up for a yearly physical a bit worried, only to find out that the news is fabulous. It might also be that you're feeling fine but you've begun to notice physical symptoms related to a bad habit you haven't put an end to just yet. The point here is to get you to notice a physical condition that's not in keeping with your spiritual beliefs. Your mission is to stop ignoring it and fix it.

Pisces | January

Relaxation and Recreation

You may need a few days to get over your New Year's celebration, but the Universe is prepared to go easy on you, Pisces. Mars, Venus, Neptune, and the Moon will spend a few days at the beginning of 2017 in your sign and your solar first house of personality, a team whose mission it is to keep you away from loud sounds, bright lights, and any part of reality that's just a tad too harsh to deal with right now.

Lovers and Friends

The Full Moon in Cancer on January 12 will set up shop in your solar fifth house of fun times, playmates, and interactions with kids, all done up in ultra-sensitive Cancer. This full-hearted lunation will work together with loving Venus and your ruler, Neptune, to inspire a certain someone to plan something special for you. Enjoy!

Money and Success

Venus will spend most of the month in your sign, Pisces, making her way through your solar first house of personality and appearance. She's a bit of a glamour gal, so it's probably fair to say that you'll spend a good amount of your hard-earned cash on your appearance. Of course, when we become ultra-interested in our appearance, it's usually because there's a delicious new reason…Nice!

Tricky Transits

What starts out as an innocent enough conversation around January 11 or 31 could turn volatile quite quickly, Pisces. If you're involved in a group endeavor and you feel the tide start to change, remove yourself—just in case. With Neptune in your sign, you're a psychic sponge. Why absorb any more negative energy than you absolutely have to?

Rewarding Days

1, 2, 3, 11, 23, 24

Challenging Days

12, 17, 19, 26, 27, 31

Pisces | February

Relaxation and Recreation

The Sun and Mercury will pass through cerebral Aquarius and your solar twelfth house, a private, secretive place. You'll be doing a bit of whispering during February, but not to worry. Looks like it's going to be for all the right reasons. Your mission is to resist the urge to hibernate for long periods of time. Given the perfect hideout, you could get far too comfy far too easily.

Lovers and Friends

Venus will storm off into Aries on February 3, putting this charming but impulsive energy in the mood to buy some presents. If you've just recently become involved with someone, it won't take much of a hint from the object of your desire to convince you to head off on safari. If you have a long-time partner, they deserve the same treatment. Don't wait for a hint. Figure out what would make them happy.

Money and Success

Aries planets have never been especially famous for their self-control or patience, Pisces, and you'll have three of them moving through your solar second house of finances this month. If you're due for a raise, bonus, or promotion, you just won't stop until you know it's in the bag—and since Mars is one of the crew members on duty, yelling isn't out of the question. Careful, though. Don't alienate anyone who's on your side.

Tricky Transits

Jupiter will stop in his tracks to turn retrograde on February 6, Pisces, right in the middle of your solar eighth house of shared finances and joint resources. If you've been working on a loan or mortgage or trying to settle an inheritance issue nicely and it hasn't happened by now—well, get comfy. This could take a while.

Rewarding Days

4, 6, 11, 12, 18, 25

Challenging Days

7, 8, 9, 21, 26, 27

Pisces | March

Relaxation and Recreation

If you suddenly get the feeling that you're on a magic carpet ride this month, Pisces, you're absolutely right. From March 4 through March 9, the Universe will see to it that you're surrounded by nothing but supportive, easygoing energies. Take advantage of every last moment. If you need to get away to clear your mind, try to do it then. Oh, and aim to spend time on or near the water.

Lovers and Friends

The opposition between mighty Jupiter and startling Uranus on March 2 will turn your attention toward matters of the heart, Pisces, possibly because someone you adore is about to make their feelings known—in only the nicest of ways. If you're the target of this adoration, wonderful. Enjoy. If you're the giver, know right now that your thoughtfulness and attention will be much appreciated.

Money and Success

Financial matters could also be a bit problematic around March 2, Pisces, especially if you've been trying to extricate yourself from a tough partnership situation with very little luck. Matters may come to a head, and ending your connection may seem inevitable. Think before you act. Matter of fact, get some professional advice before you move one muscle.

Tricky Transits

Expansive Jupiter will get into a testy square with intense, powerful Pluto on March 30, Pisces—and this is the stuff that major power struggles are made of. If a sudden dispute turns nasty and you're not directly involved, put some distance between you and the situation. There's no reason to soak up any negative feelings or energies. Excuse yourself and go find some laughter.

Rewarding Days

4, 5, 6, 7, 8, 9, 29

Challenging Days

10, 11, 17, 21, 23, 24

Pisces | April

Relaxation and Recreation

Whatever it is that you've been dying to do lately, Pisces, make some time for it. Whether it's fishing, napping, binge-watching your favorite show, or just snuggling up with your sweetheart, it's your turn to be hedonistic. Throw yourself into the project wholeheartedly—just for a little while, though. No fair ducking out permanently.

Lovers and Friends

The lovely lady Venus will spend most of the month in your sign and your solar first house of appearance, Pisces, turning up the charm on your already delightful personality. If you're single, be prepared to attract a whole lot of attention. Matter of fact, even if you're attached, you'll still be attracting appreciative glances. Your mission is to enjoy the attention and make your partner proud, not jealous.

Money and Success

If you need to have a serious chat about finances, Pisces, try to arrange it for April 16 or 17. Whether it's an elder, a higher-up, or an authority figure, the heavens will be happy to help you make the best impression possible. Oh, and if you're already acquainted, having all your paperwork in order wouldn't hurt, either.

Tricky Transits

April 8 could be a tricky day to navigate, Pisces. Two potentially nasty squares will form that day, putting money and relationships in the spotlight. If you've been doing more than your share and you're over it, this is your chance to make a break for it, take control, and stop yourself from being used or taken advantage of. Go for it. This needs to happen.

Rewarding Days
5, 6, 15, 16, 17, 24

Challenging Days
4, 7, 8, 9, 21

Pisces | May

Relaxation and Recreation

If it seems that just about everyone has finally been able to put their disputes and disagreements aside this month, Pisces—well, you may be right. Temporarily, at least. Serious Saturn will form an easy trine aspect with futuristic Uranus on May 19, and for one brief, shining moment, progressive thinkers and conservative folks will actually be able to agree on something. Enjoy the peace and quiet, and remind them that in your tribe, this is the way it's done all the time.

Lovers and Friends

As one of the three water signs, Pisces, you're a highly emotional creature with a fondness for delving deep. So when the Full Moon arrives on May 10, all done up in intense, sexy Scorpio—well, it only makes sense that if you're attached, you two may not spend much time mingling for a day or so. Alert your friends that you're staycationing and will get back to them shortly. No need to worry anyone.

Money and Success

On May 19, Venus in impulsive Aries and your solar second house will face off with excessive Jupiter. Now, this, Pisces, is the stuff that binge-spending and other financial sprees are made of. Telling you not to do that won't work—but maybe you could set yourself a limit. Take a friend along when you hit the mall to talk some sense into you.

Tricky Transits

The New Moon on May 25 will arrive with a testy square between loving Venus and all-or-nothing Pluto, possibly bringing some news you were never expecting to hear regarding the plight of a loved one who has hit rock bottom and is afraid to talk about it. Consider their pride, but not for long. Find a way to broach the subject and offer support without bruising their ego.

Rewarding Days

9, 11, 12, 23, 24, 28

Challenging Days

5, 6, 10, 14, 19

Pisces | June

Relaxation and Recreation

On June 4, fiery Mars will set off for Cancer and your solar fifth house of recreation and playmates. Mars is a high-energy fellow who inspires us to push beyond our limits in search of a sweet, sweet drug: adrenaline. For the next six weeks, you'll be a lot more liable to take risks in the name of having an adventure. Make sure they're well calculated.

Lovers and Friends

The New Moon on June 23 will set up shop in your solar fifth house of fun, all done up in home-loving Cancer. Imagine her crossing her arms in front of her apron and insisting that you have everyone over to your place for at least one impromptu feast, possibly at an unlikely time on an unlikely day. What a wonderful memory that gathering could make!

Money and Success

Talking things over with a higher-up or an authority figure whose professional support you truly need will go especially well if you plan your chat for June 1. Well, your initial chat anyway. You'll probably need to set up several more meetings this month, but once Jupiter turns direct on June 9, the wheels will be set in motion to just about guarantee your success.

Tricky Transits

Neptune will stop in her tracks on June 16, and since she's made herself comfortable in your sign—which is her sign, actually—her magic will be especially potent for you. Her favorite thing to inspire is love at first sight, of course, but adopting someone or something kind of gives you the same feeling. If you only want to help temporarily, make that clear.

Rewarding Days
1, 2, 3, 18, 25, 26

Challenging Days
13, 15, 16, 20, 24

Pisces | July

Relaxation and Recreation

The Sun, Mercury, and Mars will take turns passing through your solar fifth house of playmates and recreation during July, Pisces—which certainly could mean you'll be doing a whole lot of partying. Since they'll all be wearing home-loving Cancer for the duration of their visits, you should probably plan on a lot of those parties being at your place.

Lovers and Friends

A power struggle on July 2 or 9 that pits a loved one against a friend really can't end well, Pisces. Same thing goes for disagreements between your kids and your friends—especially if it's with regard to the amount of time you spend with them. Anyone who doesn't understand that your children will always come first in your life should be informed of that fact immediately.

Money and Success

Startling Uranus has been wreaking havoc on your second house for years now, Pisces, so to say that your financial picture has been the perfect example of feast and famine is an understatement. Still, you've learned to live with and prepare for uncertainty in this department. That trait will come in handy around July 4 and 20. Don't dip into the squirrel fund too deeply, though.

Tricky Transits

The New Moon on July 23 will occur in fiery and extremely romantic Leo and your solar sixth house of work and work-oriented relationships, Pisces. If you've been eyeing someone from across the office for some time, you'll put an end to that nonsense in short order. That's if they don't beat you to it, of course.

Rewarding Days
6, 7, 14, 18, 19, 24

Challenging Days
2, 4, 5, 13, 16

Pisces | August

Relaxation and Recreation

Generous Jupiter will get together with cautious Saturn on August 27, Pisces, and suddenly all will be right with the world and the people who inhabit it. This is an excellent time to plan a reunion, especially if you just know in your gut that a feud is finally cooling down enough to do some creative negotiations.

Lovers and Friends

Mercury will stop in his tracks to turn retrograde on August 12, Pisces. Now, he'll be in your solar seventh house of one-to-one relationships at the time, so you can expect to be in contact with at least one someone you think of often but haven't seen in far too long. Your mission is to resist the urge to romanticize the past. Remember it all—the good and the not so much.

Money and Success

If you're ready to march into so-and-so's office and demand your raise, bonus, or promotion, Pisces—well, first of all, please do make an appointment. Oh, and please do make it for as close to August 10 or 11 as possible. Mercury will turn retrograde on August 12, so you may still have to wait to hear any news, but at least the wheels will be put in motion with positive energies backing them.

Tricky Transits

If you've been trying to gradually back away from a certain relationship, a conversation around August 24 may open your eyes to the fact that they're not taking the hint. If you really want to get away, you'll have to buckle up, face them, and tell them it's over. That goes for both friendships and romances. Go ahead. You know what to say.

Rewarding Days
10, 11, 13, 20, 22, 27

Challenging Days
3, 4, 5, 16, 21, 24

Pisces | September

Relaxation and Recreation

The Full Moon in your very own sign will team up with Mercury on September 6 to bring you some quite unexpected news, Pisces—the kind that you've been waiting for and had just about given up on. See? You were right all along. It pays to keep your spirits up and your attitude positive. It's the Law of Attraction.

Lovers and Friends

No less than four planets will make their way through Virgo and your solar seventh house this month. They'll all be ready to fix you up with someone who seems to have all the right stuff. If a loved one or family member insists that you at least have coffee with someone they're sure is perfect for you, don't argue. This time out, they just might be right.

Money and Success

Venus will set off for your solar seventh house on September 19, all done up in hardworking Virgo. This is the stuff that negotiations preceding business partnerships are made of. If you're ready to strike out on your own but feel better working with a partner, broach the subject with someone you know is as qualified and determined as yourself.

Tricky Transits

Jupiter will face off with startling Uranus on September 28, Pisces, causing just about everyone's blood pressure to rise a couple of notches. If yours gets a little too high due to a pompous, unpredictable person who loves the spotlight—well, don't bother arguing. Excuse yourself and walk away. It's not worth the energy.

Rewarding Days

2, 9, 12, 15, 17

Challenging Days

3, 13, 16, 19, 25

Pisces | October

Relaxation and Recreation

Everything you do will be far more fun this month if you do it with someone else—but just one particular someone else. Yes, you're fond of kindred spirits in groups, but every now and then it's nice to hang out with someone who simply adores you and has no expectations of how your time together "should" turn out. Netflix and chill.

Lovers and Friends

If you're single, Pisces, two easy trines will make it easy for you to meet up with a new admirer, provided you actually get off the couch and go out to do some mingling—no easy feat when trines are in full swing. Give it shot, though. On October 1 and 3, you stand a very good chance of meeting someone who could turn out to be a soulmate—or at the very least, a terrific friend.

Money and Success

Five planets will make their way through partner-oriented Libra and your solar eighth house during October, Pisces, putting the issue of joint finances and shared resources at the very top of your priority list. Talk things over with anyone who isn't carrying their share of the weight—firmly, please, and no fair apologizing before you start. Enough of this, right? It's time.

Tricky Transits

Expansive Jupiter will set off for Scorpio on October 10, an intense, determined, and oh-so-passionate sign. He'll spend the coming year in your solar ninth house of politics, religion, and other belief systems, urging you to broaden your horizons—even if it means changing your mind about an issue that's important to you. Basically, your world perspective will enter a stage of growth. Enjoy!

Rewarding Days

1, 3, 12, 16, 27, 28

Challenging Days

5, 8, 9, 11, 23, 26

Pisces | November

Relaxation and Recreation

The Full Moon in earthy, grounded Taurus will arrive on November 4, training her spotlight on your solar third house of thoughts, conversations, and communications. Now, you're probably an ultra-sensitive and highly psychic soul, but any decisions to be made now will also require a strong dose of practical reality. Tap into this Moon's energy and you'll have the best of both worlds.

Lovers and Friends

The lovely lady Venus will join hands with expansive, excessive Jupiter on November 13, both of them all done up in sexy Scorpio, an emotional water-sign cousin you're easily influenced by. Your relationships—pretty much all of them you don't think of as casual, anyway—are about to deepen in ways you'd never thought possible. It's time to experience the magic of true bonding.

Money and Success

The Sun and Mercury will join no-nonsense Saturn in your solar tenth house of career matters during November, Pisces, so if you're looking to get ahead, be warned: hard work is the only way to do it. The good news is that this pack of planets will all be wearing funny, philosophical Sagittarius, so even the hours you spend working overtime could actually turn out to be educational and enjoyable.

Tricky Transits

If you have something uncomfortable or unpleasant to say and you've been waiting for astrological backup to say it, wait no more. Mercury and Saturn will get together on November 28, a team that's all about relaying just the facts, ma'am, in an eminently practical way. Buckle up, figure out what you want to say, and say it, in no uncertain terms.

Rewarding Days

3, 4, 11, 12, 21, 23

Challenging Days

13, 14, 19, 27

Pisces | December

Relaxation and Recreation

The Sun, Mercury, and Venus will take turns passing through your solar tenth house this month, Pisces, all done up in funny, philosophical and oh-so-lucky Sagittarius. If you've been trying to get on the good side of a certain higher-up, authority figure, or elder, there's truly no time like the present to spend time with them—and don't be shy about pointing out the finest of your fine character traits.

Lovers and Friends

Just in time for a splendid holiday season, loving Venus will take off for your solar eleventh house of groups on December 25, Pisces, all done up in Capricorn. Now, this sign is an historian and is extremely fond of tending to family trees. So just imagine how good it will be to spend time with your loved ones with Venus nudging you into seeing and appreciating them. Enjoy!

Money and Success

Venus will spend from December 1 until December 25 in extravagant, excessive Sagittarius—and since she's the planetary holder of the purse strings, we'll all be feeling a tad excessive this holiday season. You, however, are already famous for pulling out all the stops to make a moment memorable for a loved one. Go easy on your budget this time around.

Tricky Transits

For the first time in twenty-nine years, Saturn will be off for his home turf on December 19. He'll move into Capricorn and your solar eleventh house of groups, and suddenly all those nice people you knew casually from your gym or spiritual meeting place will be eyeing you as a possible replacement for a missing leader. Ready or not...

Rewarding Days
1, 7, 8, 10, 16, 20

Challenging Days
3, 11, 21, 22

Pisces Action Table

These dates reflect the best—but not the only-times for success and ease in these activities, according to your Sun sign.

	JAN	FEB	MAR	APR	MAY	JUN	JUL	AUG	SEP	OCT	NOV	DEC
Move	9, 10			5, 6, 7		13, 14, 15		4, 5			7, 18	
Start a class			24		24	24		27	8, 22		7, 8	
Join a club				18, 19	10, 11		8, 9		15, 16, 17	1, 3, 5		
Ask for a raise	3, 4		2, 3	8, 9	17, 18	2, 3	7, 16					11, 12
Get professional advice	19, 20, 21	20, 23			2, 3	18		26, 27		20, 21, 22		16
Get a loan		16, 17	17, 18			27, 28			22		14, 15	
New romance	23, 24				4, 5, 23		24, 25		29, 30		21	24
Vacation		17	4, 5	12, 13			26, 28	13, 24		20, 21		4, 5

Notes

Notes

Notes

Notes

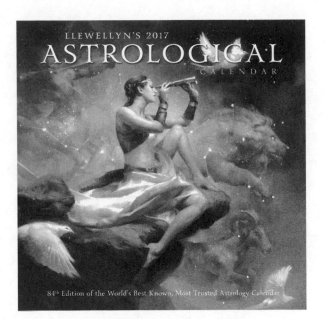

Llewellyn's 2017 Astrological Calendar
Horoscopes for You Plus an Introduction to Astrology

Llewellyn's Astrological Calendar is the best-known, most trusted astrological calendar sold today. Everyone, even beginners, can use this beautiful and practical calendar to plan the year wisely.

There are monthly horoscopes, best days for planting and fishing, rewarding and challenging days, travel forecasts, and an astrology primer. Advanced astrologers will find major daily aspects and a wealth of other essential astrological information.

This edition features Cynthia Sheppard's gorgeous artwork, inspired by the signs and symbols of astrology.

978-0-7387-3758-4, 40 pp., 12 x 12   **U.S. $14.99**

Complete Astrology At-A-Glance

LLEWELLYN'S 2017

Daily Planetary Guide

Your Best Opportunity Periods from
Jim Shawvan & Forecasts by Pam Ciampi

Llewellyn's 2017 Daily Planetary Guide
Complete Astrology At-A-Glance

Empower your life with the most trusted and detailed astrological guide available. Take advantage of cosmic forces on a daily, weekly, or monthly basis with *Llewellyn's Daily Planetary Guide*.

With exact times down to the minute, this astrological planner lists ideal times to do anything. Before setting up a job interview, signing a contract, or scheduling anything important, consult the weekly forecasts and Opportunity Periods—times when the positive flow of energy is at its peak.

Even beginners can use this powerful planner, which includes a primer on the planets, signs, houses, and how to use this guide.

978-0-7387-3760-7, 208 pp., 5 x 8¼ $12.99

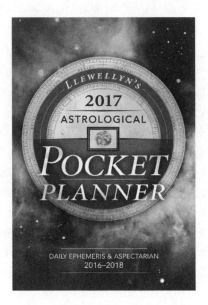

Llewellyn's 2017 Astrological Pocket Planner
Daily Ephemeris & Aspectarian 2015–2017

Empower your future—plan important events, set goals, and organize your life—with *Llewellyn's Astrological Pocket Planner*. Both beginners and advanced astrologers can use this award-winning datebook, the only one to offer three years of ephemeris and aspectarian data.

Choose optimal dates for job interviews, weddings, business meetings, and other important occasions. Pinpoint ideal times to plant a garden, begin new projects, conduct self-reflection, go fishing, and more. Avoid planetary pitfalls by following the easy-to-read retrograde and Moon void-of-course tables.

Comprehensive and compact, *Llewellyn's 2017 Astrological Pocket Planner* also contains time zone information and space to jot down your daily appointments.

978-0-7387-3759-1, 192 pp., 4¼ x 6⁵/₁₆   **$8.99**

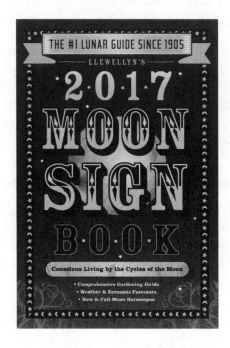

THE #1 LUNAR GUIDE SINCE 1905

LLEWELLYN'S

·2·0·1·7·

MOON
SIGN
B·O·O·K

Conscious Living by the Cycles of the Moon

• Comprehensive Gardening Guide
• Weather & Economic Forecasts
• New & Full Moon Horoscopes

Llewellyn's 2017 Moon Sign Book
Conscious Living by the Cycles of the Moon

Since 1905, *Llewellyn's Moon Sign Book* has helped millions take advantage of the Moon's dynamic energies. Use this essential life-planning tool to choose the best dates for almost anything: getting married, buying or selling your home, requesting a promotion, applying for a loan, traveling, having surgery, seeing the dentist, picking mushrooms, and much more. With lunar timing tips on planting and harvesting and a guide to companion plants, this popular guide is also a gardener's best friend. In addition to New and Full Moon forecasts for the year, you'll find insightful articles on growing a tea garden, cultivating roses, organic and natural food labeling, the Moon and earthquakes, outer planets in water signs, and Greek lunar folklore.

978-0-7387-3763-8, 312 pp., 5¼ x 8 $11.99

To order, call 1-877-NEW-WRLD
Prices subject to change without notice
Order at Llewellyn.com 24 hours a day, 7 days a week!

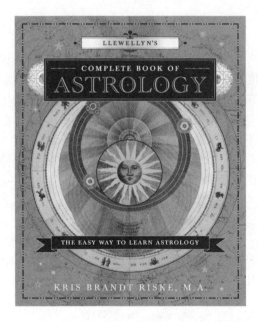

LLEWELLYN'S

COMPLETE BOOK OF

ASTROLOGY

THE EASY WAY TO LEARN ASTROLOGY

KRIS BRANDT RISKE, M.A.

Llewellyn's Complete Book of Astrology
The Easy Way to Learn Astrology
KRIS BRANDT RISKE, MA

The horoscope is filled with insights into personal traits, talents, and life possibilities. With *Llewellyn's Complete Book of Astrology*, you can learn to read and understand this amazing cosmic road map for yourself and others.

Professional astrologer Kris Brandt Riske introduces the many mysterious parts that make up the horoscope, devoting special attention to three popular areas of interest: relationships, career, and money. Friendly and easy to follow, this comprehensive book guides you to explore the zodiac signs, planets, houses, and aspects, and teaches how to synthesize this valuable information.

Once you learn the language of astrology, you'll be able to read birth charts for yourself and others, determine compatibility between two people, track your earning potential, uncover areas of opportunity or challenge, and analyze your career path.

978-0-7387-1071-6, 336 pp., 8 x 10 $19.99

HOW TO SURVIVE MERCURY RETROGRADE

[AND VENUS & MARS, TOO]

BERNIE ASHMAN

How to Survive Mercury Retrograde
And Venus & Mars, Too
BERNIE ASHMAN

Go beyond the fear and negativity of retrograde periods and achieve success. Retrogrades can present unexpected opportunities when you approach them with creativity and patience. *How to Survive Mercury Retrograde* shows you how to be better prepared for retrograde cycles and handle those areas of life that are most commonly affected.

Discover the answers to questions about getting married, accepting a new job, or buying a car during a retrograde period. Explore retrograde survival tips that will help you maintain focus and correct mistakes. Look up your sign and corresponding element to see how you can cope.

Whether you are a student of astrology or just someone wanting to know how to survive a retrograde cycle with less stress, this book will help you navigate these challenging astrological periods.

978-0-7387-4517-6, 240 pp., 5¼ x 8   **$16.99**

Bernie Ashman

SUN SIGNS

&

PAST LIVES

Your Soul's Evolutionary Path

Sun Signs & Past Lives
Your Soul's Evolutionary Path
BERNIE ASHMAN

Discover how to break free from destructive past-life patterns and reach your full potential.

Sun Signs & Past Lives offers an easy, foolproof way to pinpoint behaviors that may be holding you back from a rewarding life of peace and fulfillment. All you need to know is your birthday. Bernie Ashman divides each Sun sign into three energy zones, allowing easy access to innate strengths and the spiritual lessons for this lifetime. With his guidance, you'll discover how to transform these precious insights into action—reverse negative past-life tendencies, find healing, discover your life purpose, and get back on the road to empowerment.

978-0-7387-2107-1, 264 pp., 6 x 9 $17.99

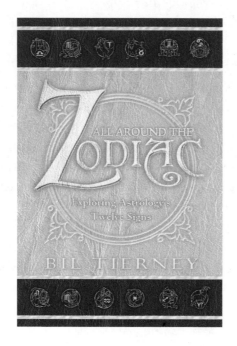

All Around the Zodiac
Exploring Astrology's Twelve Signs
BIL TIERNEY

Here is a fresh, in-depth perspective on the zodiac you thought
you knew. This book provides a revealing new look at the astrological signs, from Aries to Pisces. Gain a deeper understanding of how each sign motivates you to grow and evolve in
consciousness. How does Aries work with Pisces? What does
Gemini have in common with Scorpio? *All Around the Zodiac*
is the only book on the market to explore these sign combina-
tions to such a degree.

Not your typical Sun sign guide, this book is broken into
three parts. Part 1 defines the signs, part 2 analyzes the expression of sixty-six pairs of signs, and part 3 designates the expression of the planets and houses in the signs.

978-0-7387-0111-0, 480 pp., 6 x 9 $22.99